AF396475

IAN TWEEDY

CRISIS

CURA.BOOKS
NEW YORK • ROME

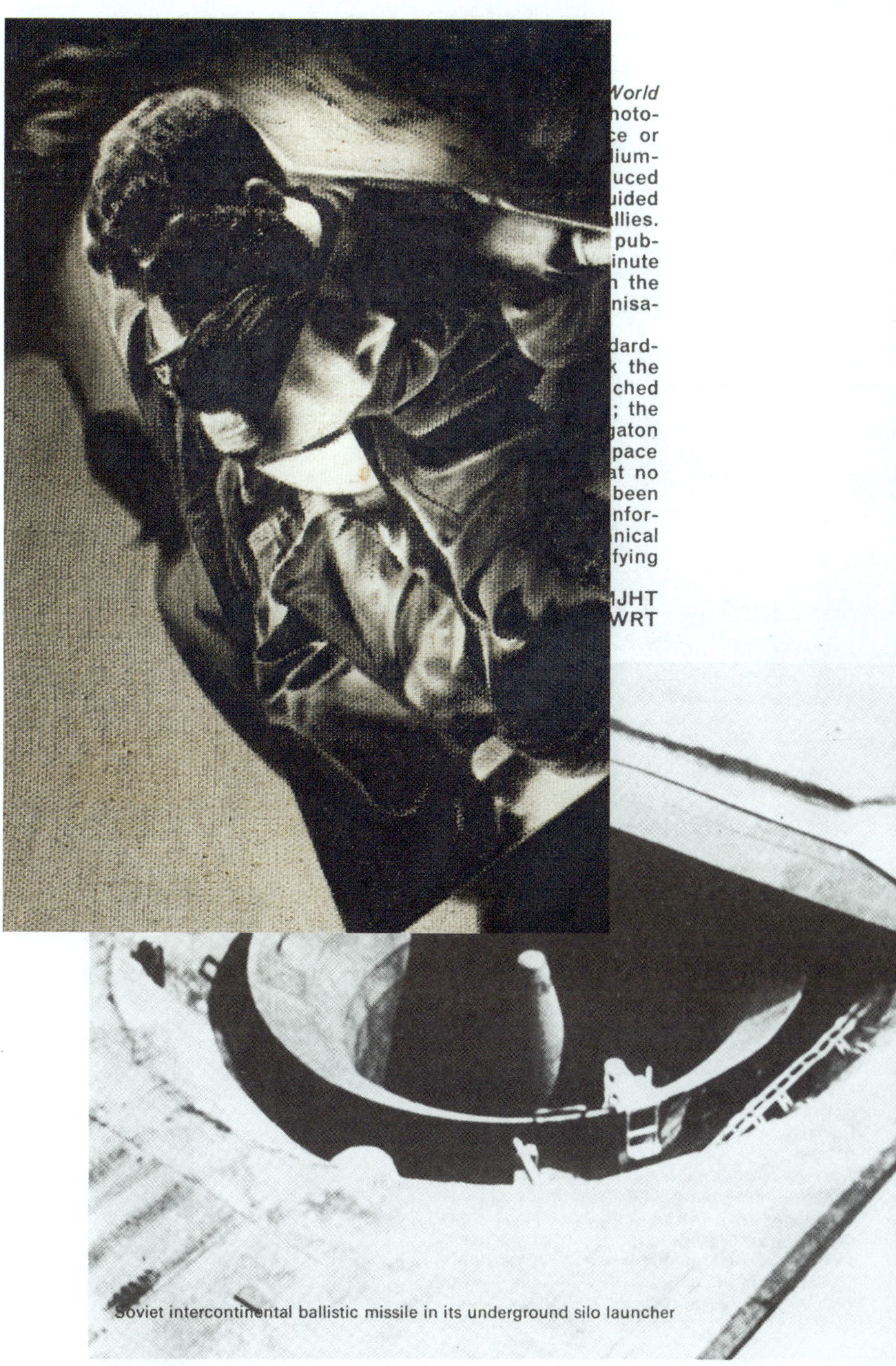

*World
hoto-
ce or
lium-
uced
uided
llies.
pub-
inute
n the
nisa-

dard-
k the
ched
; the
gaton
pace
at no
been
nfor-
nical
fying

JHT
WRT

Soviet intercontinental ballistic missile in its underground silo launcher

ally to replace th
F-104J interceptor
fence Force. Del
r 1970, and half
al of 330 missile
rvice by the begi
f the AAM-1 hav
tion, except that
n, limited to attac

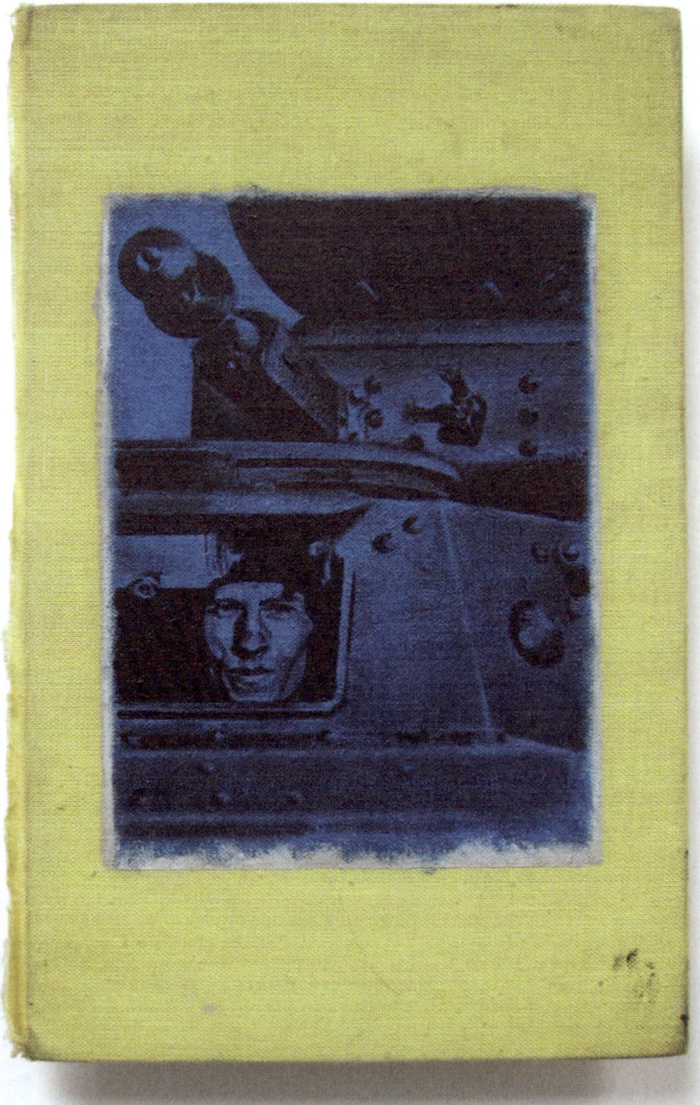

Japa

e

eloped by Mits
the AAM-1 fro
available, exce
limitations of tl
ome on the targ

Franc

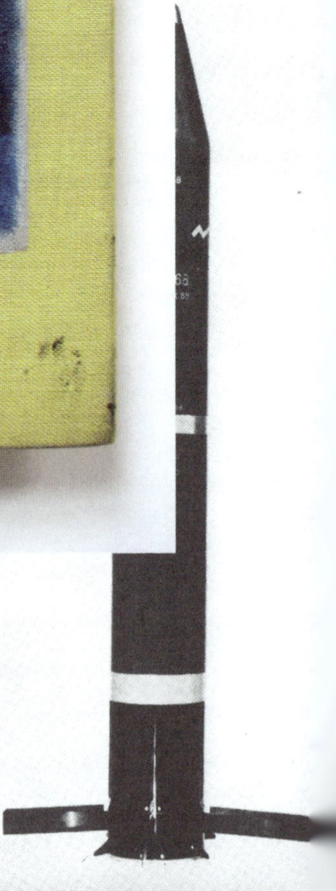

of the gun, mounted on a combat vehicle, with an initial velocity of 492ft (150m)/sec. This is increased to 1,640ft (500m)/sec by the missile's own motor, with the result that it covers its maximum range in under seven seconds. The possibility of the target taking counter-action against the ACRA launch vehicle is thus reduced to a minimum.

ACRA travels along an infra-red director

beam emitted by a laser. This beam is slaved to the operator's optical sight, which need only be held on target, with no manual steering requirement. The missile corrects its course automatically, by sensing deviations from course by comparison with the axis of the director beam—a form of guidance which is immune to jamming and offers a high degree of accuracy. Testing is scheduled for completion during 1973, ten years after development of the weapon was initiated. ACRA will then be deployed initially on AMX-10M armoured vehicles of the French Army.

Advanced Terrier (RIM-2F)   USA

Ship-based surface-to-air missile. In service

Prime contractor: General Dynamics Corporation.
Powered by: Allegany Ballistics Laboratory tandem two-stage solid-propellant rocket motors.
Airframe: Tandem two-stage design. Cylindrical missile body, with long ogival nose, cruciform long-chord wings of constant narrow span with cruciform tail control surfaces immediately to their rear. Cylindrical tandem booster, of larger diameter, with cruciform cropped-delta fins at rear, indexed in line with missile surfaces.
Guidance and Control: General Dynamics (Pomona) beam-riding guidance with semi-active terminal homing. Control by movable tail surfaces.
Warhead: Naval Ordnance Laboratory high-explosive warhead, with proximity fuse.
Length: 27ft 0in (8.23m).
Body diameter: Missile 1ft 0in (30cm) Booster 1ft 4in (40.6cm).
Wing span: 1ft 8in (0.51m).
Launch weight: 3,000lb (1,360kg).
Max range: over 20 miles (32km).

Development and Service
The original Terrier missile (RIM-2A, formerly SAM-N-7) was evolved from an experimental vehicle named Lark and became operational on ships of the US Navy in 1956. It was followed seven years later by Advanced Terrier, with new beam-riding guidance which offered greatly increased effectiveness against low-flying aircraft and multiple targets, and also gave the missile a surface-to-surface capability. Externally, the Advanced weapon differs from Terrier mainly in having

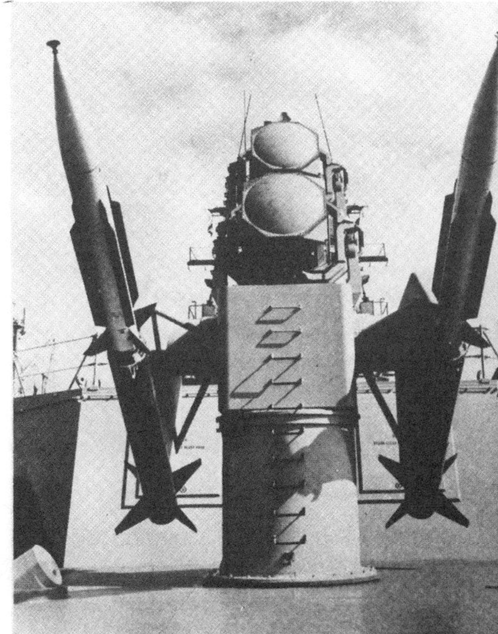

strake-like wings instead of the former small cropped-delta surfaces.

Advanced Terrier continues to arm many US attack carriers, cruisers and frigates, as well as one Dutch and four Italian cruisers. It is being replaced by Standard Missile.

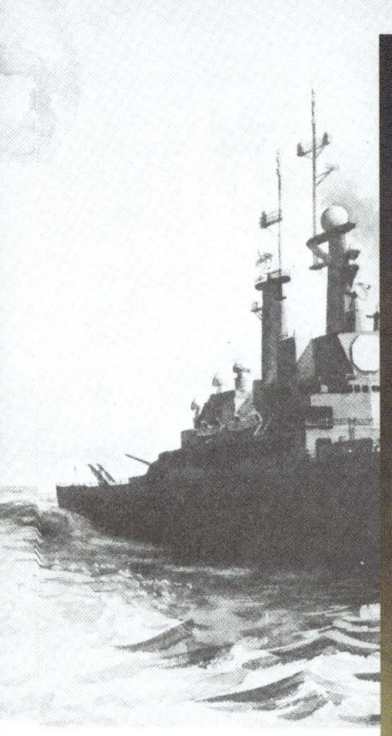

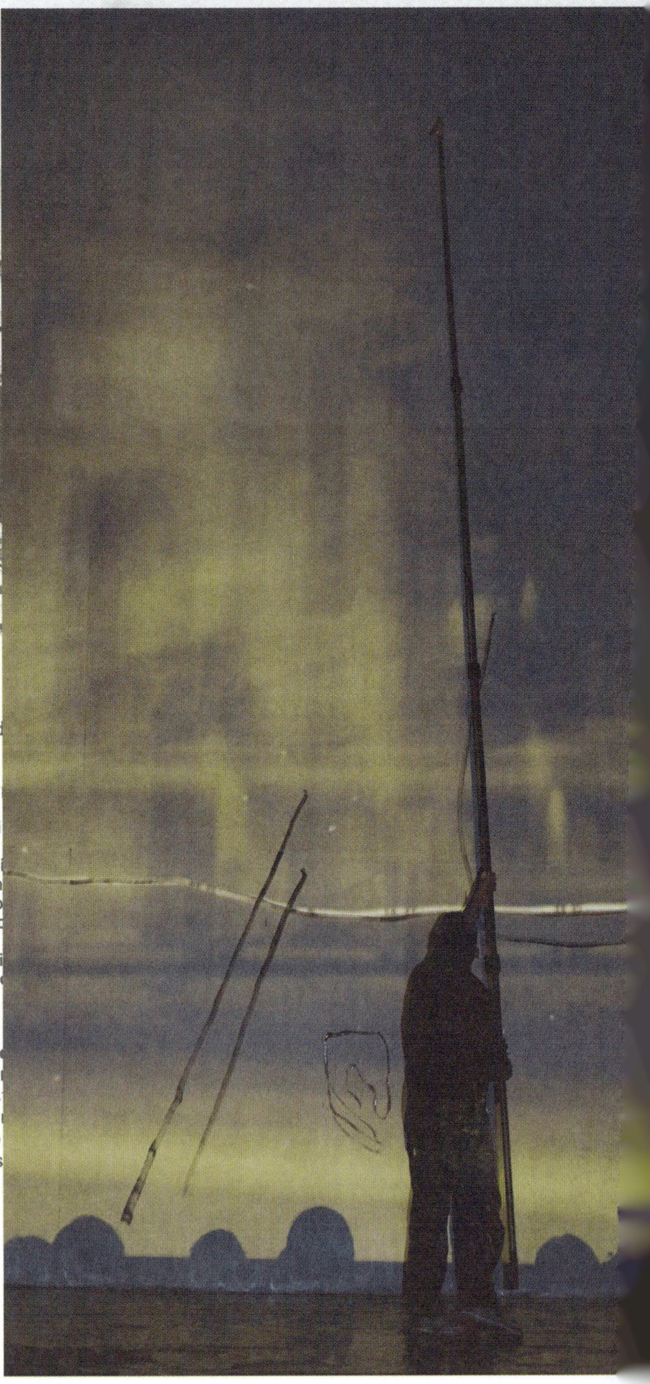

Aegis

Surface-to-air ship-based [...]
development.

Prime contractor: Radio Cor[poration of]
America.
Powered by: Dual-thrust soli[d-propellant]
motor.
Airframe: Cylindrical body, wi[th]
cruciform wings, indexed in lin[e with]
tail control surfaces. Ogival no[se, with]
four small sweptforward surfac[es and]
tip-mounted antenna.
Guidance and Control: Semi[-active radar]
guidance. Control by tail surfac[es.]
Warhead: High-explosive.

Development and Service

Aegis was known origin[ally as Ad-]
vanced surface missile sys[tem. It]
will be the US Navy's pri[ncipal air-]
defence system from abo[ut the mid-]
'80s. It is being planned as [a total]
system, able to protect an [entire fleet.]
Initial deployment will be [...]

air-to-air missile. Under
t.

Control: Infra-red guidance

ge: 3,000ft (915m).

nt and Service

dogfight' missile which the US
o develop as armament for the
14 Tomcat, following experience
types of air-to-air missile in
Vietnam. It will be highly-manoeuvrable, to deal with fast-turning enemy aircraft at close range, and may also be produced for the USAF following cancellation of the latter's AIM-82A 'dogfight' missile for the McDonnell Douglas F-15. The Naval Weapons Center, China Lake, California, is responsible for the Agile project. A contract for the infra-red seeker has been awarded to Hughes Aircraft Company.

OS

ce anti-shipping missile.
lopment.

ctors: SA Engins Matra (France)
a SpA (Italy).
Turboméca Arbizon III turbojet,
(400kg) st.
lindrical body with pointed
ur semi-circular engine air-intake
pporting a cropped-delta wing,
round body. Cruciform tail control
ed in line with wings.
Control: Thomson-CSF terminal
trol via tail surfaces.
gh-explosive.
7-50 miles (60-80km).

nt and Service
off weapon can be launched
from aircraft such as the Atlantic and Nimrod maritime reconnaissance-bombers from well outside the range of most current and projected ship-to-air defence systems. Basically, it combines the rear portion of the Otomat ship-to-ship missile (page 87) with the forward section of Martel (page 76); but, being air-launched, it does not need Otomat's boosters. After launch, it descends to a very low altitude, which is maintained by a radio-altimeter. Then, like Otomat, it climbs before making a terminal dive into the target. Albatros is expected to be ready for service by 1973 and will be suitable as armament for large anti-submarine helicopters in the class of the French Super Frelon.

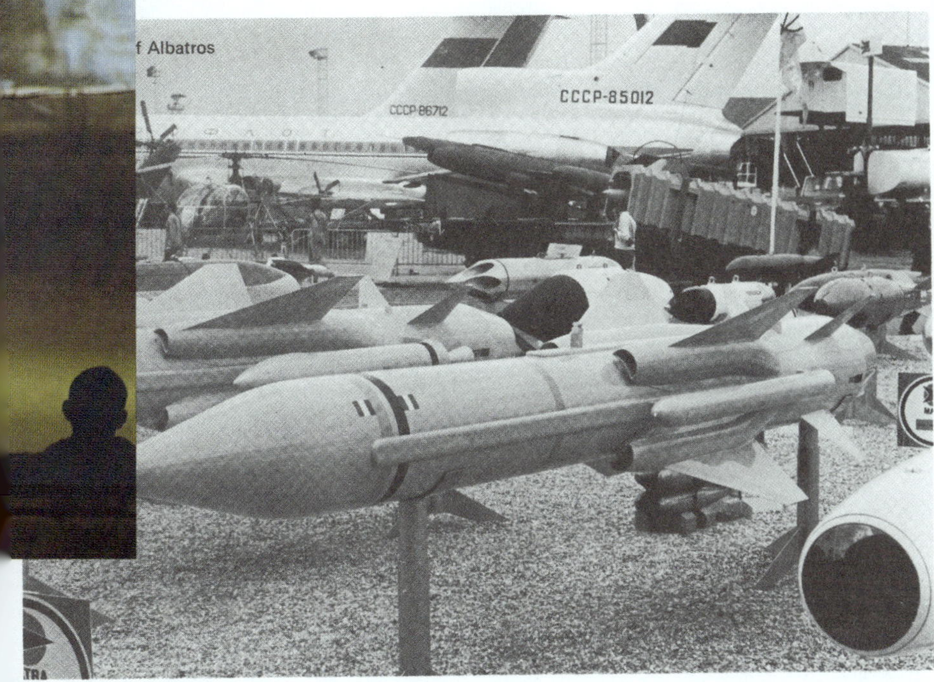
f Albatros

Albatros Italy

Surface-to-air missile system. Under development.

Prime contractor: Selenia SpA.

Development and Service

Not to be confused with the Albatros air-to-surface anti-shipping missile, Selenia's Albatros weapon system is intended to provide naval craft with all-weather point defence against attack by aircraft and missiles, down to very low altitudes. It consists of either a Ferranti GA-10 digital gun fire control system or Elsag NA-10 gun fire control system, Selenia Orion RTN 10 tracking radar, a missile launching system and one or two anti-aircraft guns, and Sparrow (AIM-7) missiles (see page 138). The missiles are modified by the use of folding wings and clipped tail-fins, to fit into the launcher, and by the addition of a rapid run-up capability. Only a single operator is required for the Albatros system, to carry out radar control functions, missile launch and gun fire control. Defensive cover is provided from the maximum range of the missiles (over 6 miles; 10km) down to the minimum effective range of the guns (about 1,000ft; 300m).

Selenia received an official contract to begin development of the Albatros system in early 1968. Successful firing trials against target drones in Sardinia are being followed by operational evaluation on board a ship of the Italian Navy. Production was expected to start in 1972.

Alkali USSR

Air-to-air missile. In service.

Powered by: Solid-propellant rocket motor.
Airframe: Basically-cylindrical body, with large rear-mounted cruciform wings of delta shape, indexed in line with small cruciform foreplanes. Control surfaces in wing trailing-edges.
Guidance and Control: Radar homing system. Control via wing trailing-edge surfaces.

Development and Service
'Alkali' continues to be carried by all-weather interceptor versions of the MiG-19, in service with some of Russia's allies and friends. It was the first-generation missile armament of this fighter and of the original version of the Sukhoi Su-9.

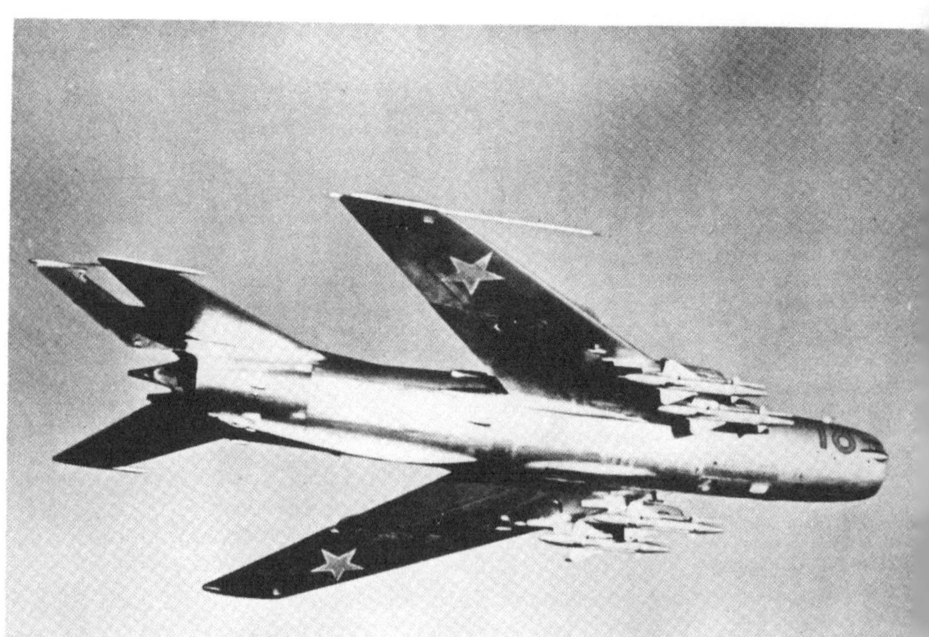

Alkali missiles under the wings of a MiG-19

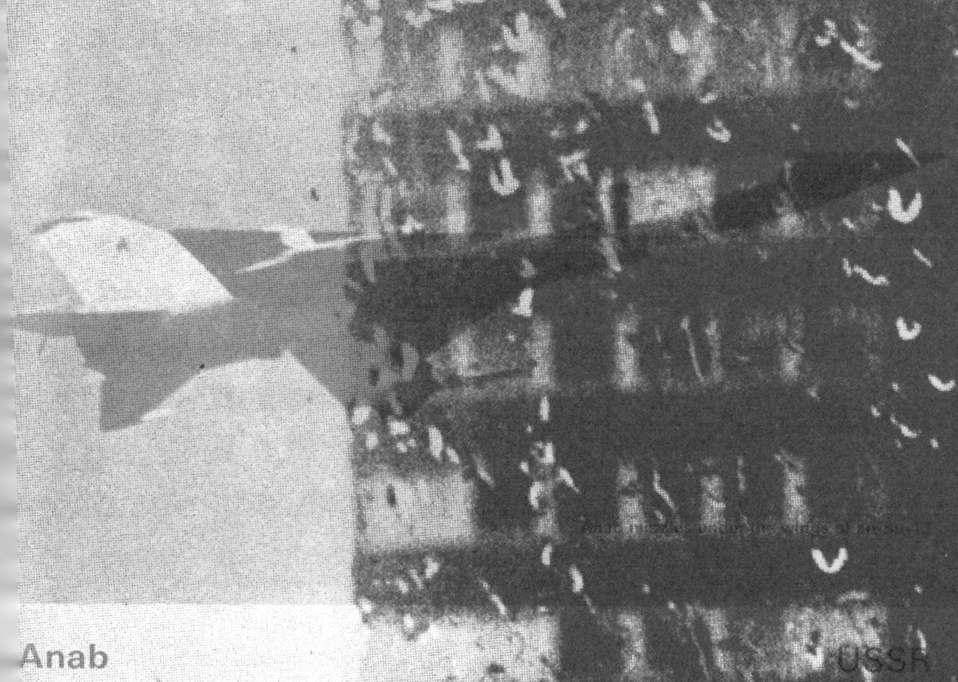

Anab missiles under the wings of an Su-11

Anab

USSR

Air-to-air missile. In service.

Airframe: Cylindrical body, fitted with large cruciform tail-fins and small canard cruciform foreplanes.
Guidance and Control: Alternative infra-red and semi-active radar homing guidance systems. Control by movable foreplanes.
Warhead: High-explosive.
Length: IR version 13ft 6in (4.1m). Radar homing version 13ft 1in (4.0m).

Development and Service
Like the USAF, the Soviet Air Force has learned by experience the value of carrying both infra-red homing and radar homing missiles on its interceptors, for use under varying weather conditions and in different tactical situations. The Sukhoi Su-9 and Yakovlev Yak-28 all-weather fighters of the Protivo Vozdushniya Oborona Strany (National Anti-Air Defence force) are thus armed usually with one 'Anab' of each type on underwing racks. So is the new single-seat twin-jet Su-11.

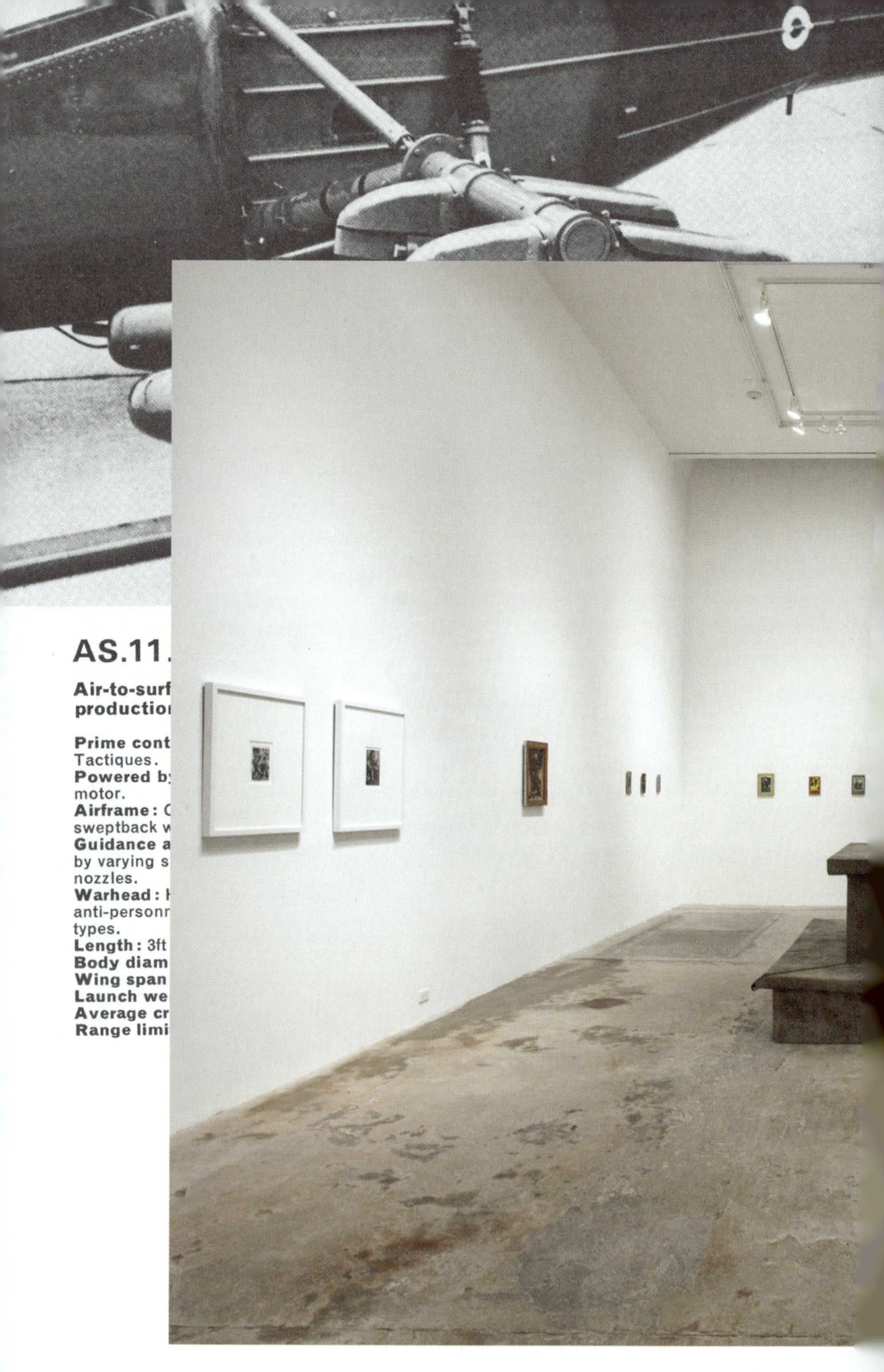
AS.11.

Air-to-surf
production

Prime cont
Tactiques.
Powered by
motor.
Airframe: C
sweptback w
Guidance a
by varying s
nozzles.
Warhead: H
anti-personn
types.
Length: 3ft
Body diam
Wing span
Launch we
Average cr
Range limi

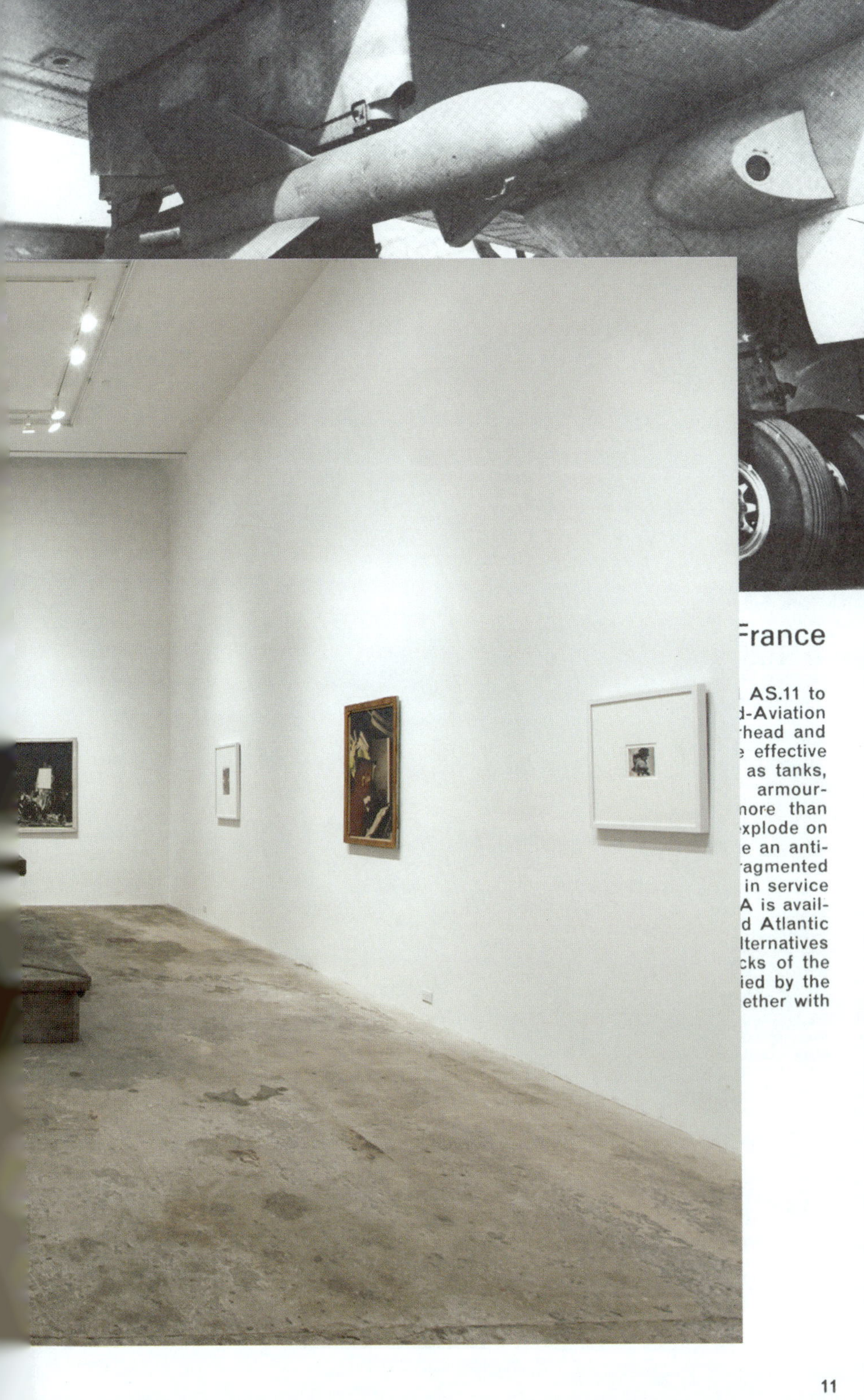
France
AS.11 to
d-Aviation
head and
effective
as tanks,
armour-
more than
xplode on
e an anti-
agmented
in service
A is avail-
d Atlantic
lternatives
cks of the
ied by the
ether with

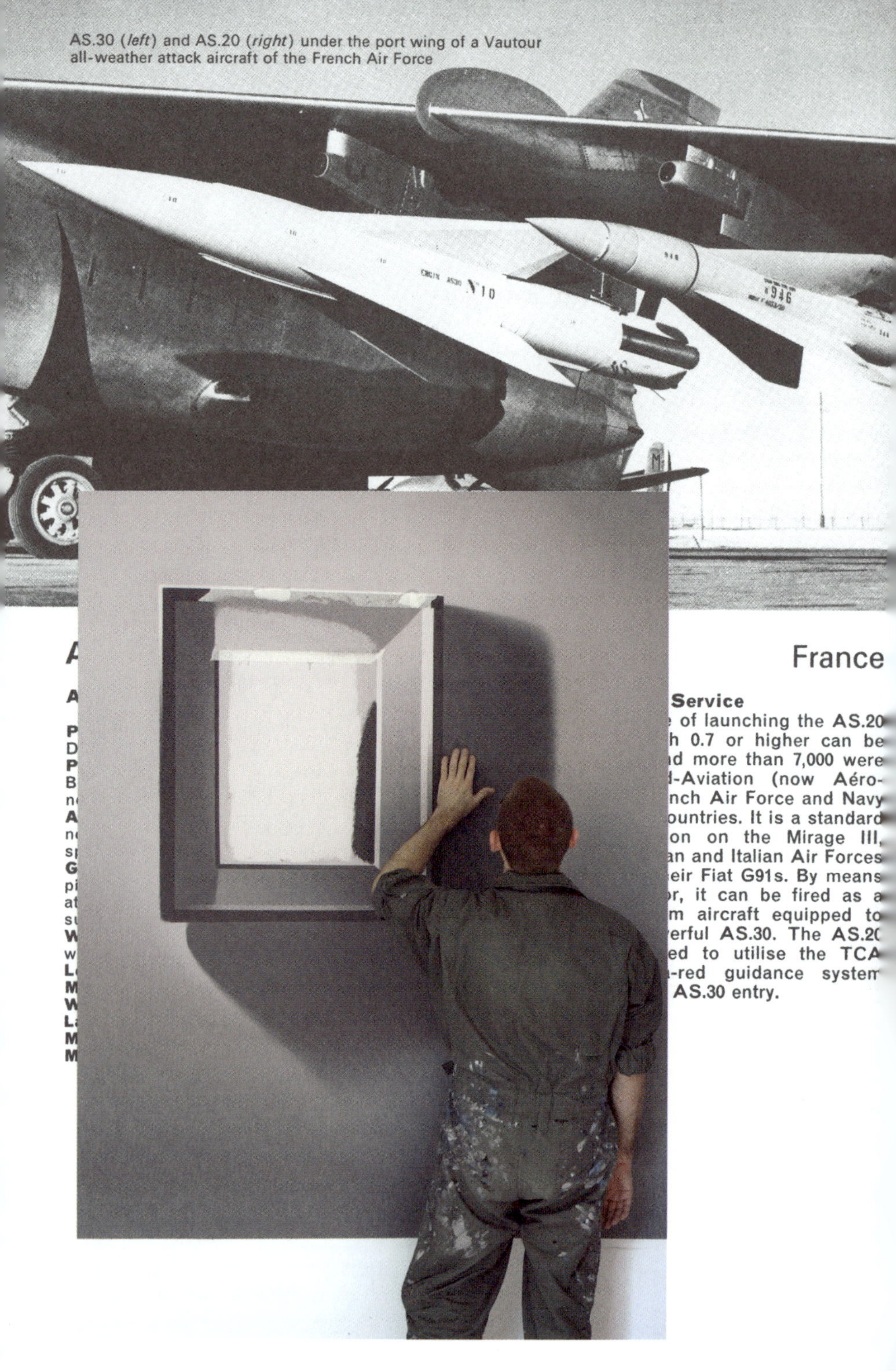

France

Service

...e of launching the AS.20
...h 0.7 or higher can be
...d more than 7,000 were
...d-Aviation (now Aéro-
...nch Air Force and Navy
...ountries. It is a standard
...on on the Mirage III,
...an and Italian Air Forces
...eir Fiat G91s. By means
...r, it can be fired as a
...m aircraft equipped to
...erful AS.30. The AS.20
...ed to utilise the TCA
...-red guidance system
... AS.30 entry.

Tactical air-to-surface missile. In service.

Prime contractor: Nord-Aviation/Aérospatiale, Division Engins Tactiques.
Powered by: Two-stage solid-propellant rocket motor.
Airframe: Cylindrical body with pointed ogival

when launched at least 6.2 miles (10km) from the target, without any need for the launch aircraft to approach within 1.8 miles (3km) of the target. This specification was exceeded by the production missiles, of which about 5,500 were delivered. They can

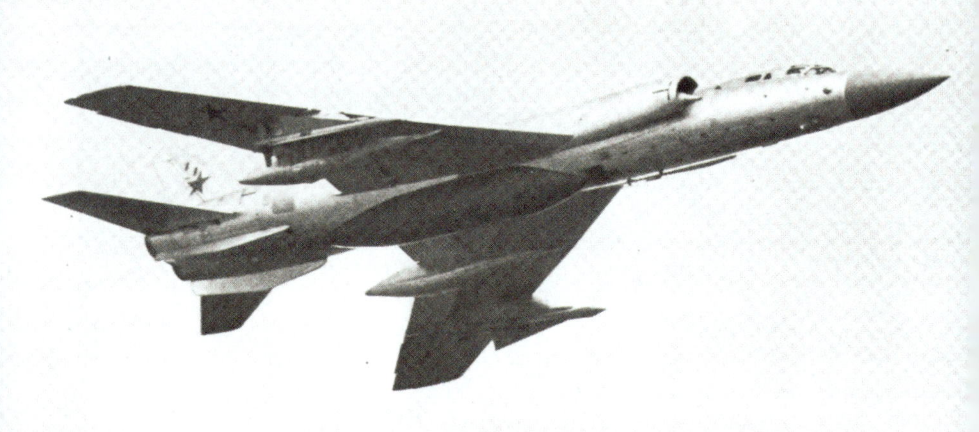

Ash missiles under the wings of an early version of the Tu-28P. Current operational Tu-28Ps each carry four missiles

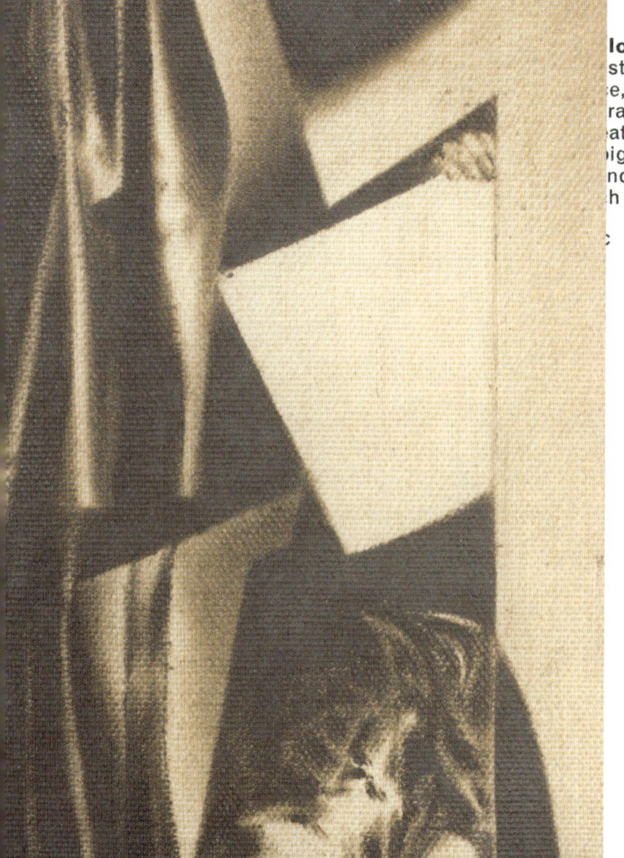

USSF

lopment and Service

st Soviet air-to-air missile in currer
e, 'Ash' is normally carried as a 'mi
ra-red and radar homing versions k
ather fighters of the Soviet Air Forc
ig Tupolev Tu-28P twin-jet intercept
nderwing attachments for two missile
h type.

Asroc (RUR-5A)

Anti-submarine rocket. In service.

Prime contractor: Honeywell Inc.
Powered by: Naval Propellant Plant
solid-propellant rocket motor.
Airframe: Cylindrical aluminium body, made in
two halves and joining torpedo at front to motor
at rear. Cruciform tail-fins.
Guidance and Control: Missile follows
unguided ballistic trajectory, after launch
towards target position predicted by shipboard
sonar. Acoustic-homing torpedo warhead, or
unguided nuclear depth charge.
Warhead: Alternative warheads include the
General Electric Mk 44 Model 0 high-speed
acoustic-homing torpedo, Aerojet-General
Mk 46 Model 0 advanced acoustic-homing
torpedo, Honeywell Mk 46 Model 1, or a nuclear
depth charge developed by the Naval Weapons
Center and Honeywell.
Length: 15ft 0in (4.57m).
Body diameter: 1ft 0in (0.30m).
Fin span: 2ft 6in (0.76m).
Launch weight: 1,000lb (450kg).
Range: 1-6 miles (1.6-9km).

Development and Service

Asroc development began in June 1956, and
production was started three years later
after successful firing trials. The weapon
has been operational on destroyers, escort
ships and cruisers of the US Navy since the
Summer of 1961 and also arms the Japanese
destroyer *Amatsukaze.*

In action, the target submarine's course,
range and speed are worked out by shipboard computer within seconds of its detection by sonar. The eight-round standard
launcher, or two-round modified Terrier
missile launcher is aligned into firing position. The ship's commander then selects
the missile with the most appropriate warhead and fires it. En route to the target, the
Asroc sheds its rocket motor at a pre-
determined signal. Later, a steel band hold-
ing the airframe together is severed by a
small explosive charge. The airframe then
falls away, allowing the depth charge to
drop into the water or the torpedo to be
lowered to the surface by parachute.

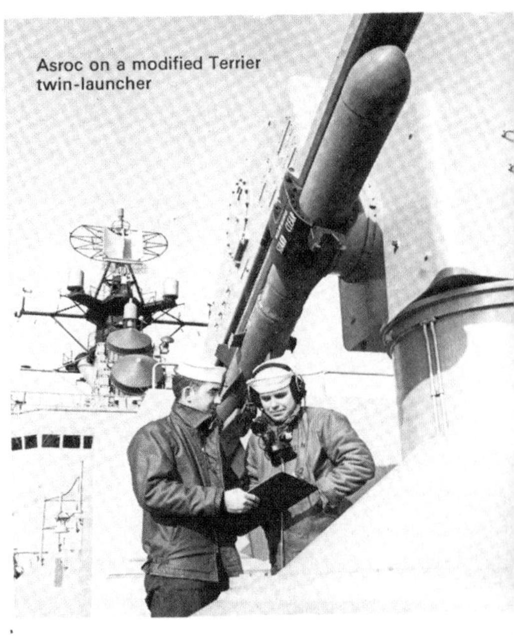

Asroc on a modified Terrier
twin-launcher

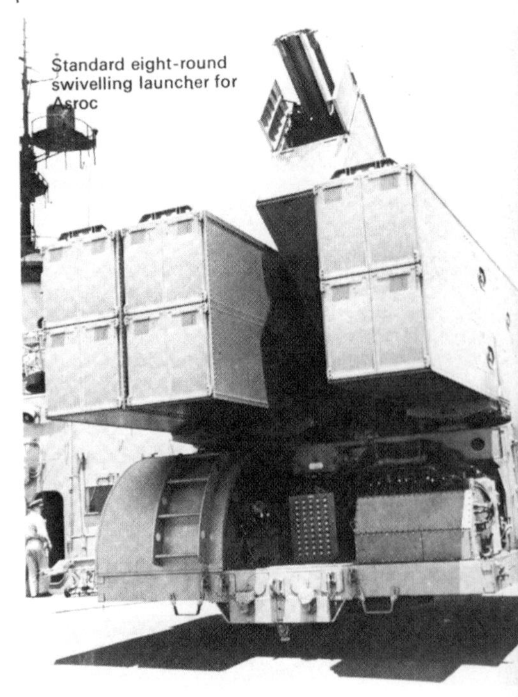

Standard eight-round
swivelling launcher for
Asroc

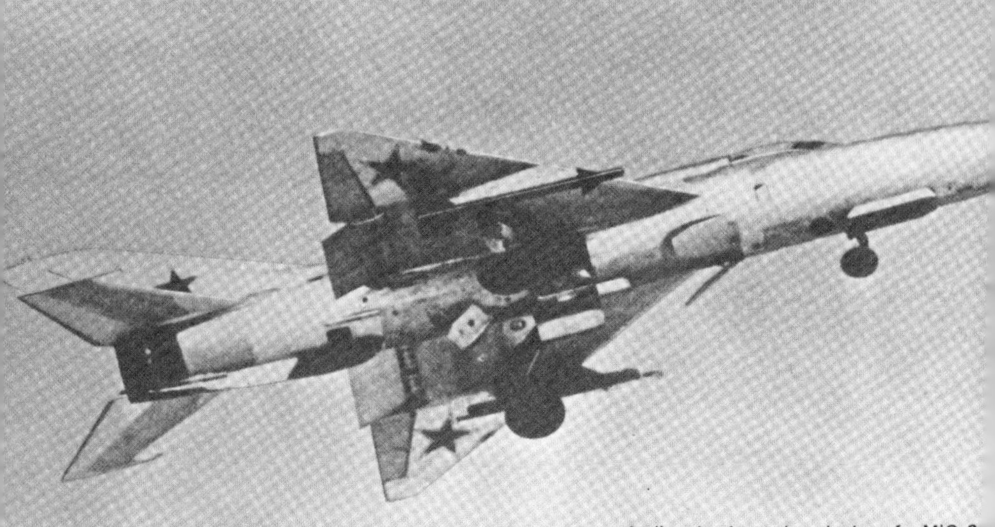

Atoll under the starboard wing of a MiG-2

Atoll

USS

Air-to-air missile. In service.

Powered by: Solid-propellant rocket motor.
Airframe: Cylindrical body. Cruciform triangular
control surfaces near nose, indexed in line with
fixed cruciform tail-fins.
Guidance and Control: Infra-red homing
guidance. Control by cruciform foreplanes and
small gyroscopically-controlled tab at tip of
trailing-edge of each tail-fin.
Warhead: High-explosive.
Length: 9ft 2in (2.80m).
Body diameter: 4.72in (12cm).
Fin span: 1ft 8¾in (0.53m).

Development and Service
Standard armament on Soviet Air Fo
and export versions of the MiG-21, 'A'
is similar to the American Sidewinder (p
133) in configuration, size and guida
system. It can be assumed that it is equ
like the US weapon in performance
operational limitations. A number of o
aircraft have been seen carrying 'Atolls'
underwing mountings, including the Y
28P.

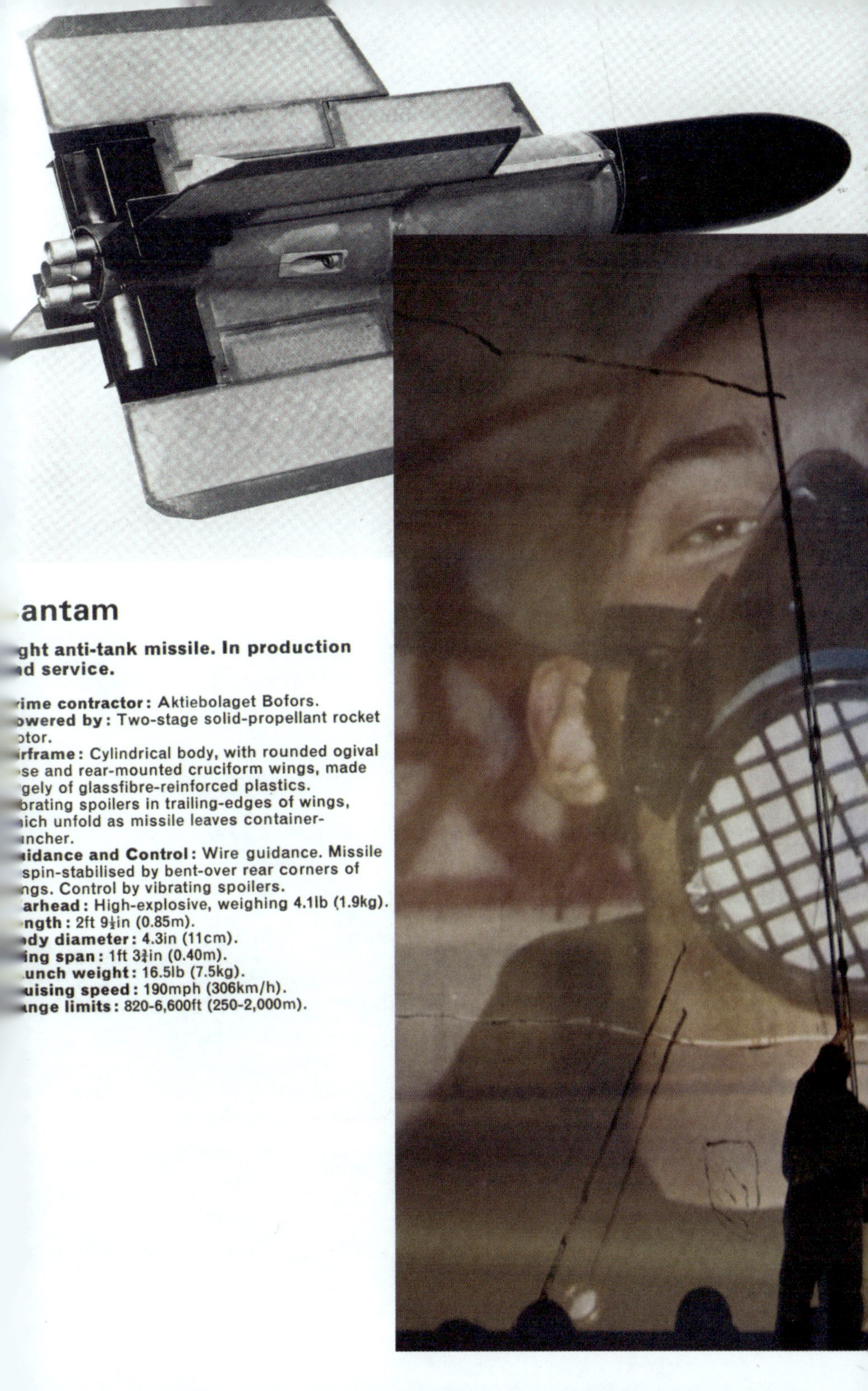

antam

**ght anti-tank missile. In production
d service.**

rime contractor: Aktiebolaget Bofors.
owered by: Two-stage solid-propellant rocket
otor.
irframe: Cylindrical body, with rounded ogival
se and rear-mounted cruciform wings, made
gely of glassfibre-reinforced plastics.
brating spoilers in trailing-edges of wings,
ich unfold as missile leaves container-
uncher.
uidance and Control: Wire guidance. Missile
spin-stabilised by bent-over rear corners of
ngs. Control by vibrating spoilers.
arhead: High-explosive, weighing 4.1lb (1.9kg).
ngth: 2ft 9½in (0.85m).
dy diameter: 4.3in (11cm).
ing span: 1ft 3¾in (0.40m).
unch weight: 16.5lb (7.5kg).
uising speed: 190mph (306km/h).
nge limits: 820–6,600ft (250–2,000m).

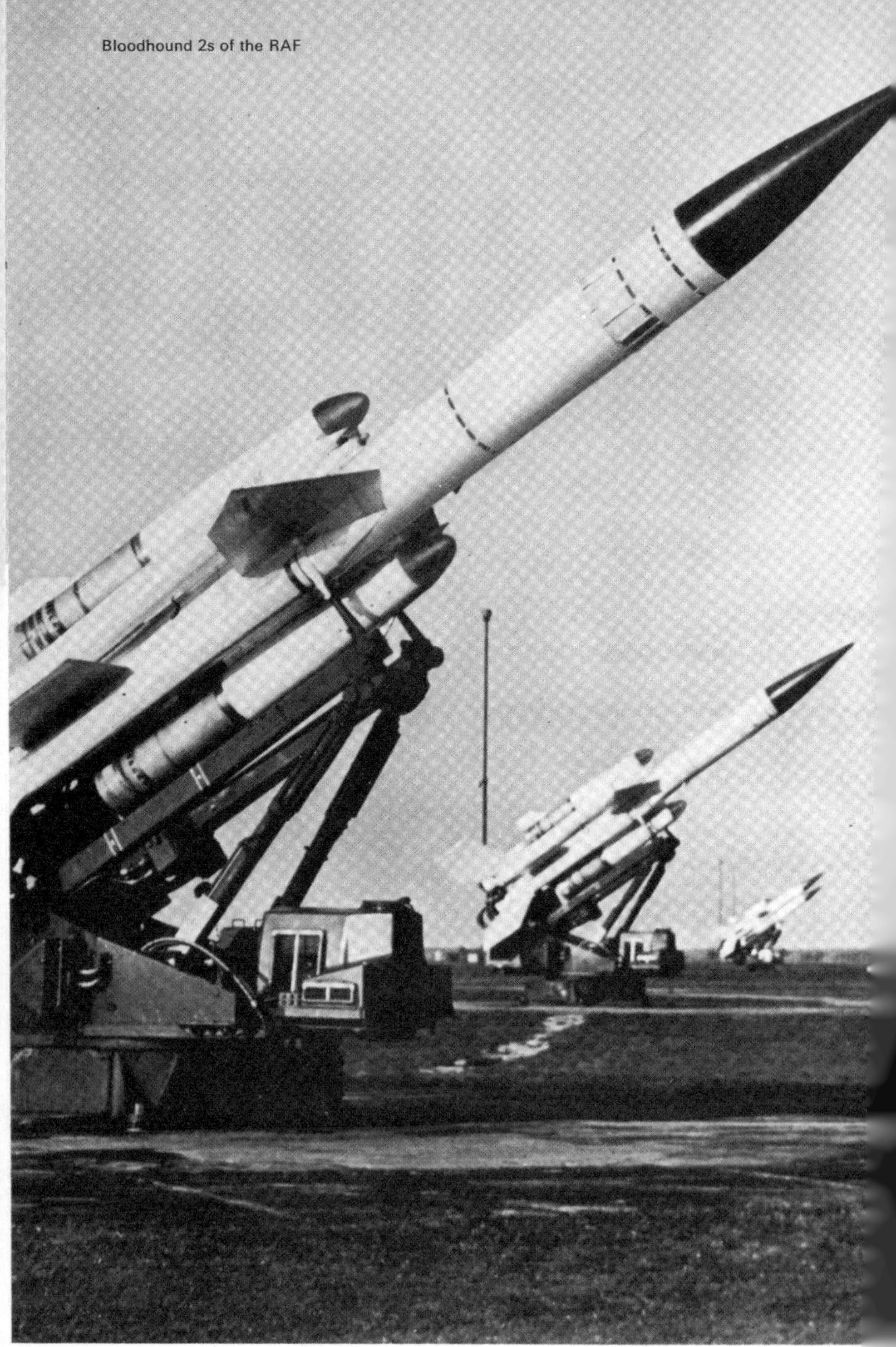
Bloodhound 2s of the RAF

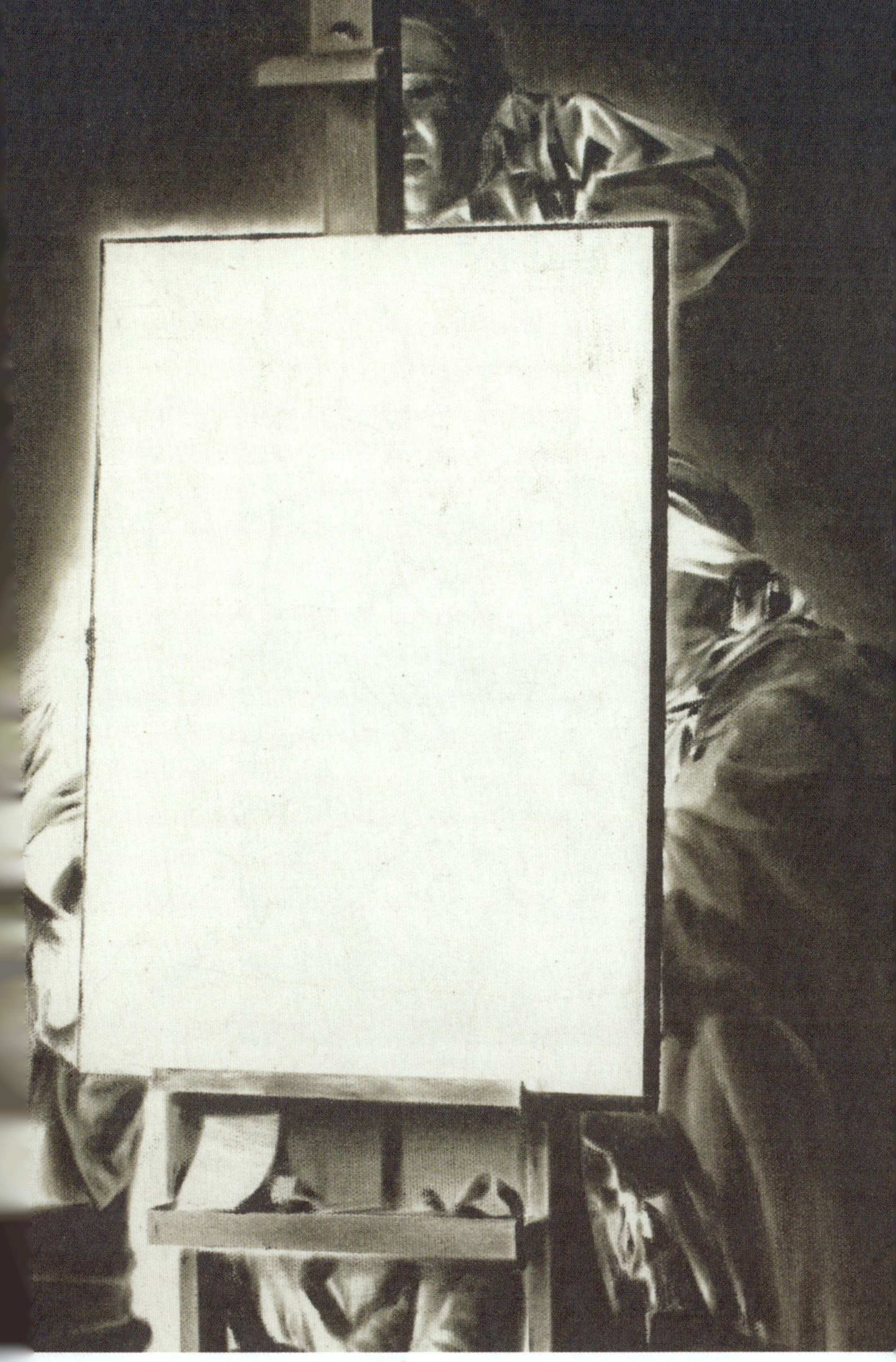

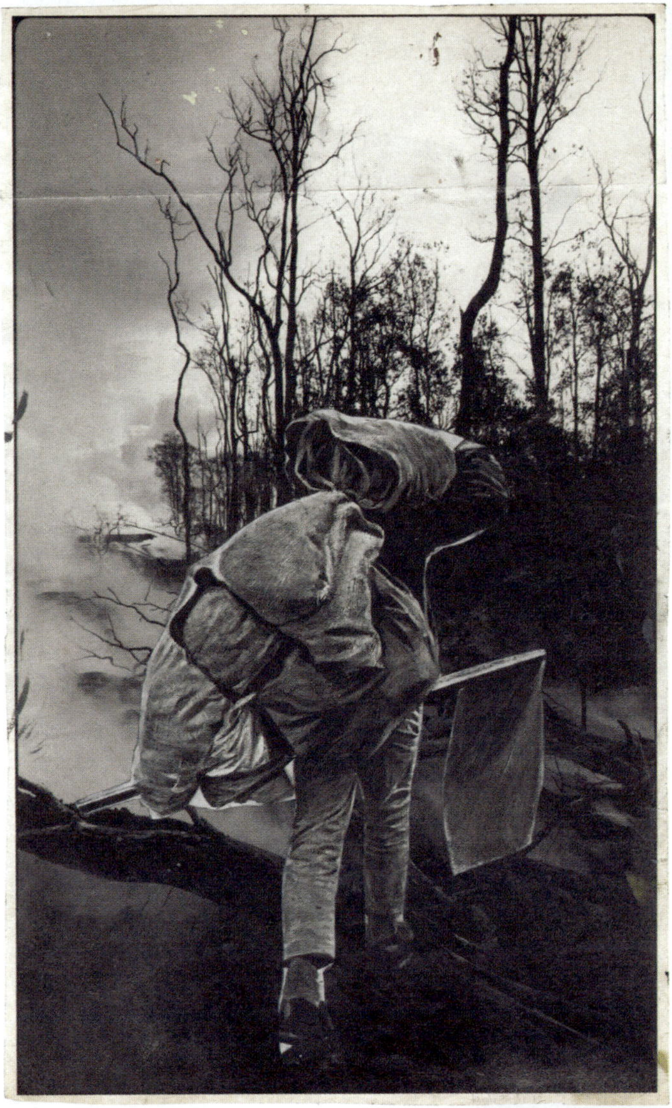

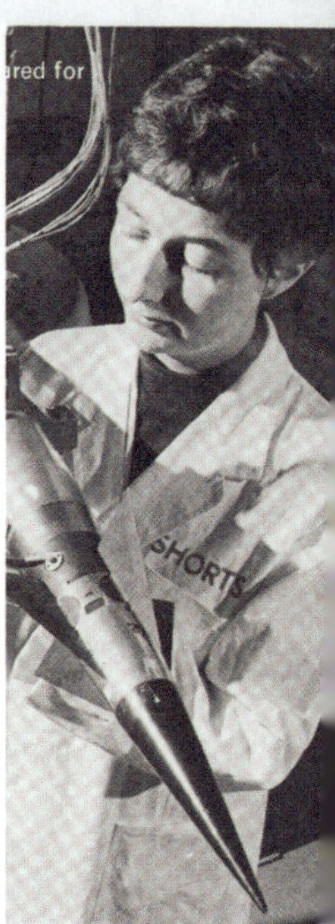

...ared for

shoulder-fired launcher

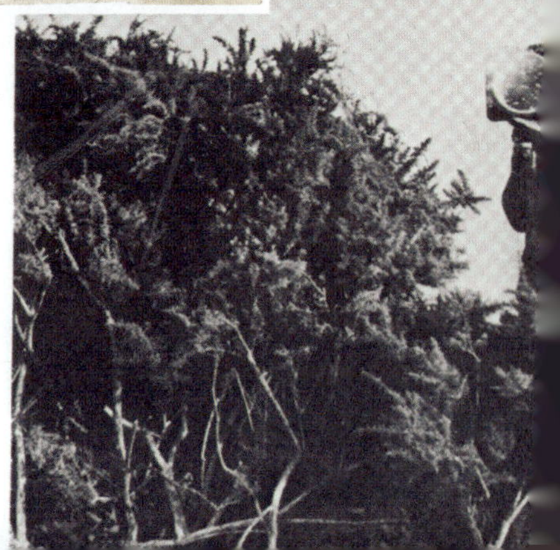

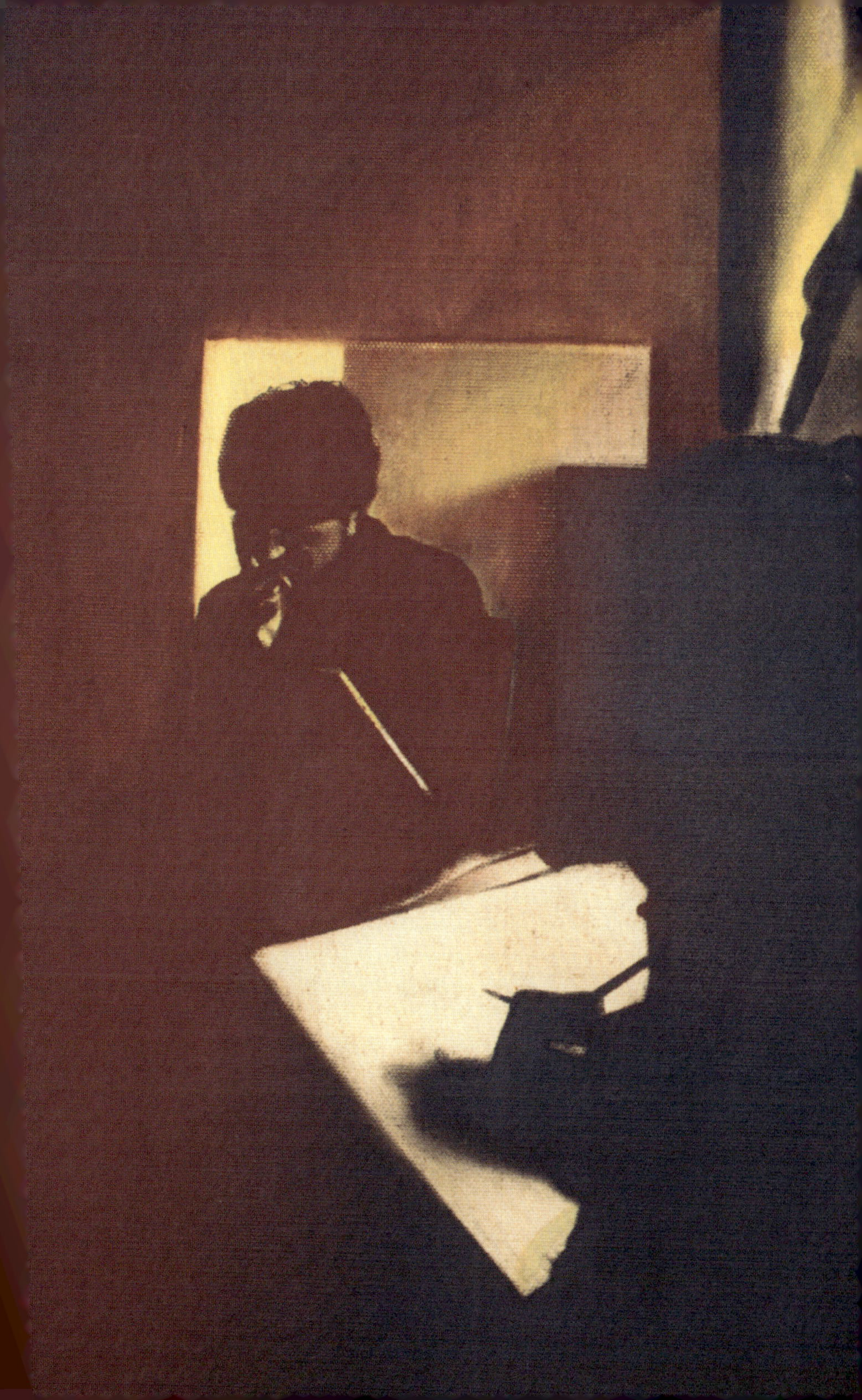

ability to penetrate to their assigned targets.
The final stage, before responsibility for the

crews being trained, for low-level penetration
'under the enemy radar cover'. By 1972, only
Nos 27 and 617 Squadrons, equipped with
campton, remained opera-
teel.

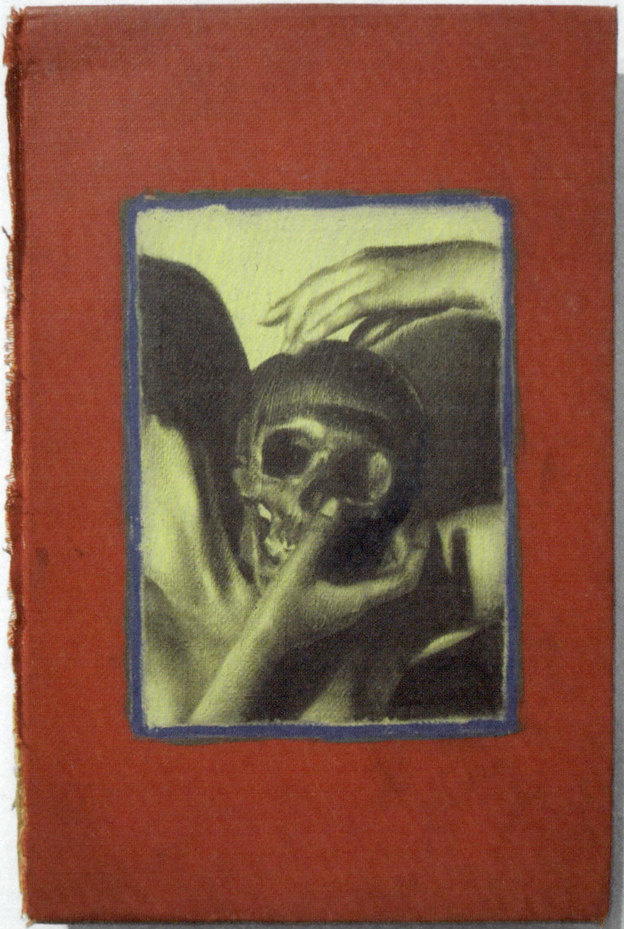

USA 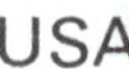

da. These demonstrated
uld be integrated into
(semi-automatic ground
nce system, which located
over the North American
directed on to them the
es most likely to ensure
and that it could intercep
at heights far above those
emporary combat aircraf
ssile operated. The origi
sion of Bomarc became
ecember 1960, but wa
five years by the muc
B, as described above
duced a solid-propellar
the former liquid-prope
werful ramjets and Wes
homing effective at a
evel to 100,000ft (30,500m
me almost instantaneou
ssile site could provid
an area of about 500,0
km²). On March 23, 196
epted a Regulus 2 supe
at a height of 100,000
rom its launcher. Missile
operational at five site
A. Two Canadian squa
ed to disband in 1972.

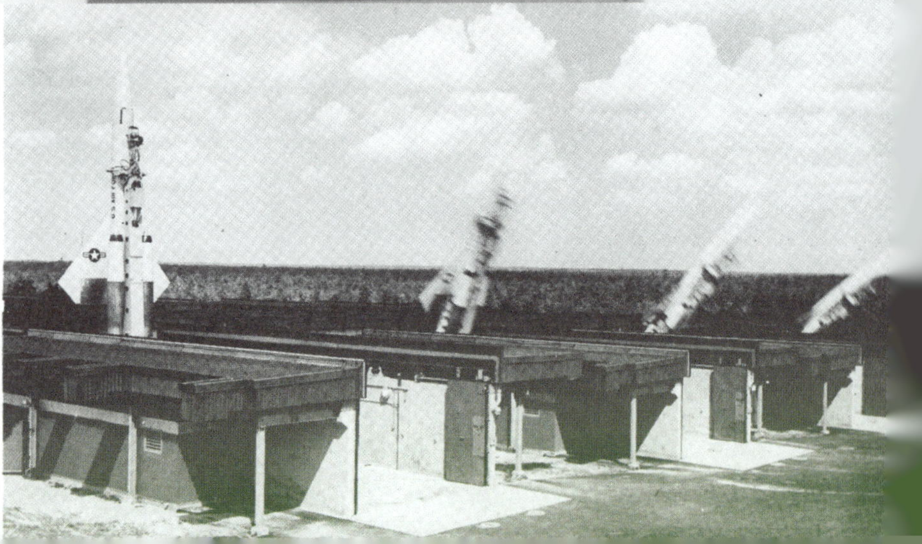

Bulldog

USA

Tactical air-to-surface missile. Under development.

Development and Service
Under US Navy contract, Texas Instruments Inc is developing guidance and control packages to adapt the Bullpup missile (page 23) into a laser-guided weapon named Bull-dog. In operation, the target would be 'illuminated' by a laser device. An electro-optical seeker in the Bulldog would then pick up and home on laser energy reflected from the target. The Naval Weapons Center, China Lake, is responsible for flight tests of the missile.

Bullpup A (AGM-12B/E)

USA

Air-to-surface tactical missile. Inservice.

Prime contractors: Martin Marietta Corporation/ Maxson Electronics Corporation/Kongsberg Vaapenfabrikk.
Powered by : Thiokol LR58-2 storableliquid-propellant rocket motor, of 12,000lb (5,440kg) st.
Airframe: Cylindrical body with pointed ogival nose and tapered tail. Rear-mounted cruciform wings indexed in line with cruciform delta control surfaces on nose-cone.
Guidance and Control: Radio command guidance. Control by foreplanes.
Warhead: High-explosive, weighing 250lb (113kg).
Length: 10ft 6in (3.20m).
Body diameter: 1ft 0in (30cm).
Wing span: 3ft 1in (0.94m).
Launch weight: 571lb (260kg).
Cruising speed: Mach 1.8.
Max range: 7 miles (11km).

Development and Service
Bullpup was conceived originally, under the US Navy designation ASM-N-7, as a simple weapon built around a standard 250lb bomb and powered by a solid-propellant motor developed by the Navy. The pilot of the launch aircraft steered it in flight by movements of a hand switch in the cockpit, using tracking flares above and below the rocket nozzle as a reference in order to keep Bullpup on a line-of-sight path to the target. This original version became operational on April 25, 1959, and was later redesignated AGM-12A. It was superseded by the AGM-2B (formerly ASM-N-7A) for the US Navy, with storable liquid-propellant engine, improved warhead and extended range control; and the USAF AGM-12B (GAM-83A) with a modified guidance system which permitted pilots to make their attacks from an offset position in relation to the target.

Production was undertaken initially by Martin Marietta, who had developed Bullpup A from design study to flight test in under two years. Maxson was brought in as second-source supplier to meet demands for the weapon, and eventually took over all US Bullpup production. Licence manufacture in Europe was handled by a consortium led by AS Kongsberg Vaapenfabrikk of Norway,

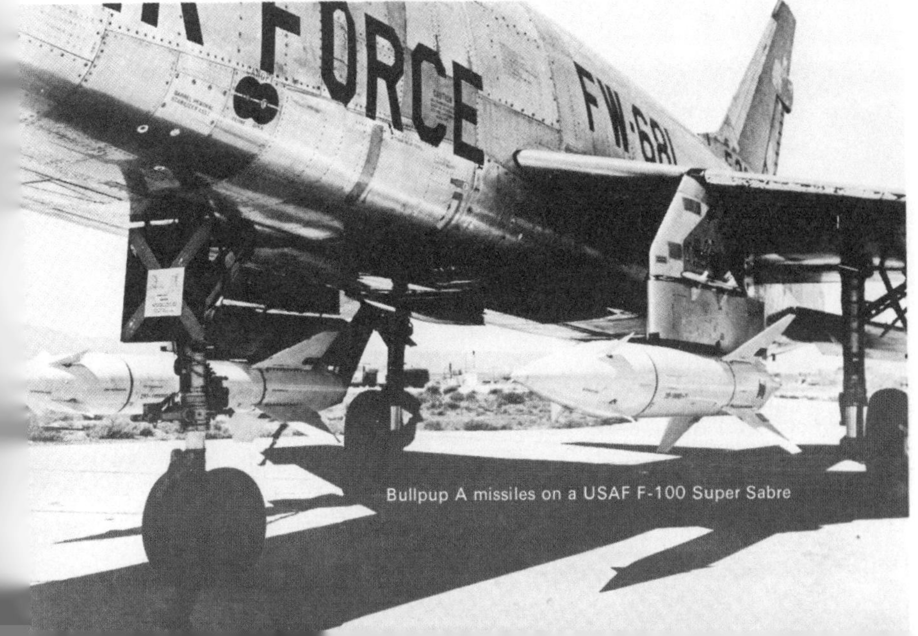
Bullpup A missiles on a USAF F-100 Super Sabre

for the armed services of Denmark, Greece, Norway, Turkey and the UK. Aircraft armed with Bullpup have included the US Navy's A-4, A-5, A-6, A-7, F-8E and P-3B; the USAF's F-4, F-100 and F-105, and the Royal Navy's Scimitar and Buccaneer aircraft.

The final version of Bullpup, produced on a limited basis by Martin Marietta for the USAF, was the AGM-12E with an anti-personnel warhead for use in Vietnam.

Bullpup B (AGM-12C/D) USA

Air-to-surface tactical missile. In service.

Data apply to AGM-12C.
Prime contractor: Martin Marietta Corporation/Maxson Electronics Corporation.
Powered by: Thiokol LR62 storable liquid-propellant rocket motor.
Airframe: Basically-cylindrical body, tapering towards nose and tail. Pointed ogival nose-cone, with cruciform delta control surfaces, mounted on front of body. Rear-mounted cruciform wings indexed in line with foreplanes.
Guidance and Control: Radio command guidance. Control by foreplanes.
Warhead: High-explosive (AGM-12C), or alternative high-explosive or nuclear (AGM-12D).
Length: 13ft 7in (4.14m).
Body diameter: 1ft 6in (45cm).
Wing span: 4ft 0in (1.22m).
Launch weight: 1,785lb (810kg).
Range: 10 miles (16.5km).

Development and Service
Bullpup A proved such an effective weapon that the US Navy sponsored the development of a version with much extended capabilities, built around a 1,000lb (454kg) high-explosive warhead. Known as Bullpup B, this went into production for the Navy under the designation ASM-N-7B, changed after a time to AGM-12C, and augmented rather than replaced Bullpup A. The USAF acquired a version designated AGM-12D (originally GAM-83B), with interchangeable nuclear and high-explosive warheads.

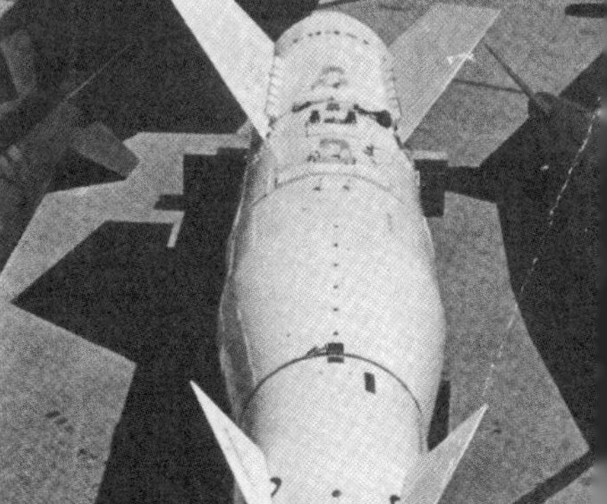

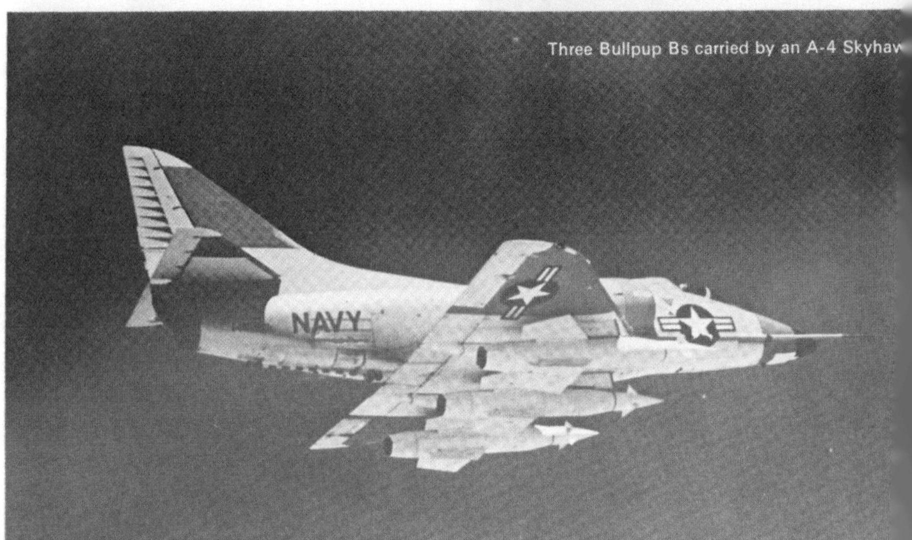

Three Bullpup Bs carried by an A-4 Skyhaw

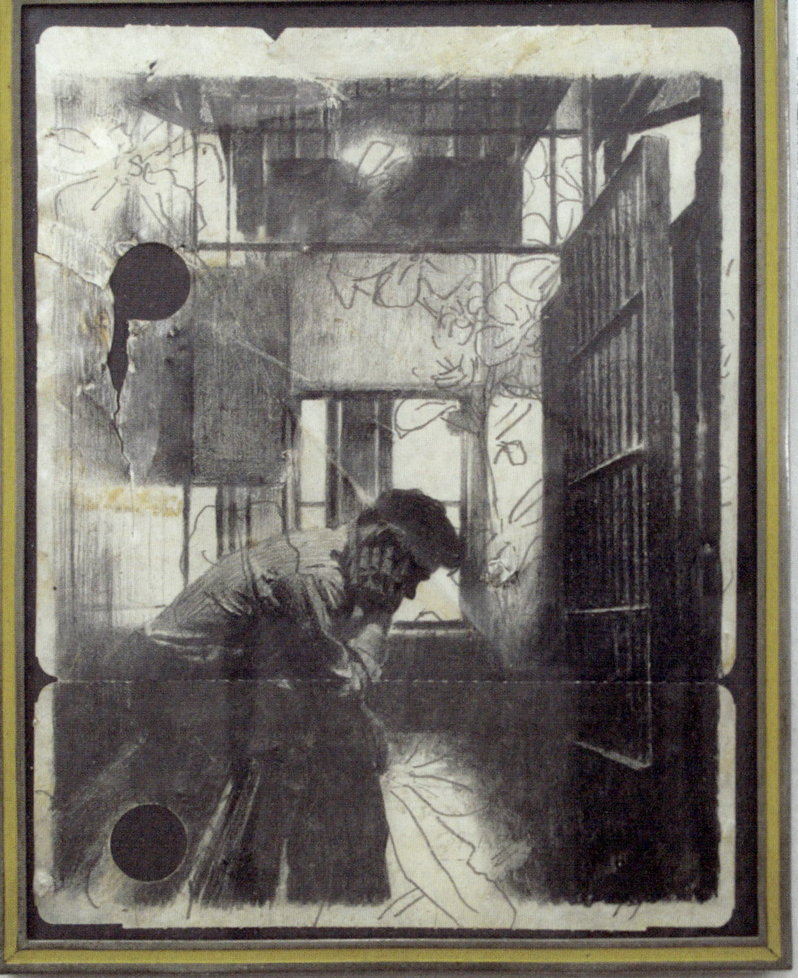

Chapa

**Surface-‍
roductio**

Prime co
Aeronutro

Develop
 Chapar
veapon
missiles
ir role.
eady-to-
s norma
Army   M
ehicle);
railer-m
 semi-m
done by

Chinese ICBM

Land-based intercontinental ballistic missile. Under development.

Powered by: Liquid-propellant rocket motors.
Warhead: Nuclear.
Range (estimated): 6,000 miles (9,600km).

Development and Service

China achieved its first, successful test firing of an ICBM late in 1970. The range of the missile, which carried an inert warhead, was restricted deliberately to 2,000 miles (3,200km), so that the test could be confined within the nation's own borders; but the eventual production version is expected to have a range of at least three times that distance. Its engines will probably be liquid-propellant rockets, although a factory has already been established to produce solid-propellant motors for second-generation long-range missiles. The US Defense Department has remarked that China is unlikely to begin deployment of ICBMs before 1973-75, and that even then the missiles are not expected to carry penetration aids. Such aids would require a detailed knowledge of the operating characteristics of America's Safeguard ABM system (page 104). An extensive radar and instrumentation system would also be needed for even the simple technique of in-flight fragmentation of the missile's fuel tanks. Nonetheless, it is estimated that China could have a force of 10-25 nuclear-tipped ICBMs operational two or three years after the initial deployment. Twenty-five such missiles launched against the USA with 3-megaton warheads would have the potential to cause 11 or 12 million fatalities in the absence of an efficient ABM system, assuming 40 per cent reliability in reaching their objectives.

Chinese MRBM

Medium-range ballistic missile. In production and service.

Warhead: Nuclear.
Range: over 1,000 miles (1,600km).

Development and Service

US Secretary of Defense Melvin R Laird said in February 1970 that China was expected to deploy its first medium-range ballistic missiles (MRBMs) at any time' and that 80-100 of the weapons would probably be operational by the mid-seventies. Subsequent reports have suggested that such missiles are emplaced at three operational sites in Tibet, with two more sites under construction in the Winter of 1970-71, some 15,000ft (4,575m) above sea level. The warheads for long-range rockets have been under rapid development since the first Chinese explosion of a 20-kiloton nuclear device at Lop Nor in the Sinkiang desert on October 16, 1964. The fourth such test, in October 1966, was claimed to involve delivery of the warhead to a target area by a missile—thought to have been based on a Soviet weapon like 'Sandal' (page 109). The satellites put into orbit by China in 1970-71 were probably launched by vehicles related to the now-operational MRBM.

Cobra 2000 (BO 810)

Lightweight anti-tank missile. In production and service.

Prime contractor: Messerschmitt-Bölkow-Blohm GmbH.
Powered by: Solid-propellant rocket motor. Non-jettisonable solid-propellant booster rocket.
Airframe: Cylindrical fibre-paper body, with pointed conical nose. Large plastic cruciform wings, each with spoiler. Booster mounted under body.
Warhead: Hollow charge, weighing 5.5lb (2.5kg) and able to penetrate more than 18.7in (475mm) of steel armour.
Length: 3ft 1½in (0.95m).
Body diameter: 3.9in (10cm).
Wing span: 1ft 7in (0.48m).
Launch weight: 22.5lb (10.2kg).
Max speed: 190mph (306km/h).
Range limits: 1,310–6,560ft (400–2,000m).

Development and Service

This typical one-man anti-tank weapon system comprises the Cobra missile, a control box and cable links; up to eight rounds can be fired selectively from a single control box. No launcher is required, as the missile is supported on the ground by the lid which covers its rear end during transport. The control box is completely self-contained and carries the firing button and control stick.

More than 120,000 Cobras have been delivered to the Danish, German, Italian, Pakistani and Turkish armies, the current version being known as the Cobra 2000 to indicate the extension of its maximum range to 2,000m.

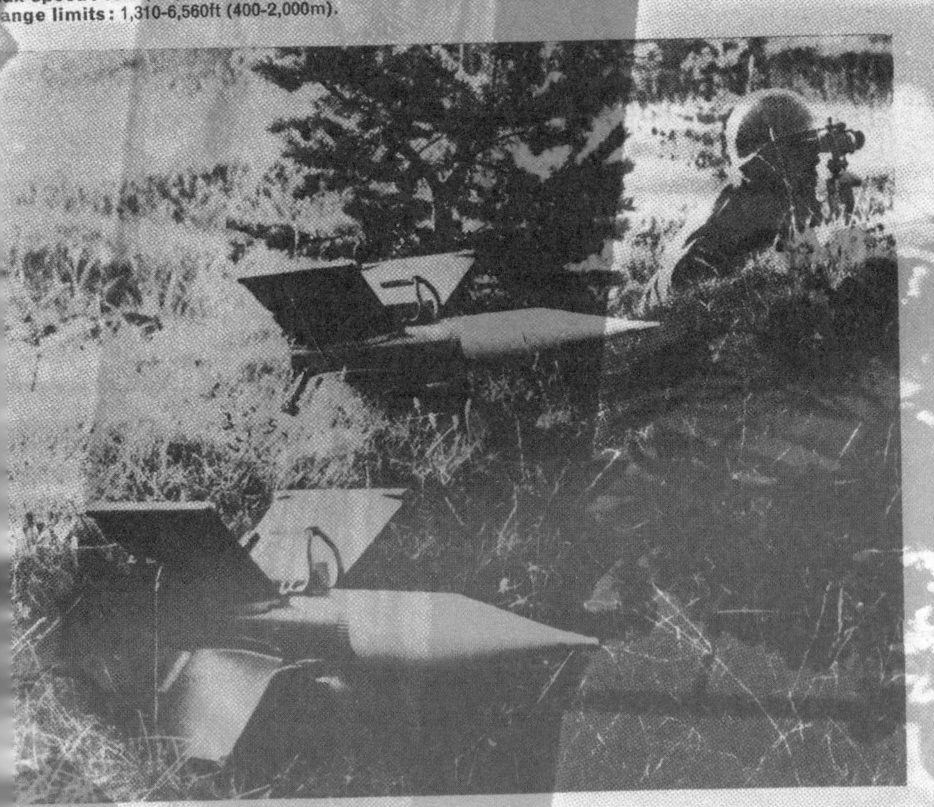

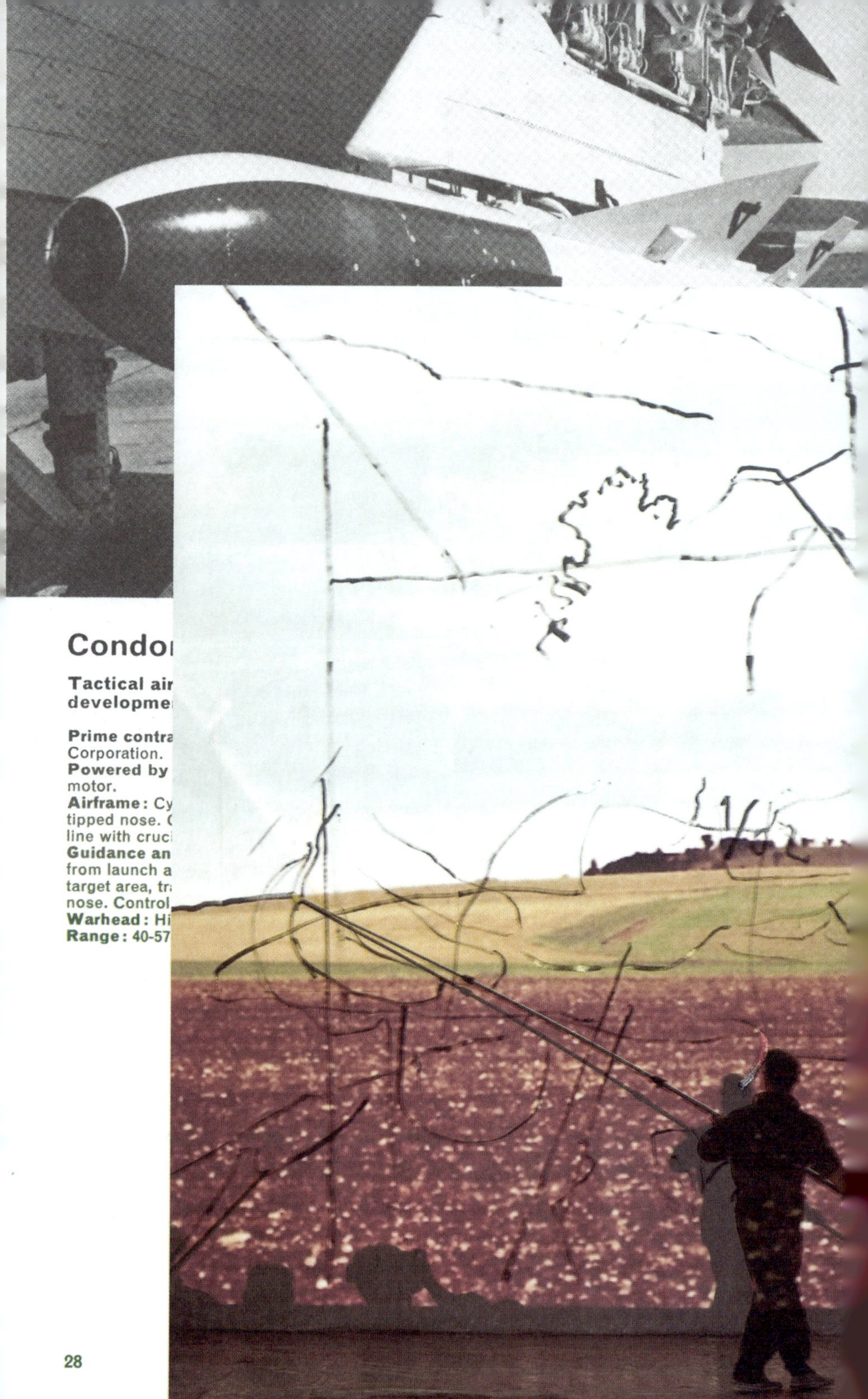

Condo

Tactical air
developme

Prime contra
Corporation.
Powered by
motor.
Airframe: Cy
tipped nose. C
line with cruci
Guidance an
from launch a
target area, tra
nose. Control
Warhead: Hi
Range: 40-57

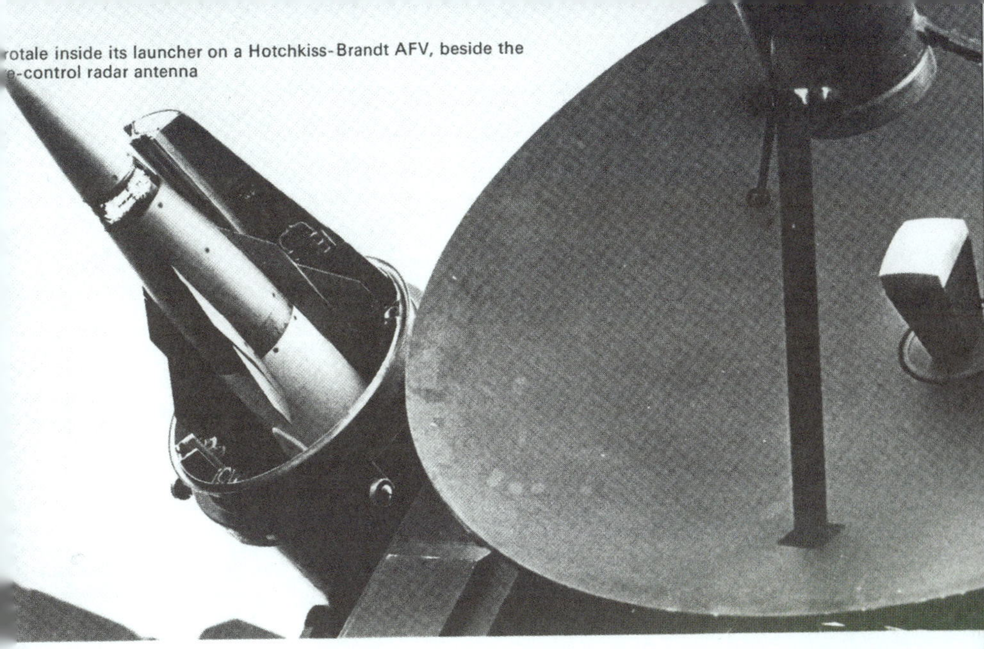

Crotale/Cactus

France

Close-range surface-to-air missile. In production

Prime contractor: SA Engins Matra.
Powered by: Single-stage solid-propellant rocket motor.
Airframe: Slim cylindrical body, with cruciform wings mounted on ogival nose-cone and indexed in line with cruciform tail control surfaces.
Guidance and Control: Radio command guidance. Control by tail surfaces.
Warhead: High-explosive, weighing 33lb (15kg), with infra-red proximity fuse.
Length: 9ft 5¾in (2.89m).
Body diameter: 5.9in (15cm).
Wing span: 1ft 9¼in (0.54m).
Launch weight: 176lb (80kg).
Max speed: Mach 2.3.
Range limits: 1,640ft-5.3 miles (500m-8.5km).

Development and Service

Matra designed this highly-mobile all-weather missile to deal with aircraft flying at speeds up to Mach 1.2 at any height from 165ft (50m) to 9,850ft (3,000m), with a reaction time of only six seconds. First news of the system was given in May 1969, when the South African Defence Minister announced that French companies were developing for his country a surface-to-air weapon known as Cactus. It was revealed subsequently that the prime contractor was Matra and that the same weapon system was known as Crotale in France. Integration with land vehicles was under way by 1969, in which year successful launches were made against target drones. Full production for South Africa and Lebanon was planned for 1972, and the French Government will also take delivery of Crotale systems for airfield defence. The US Army Missile Command is evaluating Crotale as a possible replacement for Chaparral, and Thomson-CSF is adapting the weapon for a ship-based role as part of its Murène system (page 84).

Four Crotale/Cactus missiles are carried in ready-to-fire condition on the standard Hotchkiss-Brandt all-terrain launch vehicle. This carries also a monopulse fire control radar which can track and transmit command signals simultaneously to two missiles. Acquisition after launch is facilitated by an infra-red device which locks on to the missile exhaust. A second vehicle of the same type carries a pulse-Doppler surveillance and target acquisition radar with a range of 11.5 miles (18.5km), and can serve three launch vehicles. Twelve targets can be tracked simultaneously, and 12 missiles can be launched in pairs at six targets in 11 seconds.

Dragon (M47)

Light anti-tank and assault missile. In production.

Prime contractor: McDonnell Douglas Astronautics Company.
Powered by: Several pairs of small solid-propellant rocket motors, in rows around body.
Airframe: Cylindrical body, tapering towards tail and with short ogival nose. Three curved tail-fins which flip open after launch.
Guidance and Control: Wire-guidance, by automatic command-to-line-of-sight system. Control by side-thrusters around body.
Warhead: High-explosive.
Length: 2ft 5.3in (0.74m).
Fin span: 1ft 1in (33cm).
Launch weight: 13.5lb (6.13kg).

Development and Service

Dragon was projected to replace the 90 mm recoilless rifle, to which it is superior in range and accuracy. It was known initially as MAW (Medium Anti-tank/assault Weapon) and is claimed to carry a warhead large enough to destroy most armoured and other infantry targets, while being light enough to be carried and shoulder-fired by one man. In operation, the infantryman first mounts on the missile launch-tube a tracker, embodying the telescopic sight, a sensor device and electronics package. The glass-fibre launch tube forms a sealed container for the missile during transport and storage, and is enlarged at the aft end to accommodate a propellant container and breech. After acquiring the target in the sight, the operator launches the Dragon missile. As long as the sight remains on the target, the tracker will sense the position of the missile relative to the line of sight and transmit signals to maintain or correct the flight path. 'Steering' is achieved by causing the appropriate pairs of rocket motors, or side thrusters, to fire for both propulsion and guidance.

Development of the Dragon weapon system was started in 1964. Manned shoulder-fired tests began in mid-1968, and service testing in 1971. Dragon was expected to enter full production in the 1972 fiscal year, and will probably equip the US Marine Corps as well as the Army.

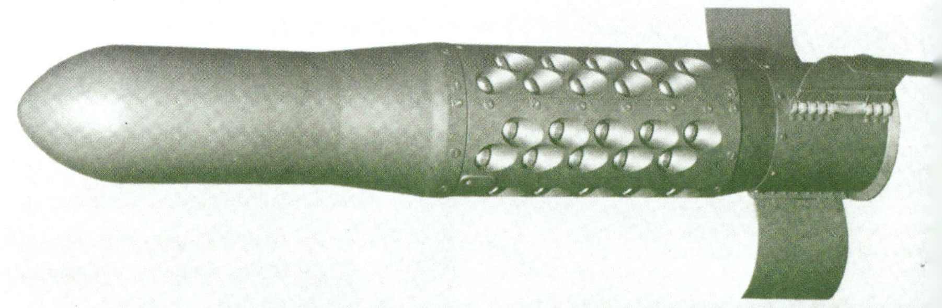

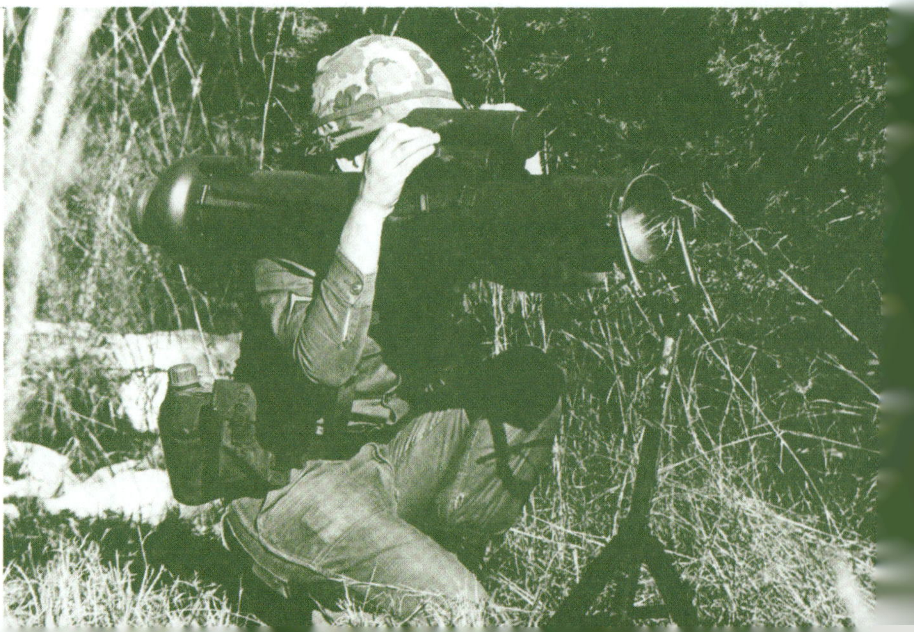

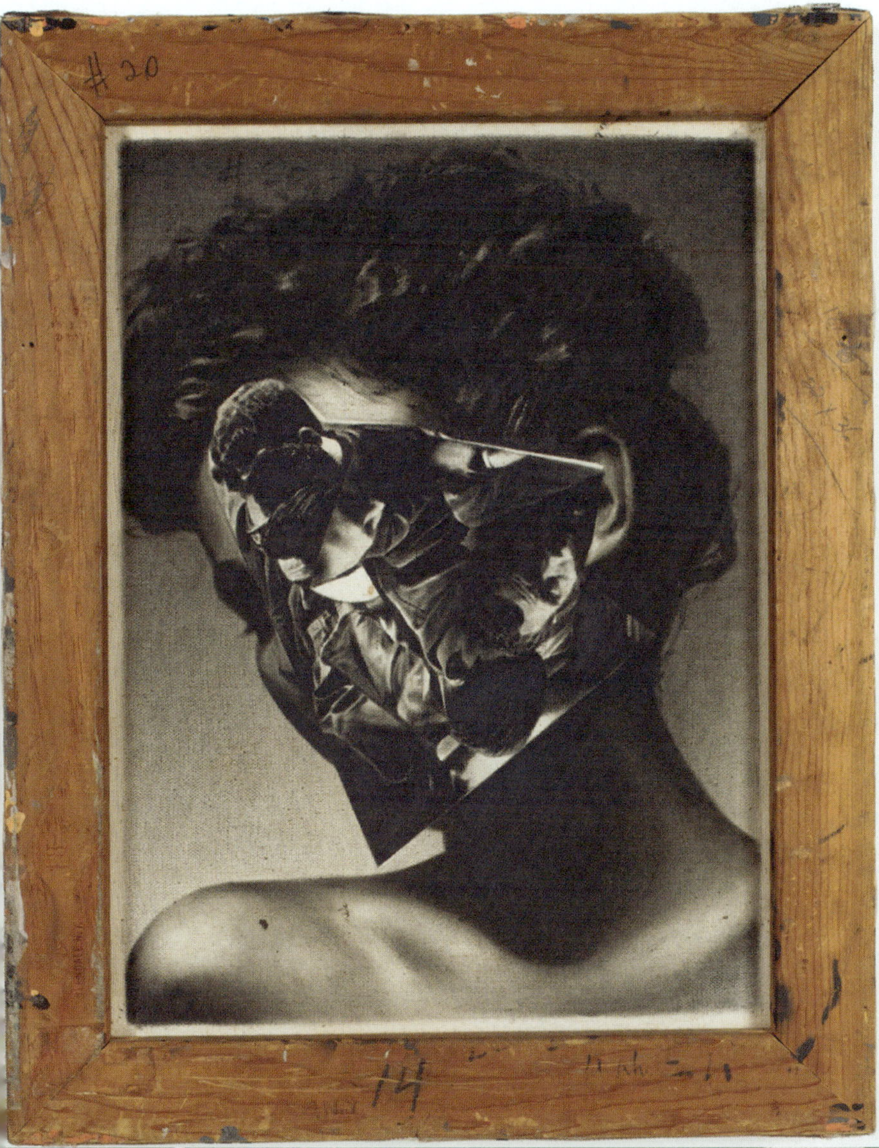

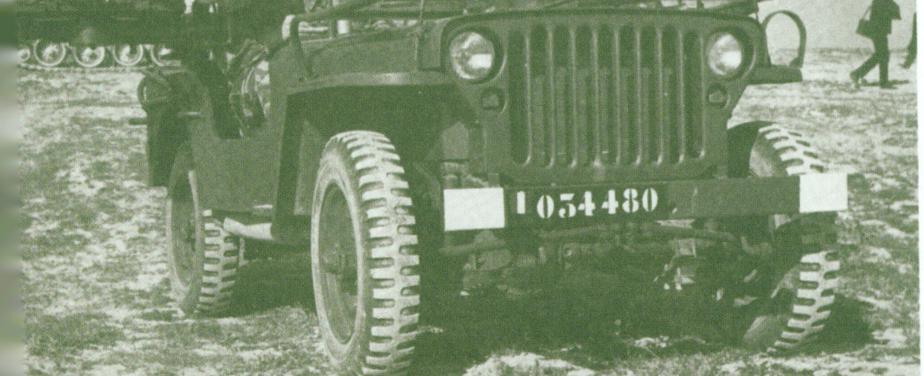
1 054480

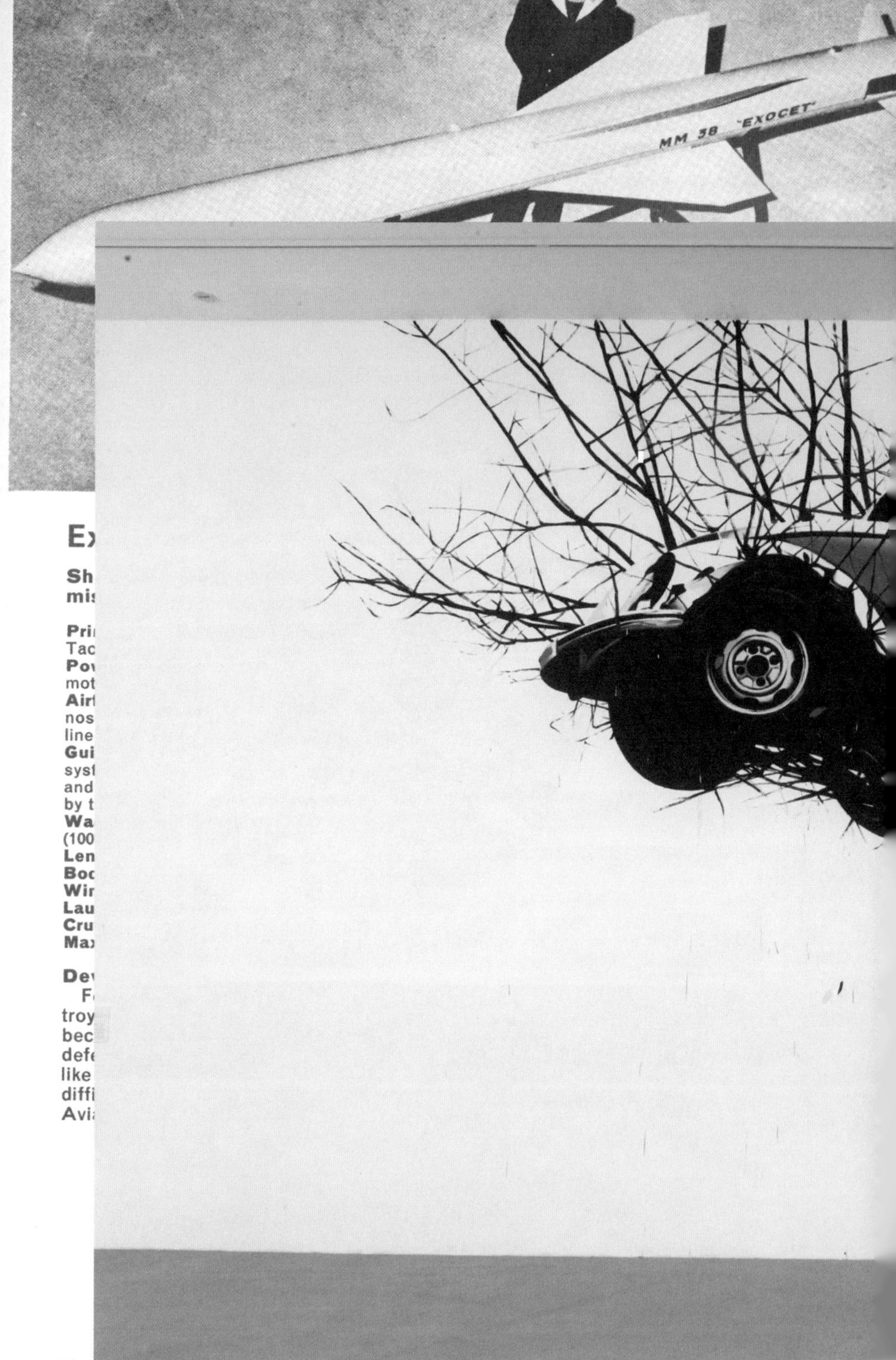

Ex

Sh
mis

Pri
Tac
Pov
mot
Airf
nos
line
Gui
syst
and
by t
Wa
(100
Len
Bod
Win
Lau
Cru
Max

Dev
F
troy
bec
defe
like
diffi
Avi

Falcon (AIM-4A/C/D/H)

Air-to-air missile. In service.

Data apply to AIM-4D
Prime contractor: Hughes Aircraft Company.
Powered by: Thiokol M58-E4 solid-propellant
rocket motor of 6,000lb (2,720kg) st.
Airframe: Cylindrical body with tapered and
rounded glass-tipped nose. Cruciform vanes aft
of nose, indexed in line with long-chord

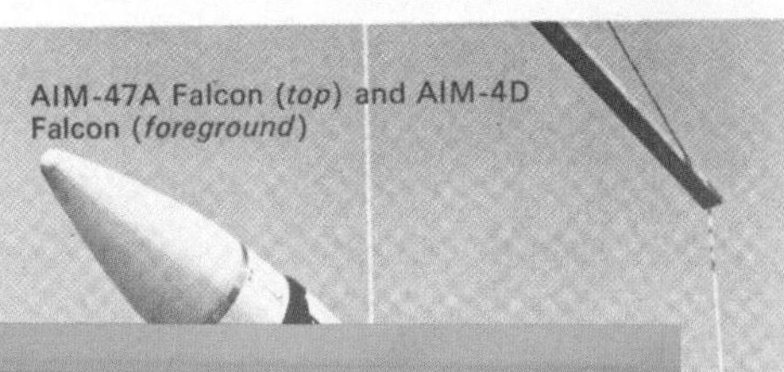

AIM-47A Falcon (*top*) and AIM-4D
Falcon (*foreground*)

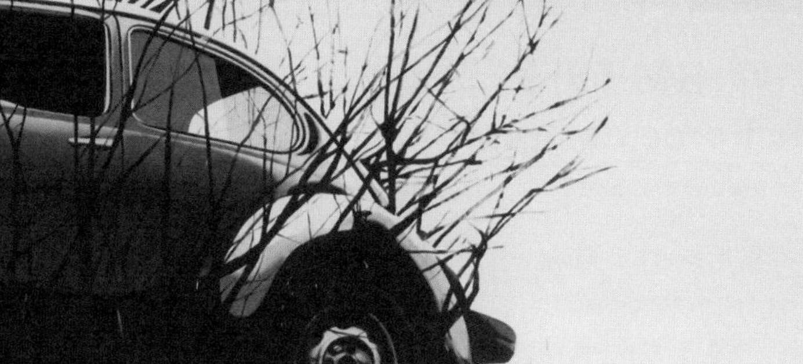

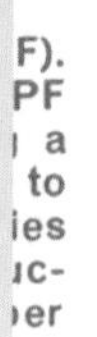

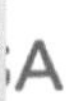

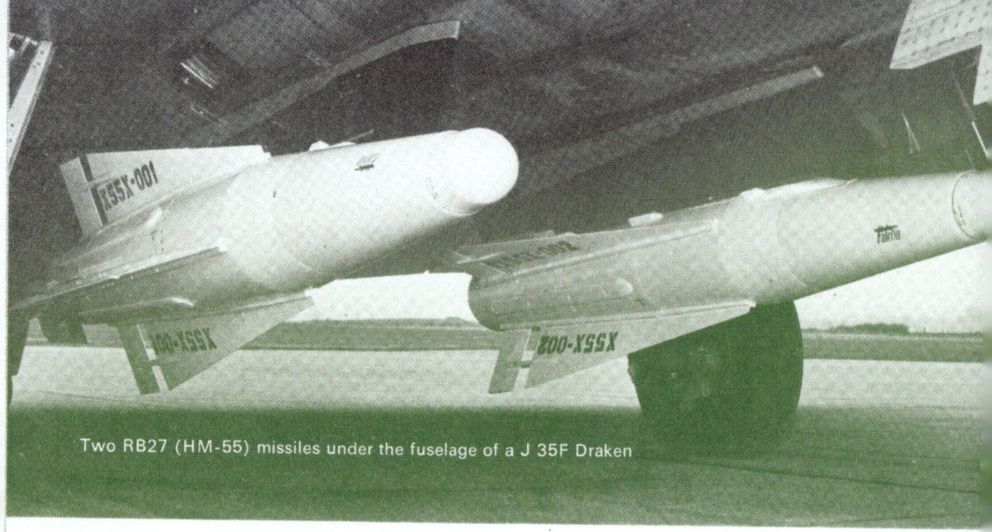
Two RB27 (HM-55) missiles under the fuselage of a J 35F Draken

Falcon (HM-55/HM-58)
(Swedish Air Force designations RB27 and RB28)

USA

Air-to-air missiles. In production and service

Prime contractors: Hughes Aircraft Company/ Saab-Scania Aktiebolag.
Powered by: Single-stage solid-propellant motor.
Guidance and Control: HM-55 has Hughes semi-active radar homing guidance; HM-58 uses infra-red homing system.
Warhead: High-explosive, with proximity fuse.
Length (RB27): 7ft 1in (2.16m).
Max body diameter (RB27): 11in (28cm).
Wing span (RB27): 2ft 0in (0.61m).
Launch weight: RB27: 262lb (119kg), RB28: 134lb (61kg).
Max speed: Mach 3.
Max range: 6.2 miles (10km).

Development and Service
The HM-55 and HM-58 export versions of the Falcon are built under licence in Sweden by Saab-Scania, under the Swedish Air Force designations RB27 and RB28 respectively. In general appearance the HM-55 resembles the AIM-26A Nuclear Falcon (page 86), but has a conventional warhead. Its all-weather guidance system makes possible attack from any direction, including head-on, and its launch speed makes it compatible with Mach 2 aircraft. The Swedish Air Force deploys it on J 35F Draken interceptors in combination with the HM-58. This is an infra-red pursuit-course weapon generally similar to the AIM-4C Falcon (page 33). The Swiss Air Force has also adopted the HM-55 as standard armament for its Mirage III-S fighters.

Firestreak

Air-to-air missile. In service.

Prime contractor: Hawker Siddeley Dynamics Ltd.

Powered by: Solid-propellant rocket motor.

Airframe: Cylindrical metal body, with cruciform wings mounted more than half-way back from nose and indexed in line with cruciform tail control surfaces. Pointed eight-sided glass nose, with two narrow rings of small windows over infra-red optics on fore-part of body.

Guidance and Control: Infra-red homing guidance. Control by tail-fins.

Warhead: High-explosive, weighing 50lb (22.7kg), with proximity fuse.

Length: 10ft 5½in (3.19m).

Body diameter: 8¾in (22.5cm).

Wing span: 2ft 5½in (0.75m).

Launch weight: 300lb (136kg).

Cruising speed: above Mach 2.

Range limits: 0.75-5 miles (1.2-8km).

Development and Service

Although Firestreak is a comparatively complex and expensive weapon, few other air-to-air missiles can offer such a high single-round kill probability. It is said to have achieved a success rate of more than 85 per cent in trials by the RAF and Royal Navy at all altitudes and in all weather conditions. Control is by a proportional navigation system. After the nose-mounted infra-red unit has brought the missile close to the target, two rings of infra-red optics lock on to the enemy aircraft and feed in angular readings to give bearing and range data during the final stage of interception. Firestreak's only limitation is that it must be fired from astern the target—a shortcoming that does not apply to the further-developed Red Top (page 103). It is standard armament on RN Sea Vixen and RAF Lightning interceptors.

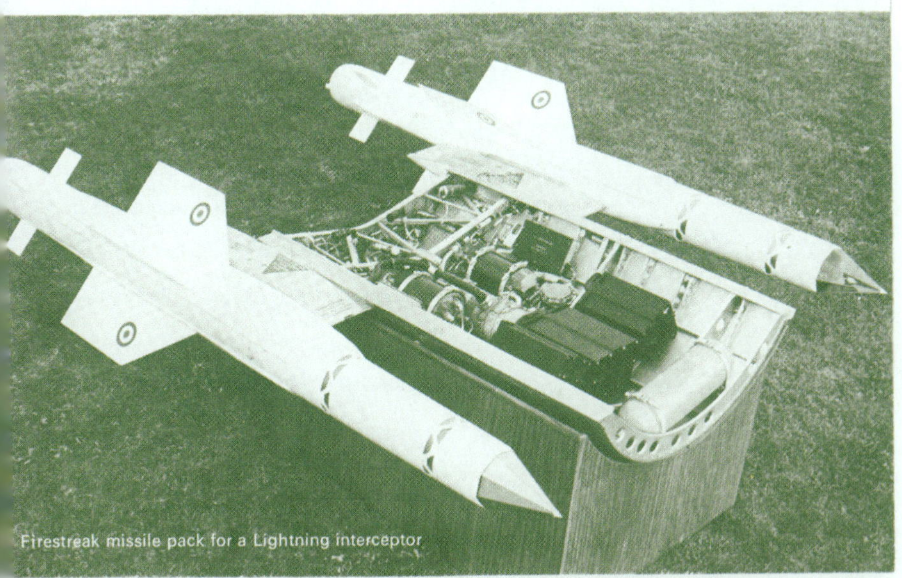

Firestreak missile pack for a Lightning interceptor

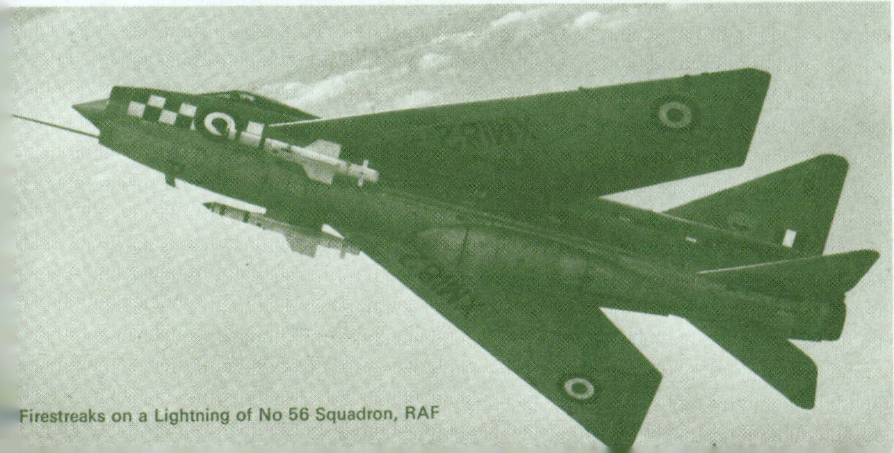

Firestreaks on a Lightning of No 56 Squadron, RAF

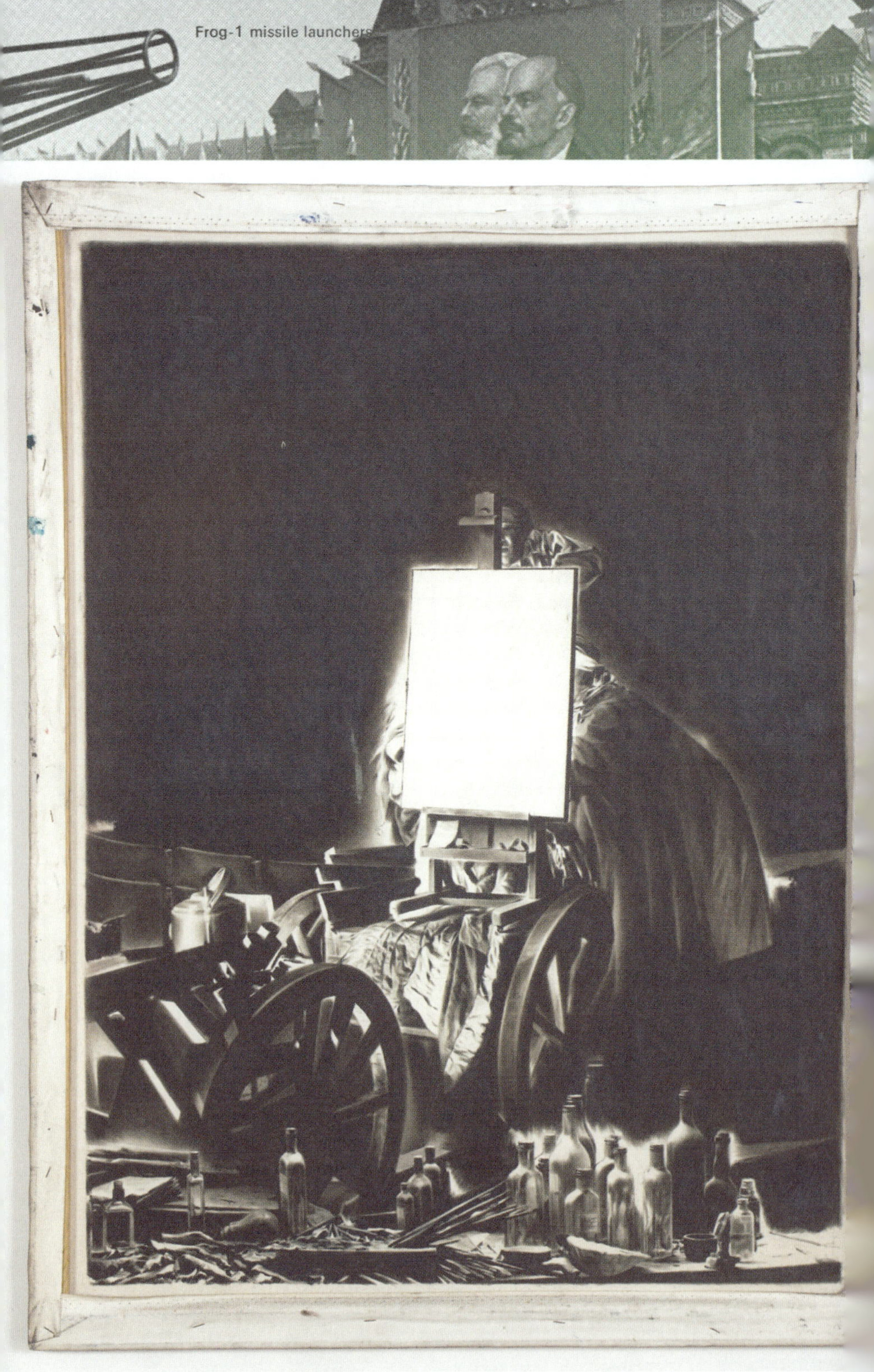

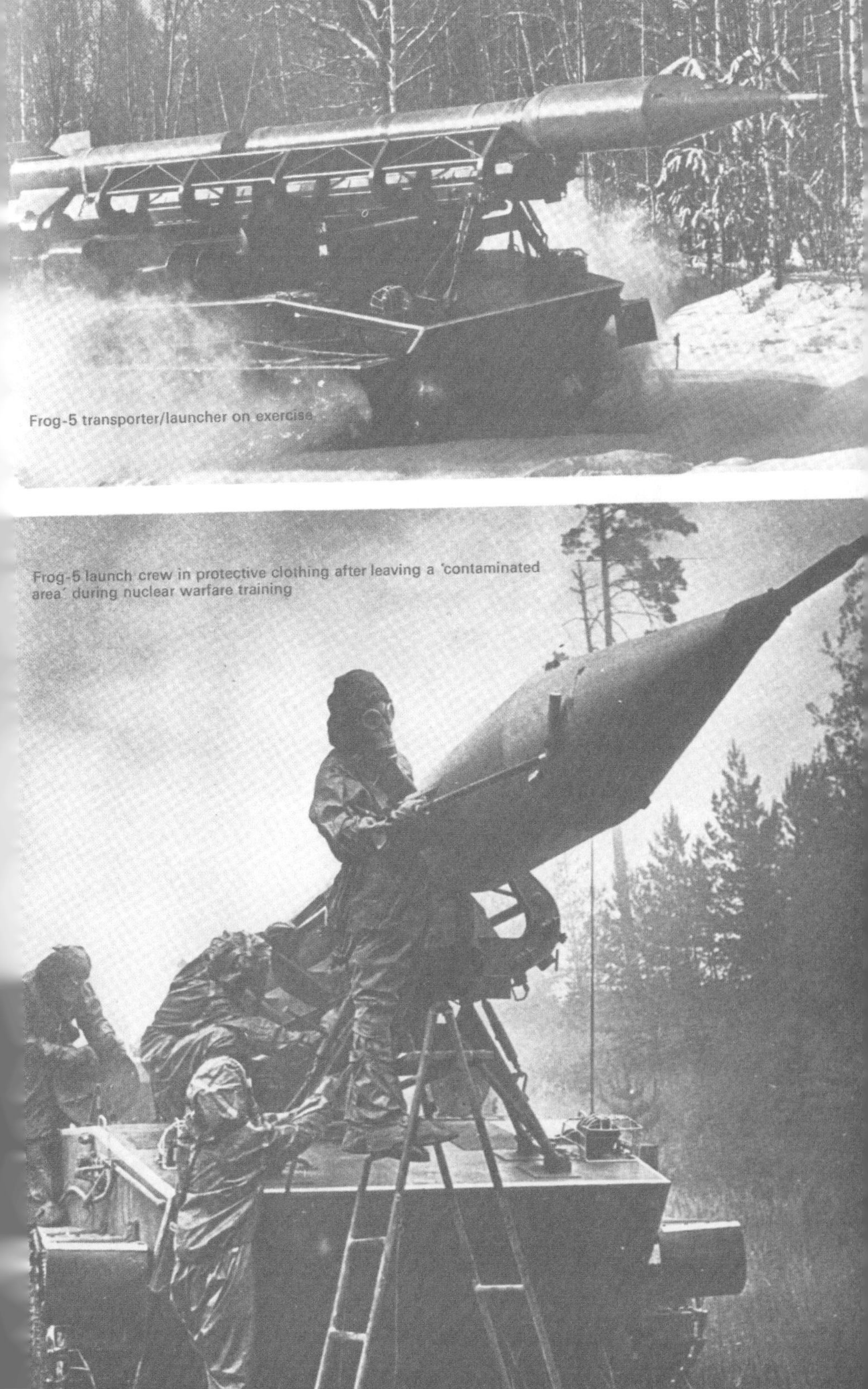

Frog-5 transporter/launcher on exercise

Frog-5 launch crew in protective clothing after leaving a 'contaminated area' during nuclear warfare training

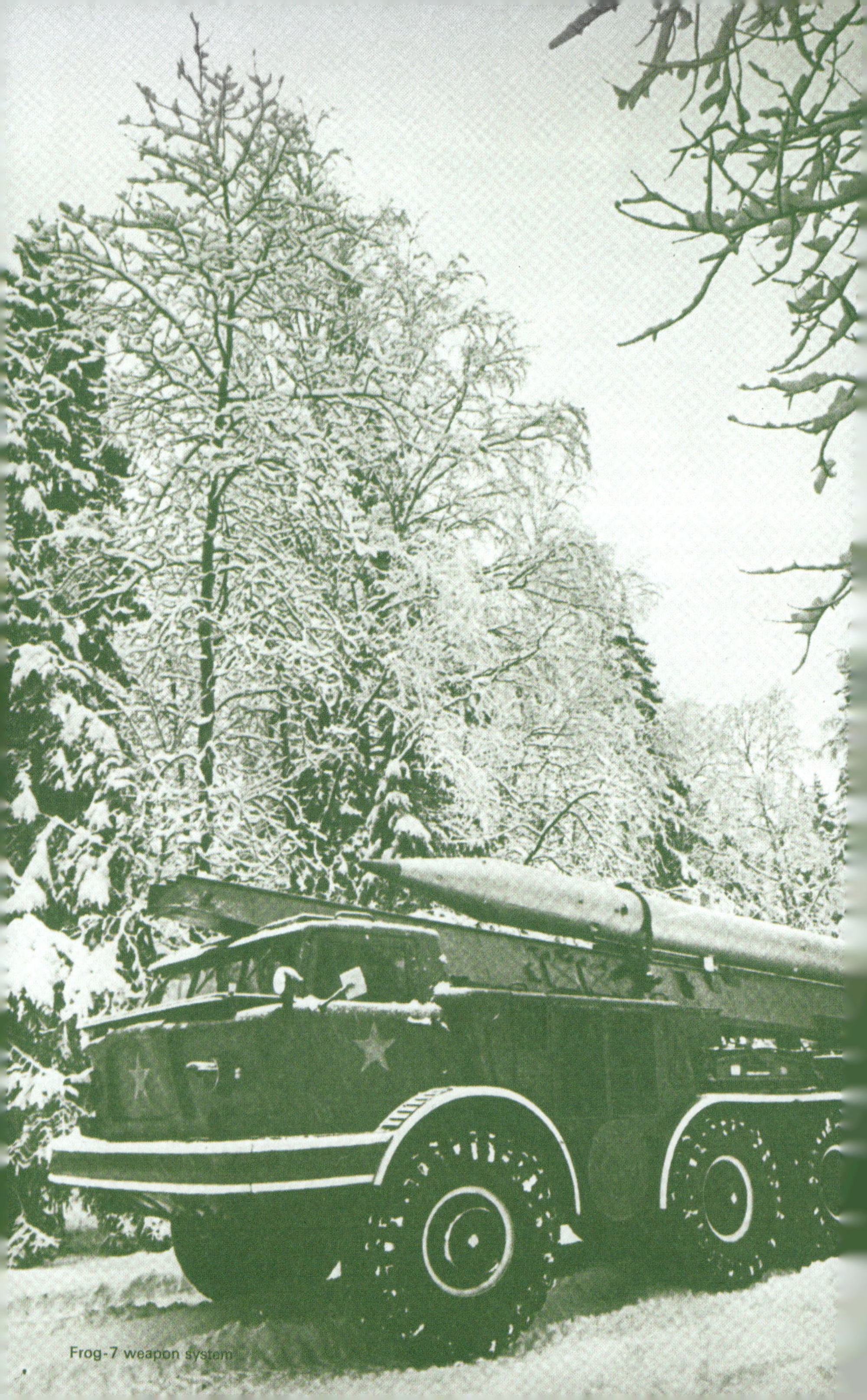

Frog-7 weapon system

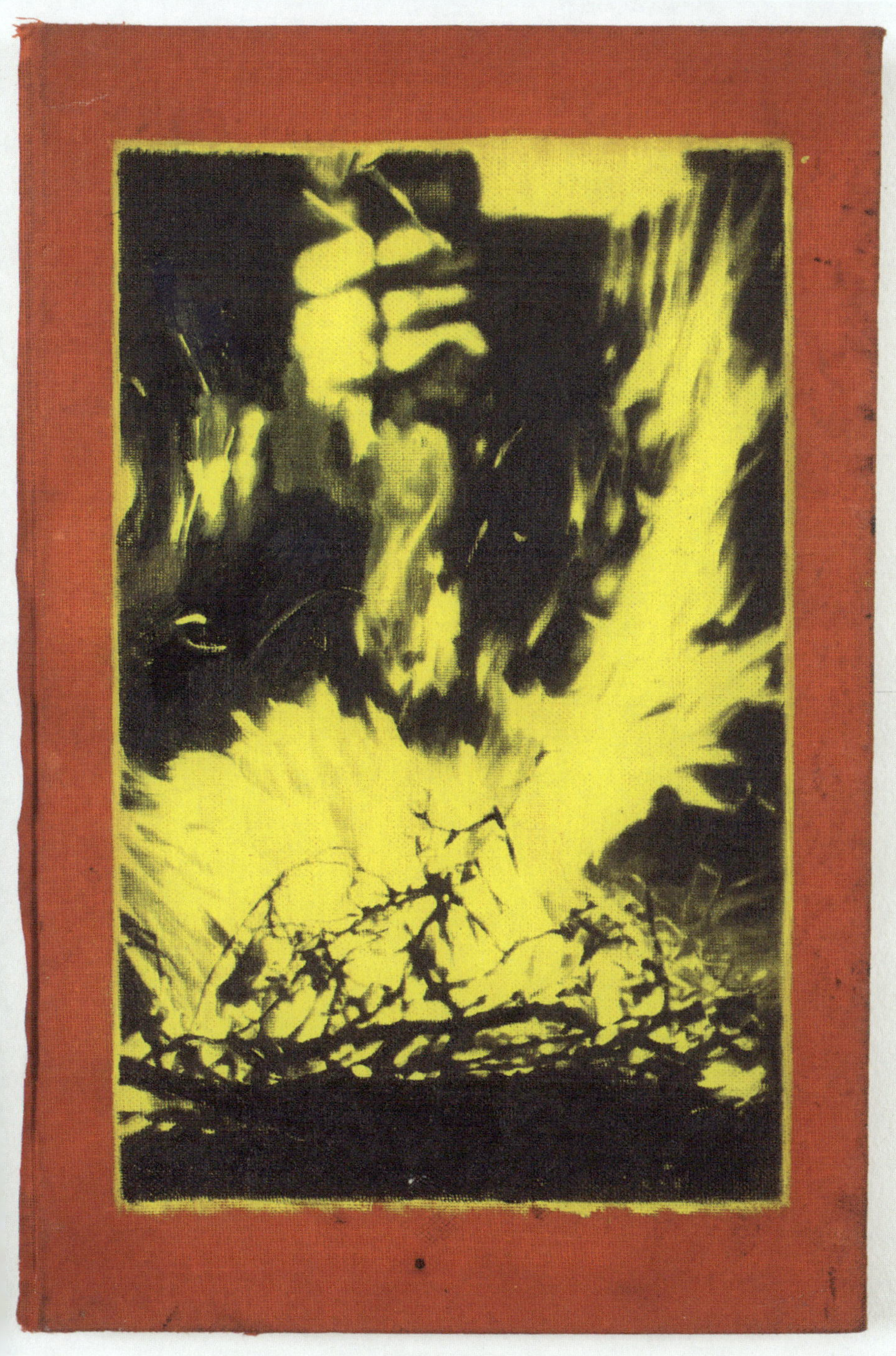

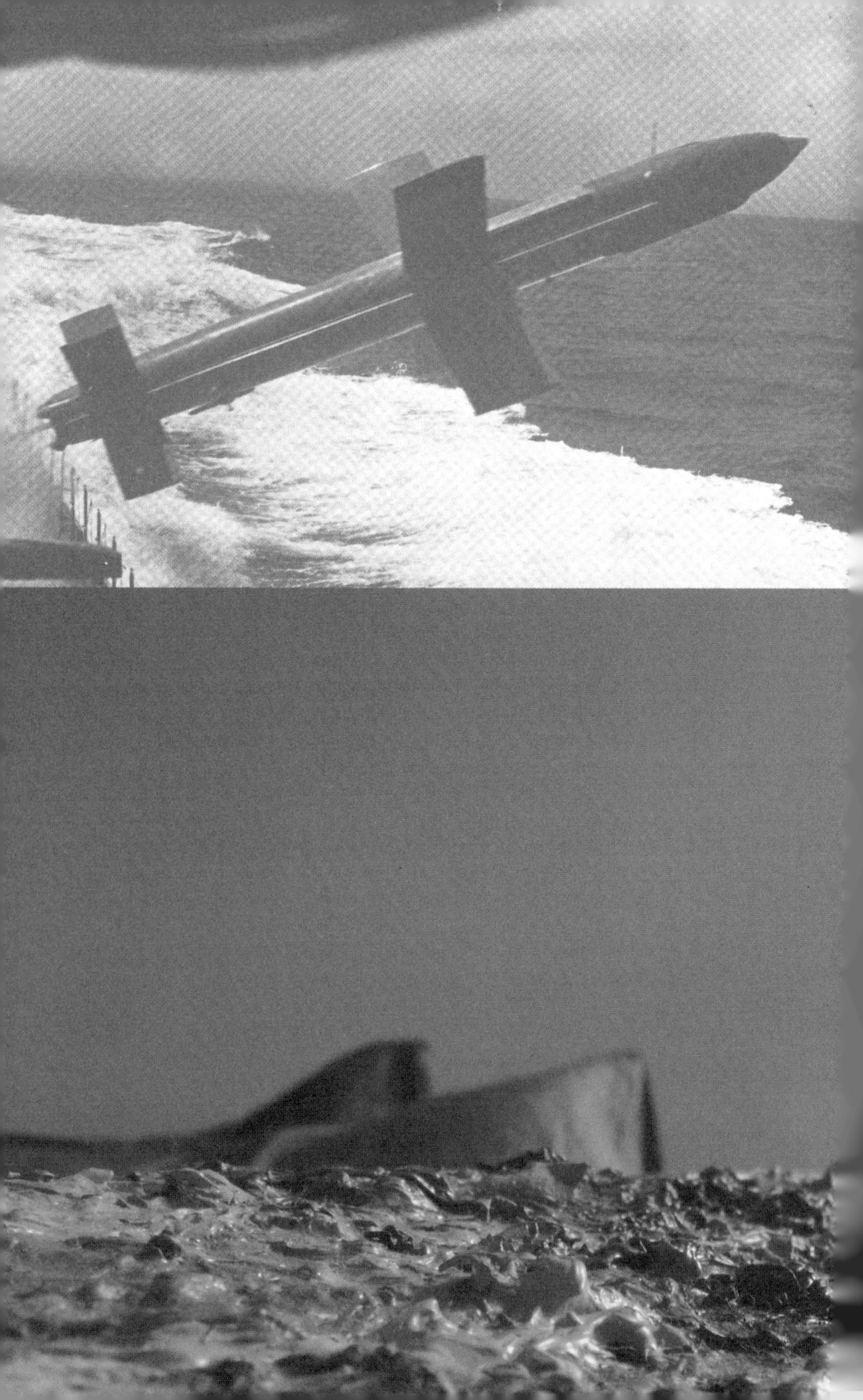

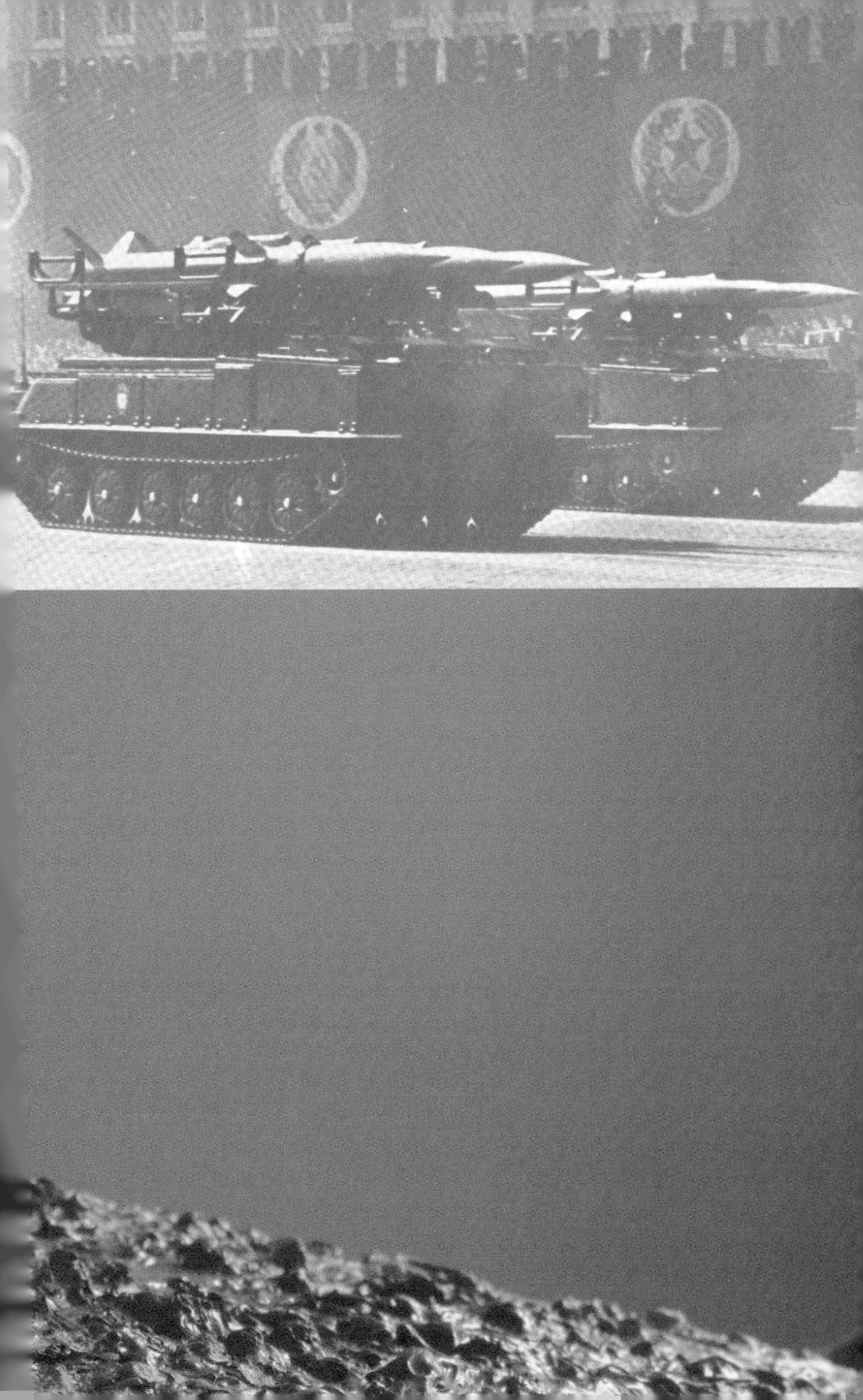

Galosh

Anti-ballistic missile. In service.

Powered by: Rocket motors with four first-stage nozzles.

Development and Service

'Galosh' has been under development at least as long as its US counterparts of the Safeguard ABM system. The ribbed cylindrical container in which it is transported (and from which it is, presumably, fired) was first displayed on a tractor/trailer in a Moscow parade on November 7, 1964. On that occasion the Soviet commentator referred to 'Galosh' as an anti-ballistic-missile (ABM) weapon. More recent American official statements have suggested that 'Galosh' is the missile installed at 64 ABM launch sites around Moscow, each with very advanced early warning radars and tracking equipment. One radar, known to NATO as 'Hen House', is described as being 'the size of three football fields lined up end-to-end and standing on their sides . . . providing the same radar coverage that the US will have by 1978 if all of the Safeguard programme is completed.'

Nothing is known of the 'Galosh' missile itself, except that four first-stage nozzles have been visible inside the container, which is 67ft (20.4m) long with a diameter of 9 (2.75m). A newsreel film shown in Moscow 1965 claimed to depict an ABM launching and may have portrayed an early 'Galosh' test round. This appeared to have a somewhat similar shape to the American Sprint (page 140) with less taper on the main body and a conventional conical nose-cone. suggested that the missile breaks through the spherical end-cap on the launch-tube when it is fired.

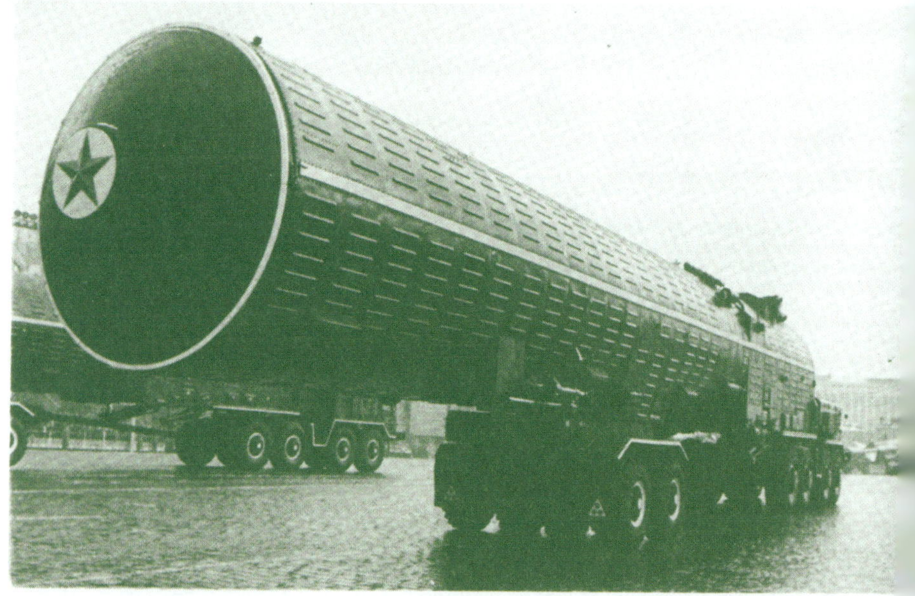

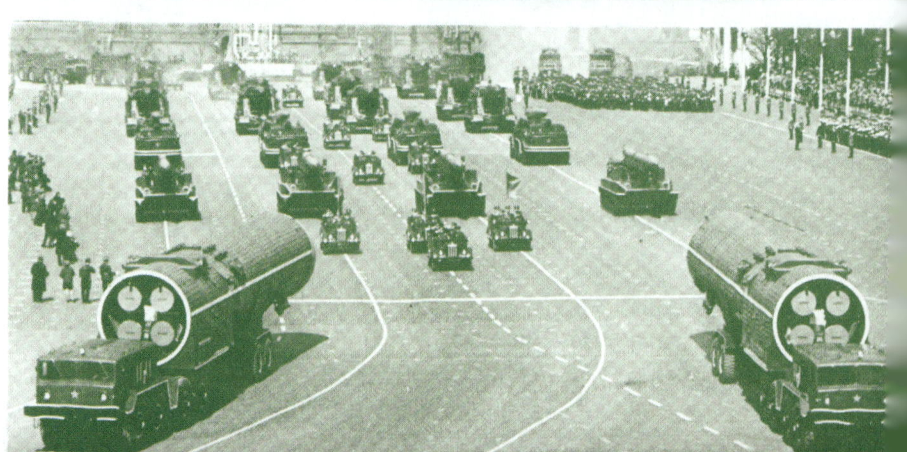

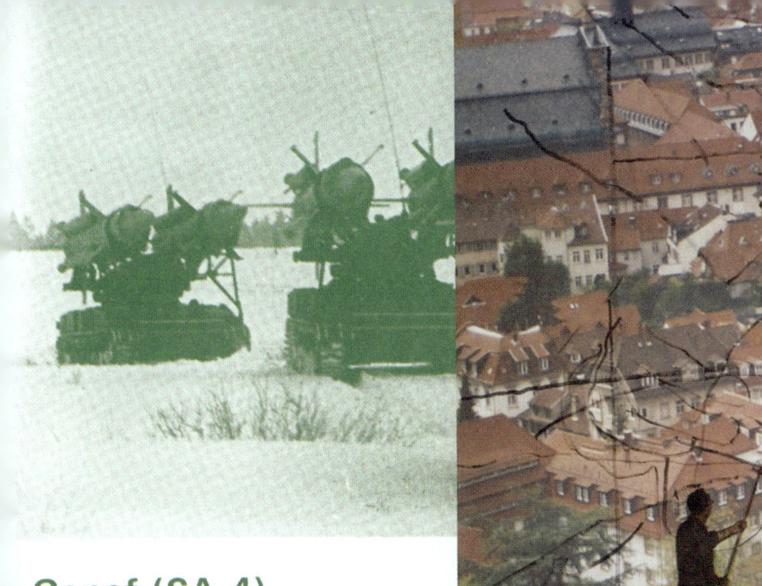

Ganef (SA-4)

Surface-to-air missile. In service.

Powered by: Ramjet sustainer. Four solid-propellant wrap-round boosters, with canted nozzles, which jettison after burn-out.
Airframe: Cylindrical main body, with smaller-diameter centre-body carrying pointed conical warhead. Cruciform pivoted wings on fore-part of main body, indexed at 45 degrees to fixed cruciform tail-fins. Boosters equi-spaced around body aft of wings.
Guidance and Control: Command guidance system. Control via pivoted wings.
Warhead: High-explosive.
Length: 30ft 0in (9.15m).
Max body diameter: 2ft 8in (0.80m).
Wing span: 7ft 6in (2.30m).
Ceiling: 80,000ft (24,400m).

main body and the centre-body suggests the use of a ramjet sustainer engine, which would be consistent with long range. The twin-round tracked launcher carrying 'Ganef' was first shown in a Moscow parade in May 1964. Since then this missile system has been deployed widely in the Soviet Union and is reported to have been despatched to Egypt as an element of the Soviet forces supporting that nation. 'Ganef' can be transported on its launch vehicle by the An-22 freight aircraft. It may have a surface-to-surface capability.

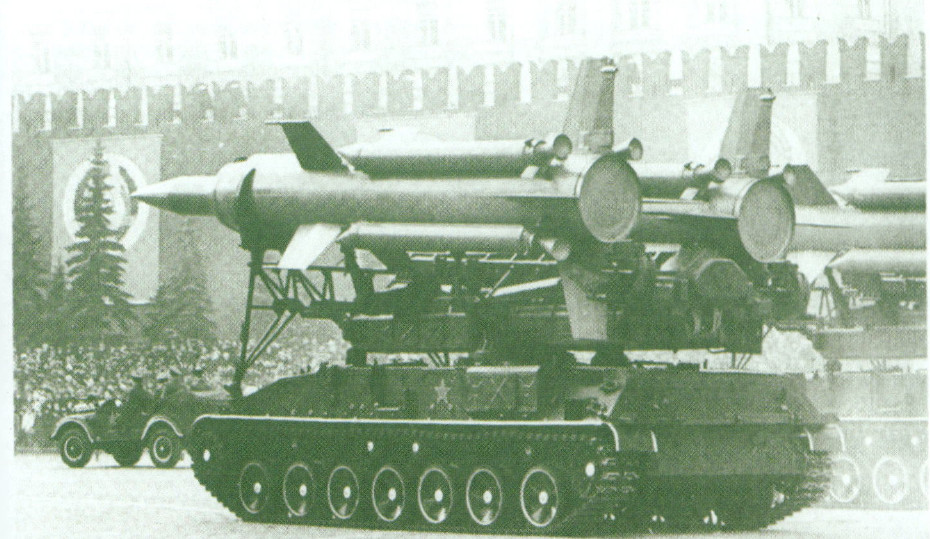

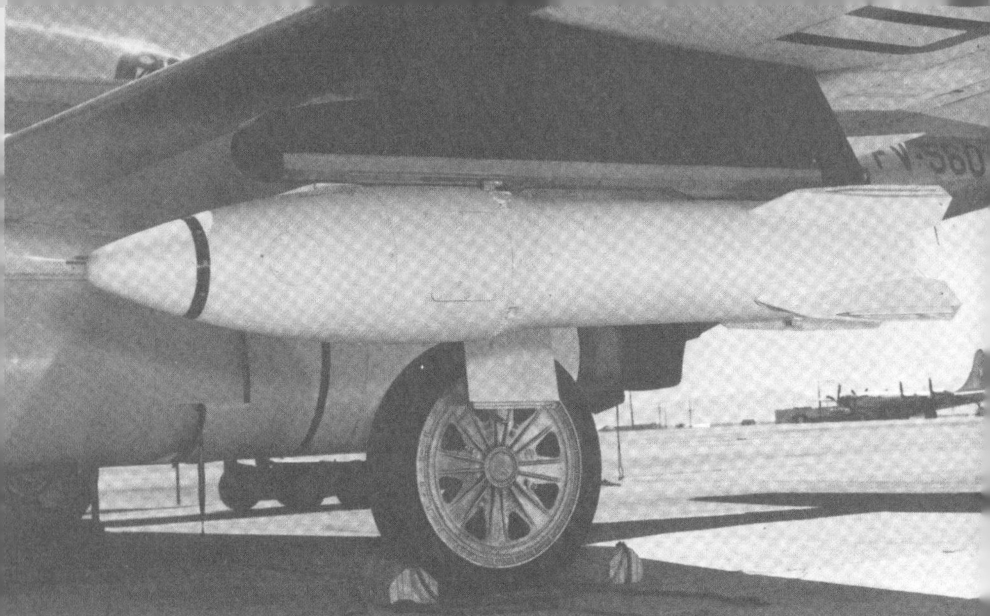

Genie (AIR-2A)   USA

Unguided air-to-air nuclear missile. In production and service.

Prime contractor: McDonnell Douglas Astronautics Company.
Powered by: Thiokol SR49-TC-1 solid-propellant rocket motor of 36,000lb (16,330kg) st.
Airframe: Cylindrical body with cruciform tail-fins, each with movable tip, and an ogival nose of greater basic diameter than body.
Guidance and Control: No guidance system. Trajectory stabilised by fins and gyroscope.
Warhead: Nuclear, with yield reported as 1.5 kilotons.
Length: 9ft 7in (2.91m).
Body diameter: 1ft 5.35in (0.44m).
Fin span: 3ft 3½in (1.00m).
Launch weight: 820lb (372kg).
Max speed: Mach 3.
Max range: 6 miles (9.6km).

Development and Service

Although Genie is an unguided rocket, it justifies inclusion in this book by reason of its nuclear warhead. It was the first nuclear-tipped air-to-air missile ever tested in a live firing when, on July 19, 1957, it was launched from a Northrop F-89J Scorpion at Indian Springs, Nevada. Immediately after launch, at a height of 15,000ft, the pilot of the fighter turned sharply to escape the blast and the missile was detonated from the ground after travelling 3 miles (4.8km). USAF observers who stood directly under the point of detonation for an hour suffered no ill effects.

Many thousands of Genies have been delivered and continue in first-line service with F-101B and F-106 squadrons of the USAF and CF-101F squadrons of the Canadian Armed Forces. They are designed to be fired automatically and detonated by the Hughes fire-control system fitted in each aircraft. A training version, without nuclear warhead, is also in service.

Goa (SA-3/SA-N-1)

Surface-to-air close-range missile. In service.

Powered by: Two-stage rocket motors. Booster is solid-propellant.
Airframe: Two basically-cylindrical stages, in tandem. Booster fitted with large rectangular cruciform fins. Second stage has cruciform fixed wings at rear and cruciform cropped-delta control surfaces on the tapered nose-cone.
Guidance and control: Control by movable foreplanes.
Warhead: High-explosive.
Length: 19ft 4in (5.90m).
Body diameter: Booster 2ft 3in (0.70m). 2nd stage 1ft 6in (0.45m).
Wing span: 4ft 0in (1.22m).
Max range: 15 miles (24km).

Development and Service

Russia's early counterpart to the American Hawk, 'Goa' is the anti-aircraft missile which caused much concern to the Israeli Air Force when 14 batteries supplemented earlier 'Guidelines' near the Suez Canal by early 1971. It is effective over a slant range of about 15 miles (24km), to a height of 40,000ft (12,200m), and is known in America as the SA-3 or SAM-3 in its land-based version. Its compact form is evident from the fact that pairs of 'Goas' can be transported on the truck that is used as a tractor for the 'Guideline' and 'Guild' trailer-transporters.

In its ship-based form (SA-N-1), 'Goa' is standard armament in the Soviet Navy, on a twin-round launcher very like that used for the American Tartar missile. Six cruisers of the *Kresta* class and 15 destroyers of the *Kashin* class each carry two launchers, fore and aft. Four cruisers of the *Kynda* class have a single twin-launcher on their fore-deck; three destroyers of the *Kanin* class and seven of the *Kotlin* class have a similar launcher on their after deck.

A photograph of a twin-launcher on a destroyer, issued by *Tass* in 1971, showed missiles of the 'Goa' type with an additional set of small tail-fins between the booster and second-stage wings. The wings also appear to carry trailing-edge control surfaces. These missiles may be similar to the new SAM (SA-N-3) carried by the helicopter cruisers *Leningrad* and *Moskva*

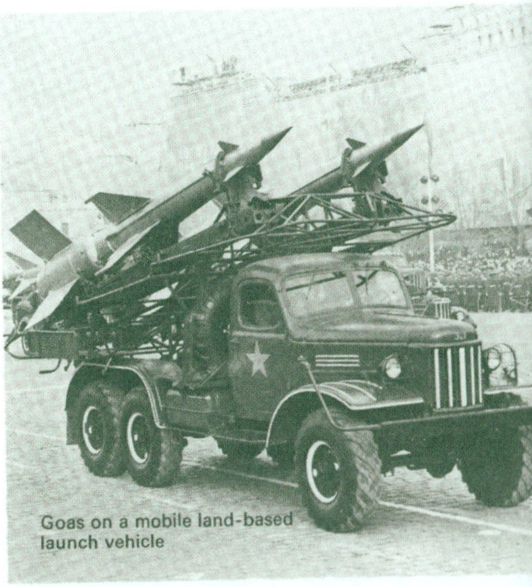

Goas on a mobile land-based launch vehicle

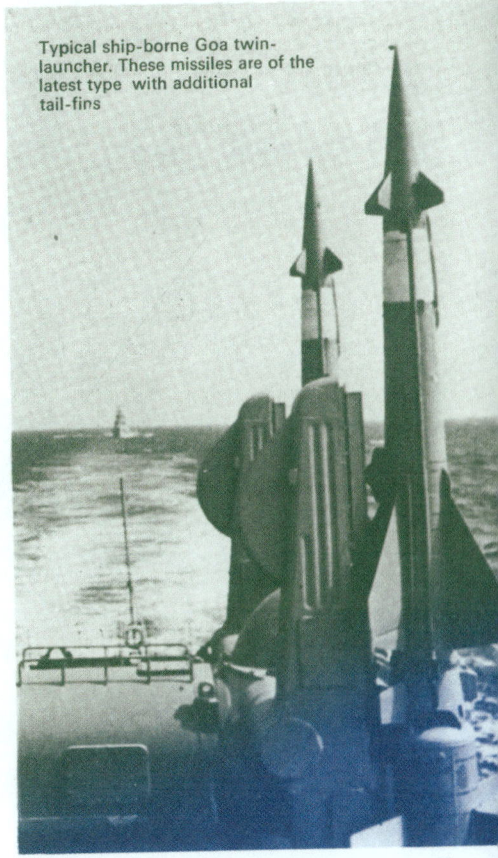

Typical ship-borne Goa twin-launcher. These missiles are of the latest type with additional tail-fins

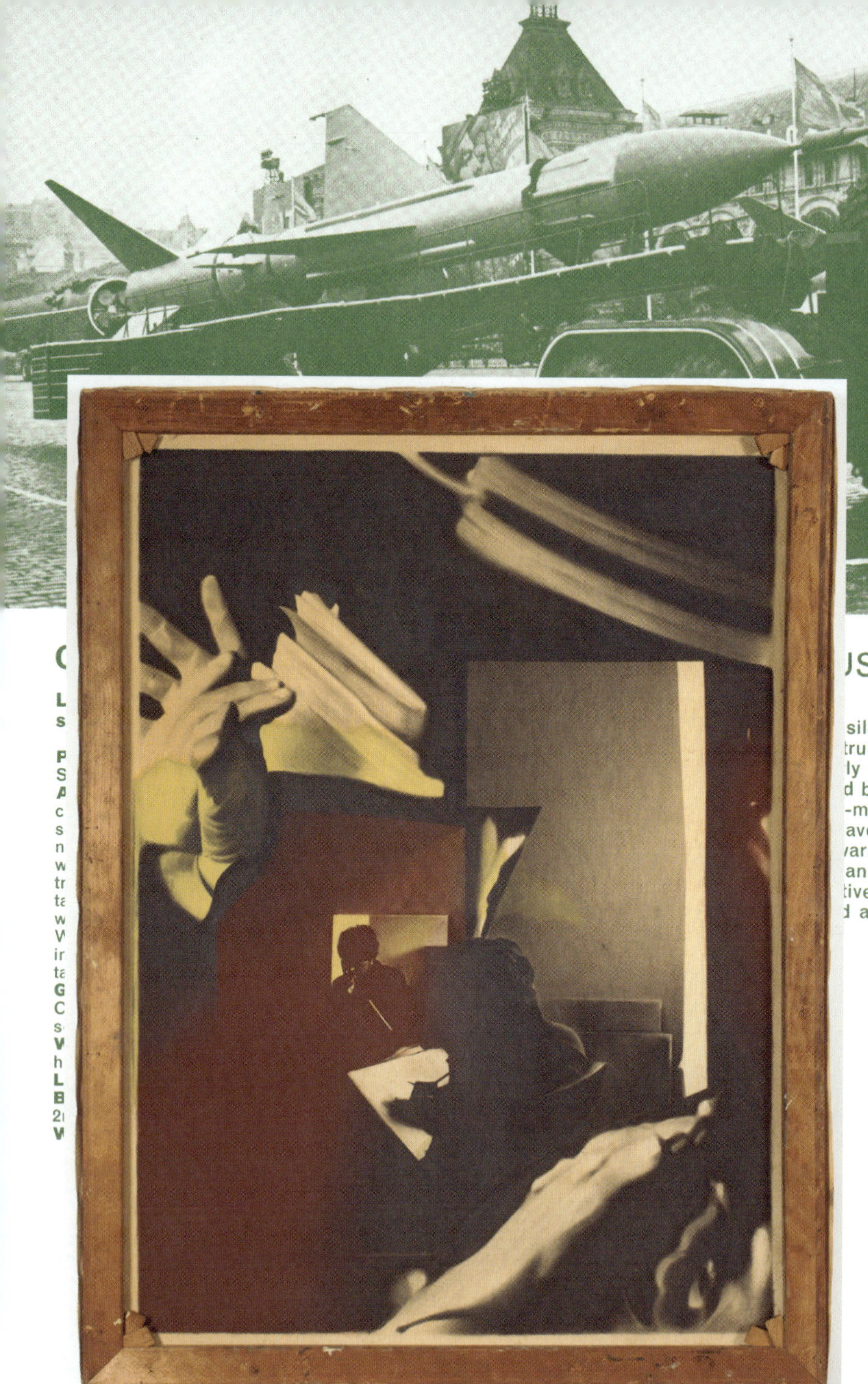

Guideline (V750VK) (SA-2/SA-N-2)

Surface-to-air missile. In service.

Data apply to 'Mk 2' version.
Powered by: Liquid-propellant sustainer;
solid-propellant booster.
Airframe: Tandem two-stage missile. Booster is
cylindrical with cruciform cropped-delta fins, two
of which have trailing-edge control surfaces.
Smaller-diameter second stage has cylindrical
body with flared skirt, fixed cruciform wings about
mid-way between nose and tail, and small
cruciform tail control surfaces, all indexed in line
with booster fins. Small cruciform vanes on nose.
Guidance and Control: Automatic radio
command. Control by movable tail surfaces and
control surfaces on booster fins.
Warhead: High-explosive, weighing 288lb
(131kg) with contact or proximity fuse, or
detonated by command.
Length: 34ft 9in (10.60m).
Body diameter: Booster 2ft 2in (0.66m).
2nd stage 1ft 8in (0.51m).
Wing span: 5ft 7in (1.70m).
Launch weight: 5,000lb (2,270kg).
Max speed: Mach 3.5.
Max range: 25 miles (40km).

Development and Service

Most widely used of all Soviet anti-aircraft
missiles, 'Guideline' was first displayed in
Moscow in 1957. It serves throughout the
Soviet Union and the Warsaw Pact countries, and has been supplied in vast numbers
to Cuba, Egypt, Indonesia, Iraq, North Vietnam and other countries. At least 28 batteries
were reported to be operational near the
Suez Canal in the Spring of 1971.

'Guidelines' captured by Israeli forces
during the 1967 war were said to bear the
Soviet designation V750VK, with the designation V75SM applicable to the entire weapon
system. This includes a Zil 157 semi-trailer
transporter-erector vehicle, radar van and
generators. The US designation is SA-2,
or SAM-2; while the version carried on a
twin-launcher by the Soviet Navy cruiser
Dzerzhinski is known as SA-N-2. 'Guideline'
has undergone considerable development.
The original version, which might be referred
to for convenience as the 'Mk 1', was similar
to the first-generation US Nike-Ajax in many
design features and probably had a com-
parable performance. Initially the nose vanes
were rectangular, but the 'Mk 2' version
captured by the Israelis had cropped-delta
vanes. The latest 'Mk 4' version, first displayed in Moscow in 1967, is about 15in
(40cm) longer than the 'Mk 2', and lacks the
latter's nose vanes and booster control
surfaces. It was described by the Soviet
commentator as being far more effective than
earlier versions, which may imply use of a
nuclear warhead in the bulged, white-painted
nose-cone.

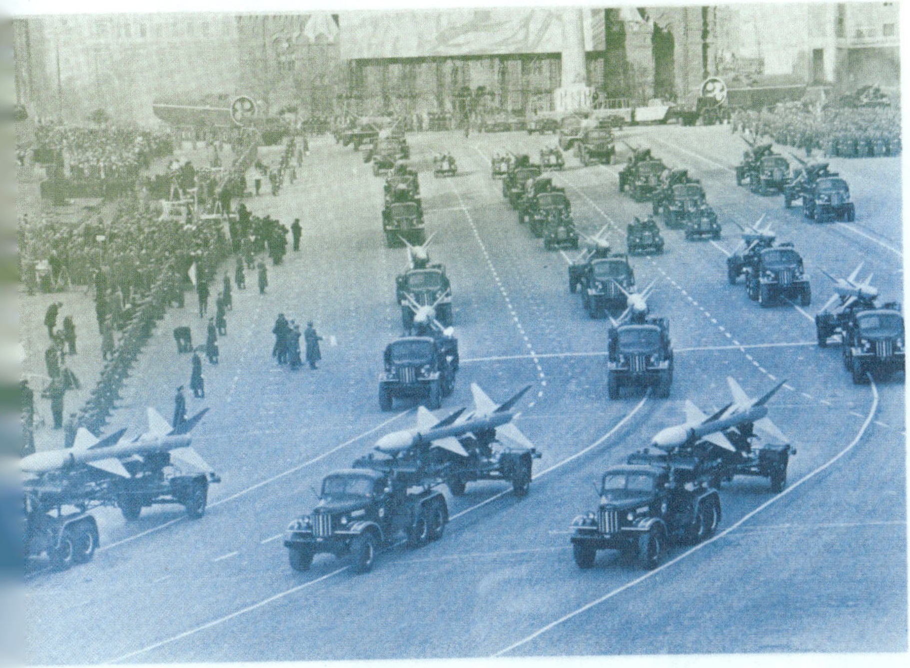

Three 'Mk 4' Guideline missiles (*foreground*)

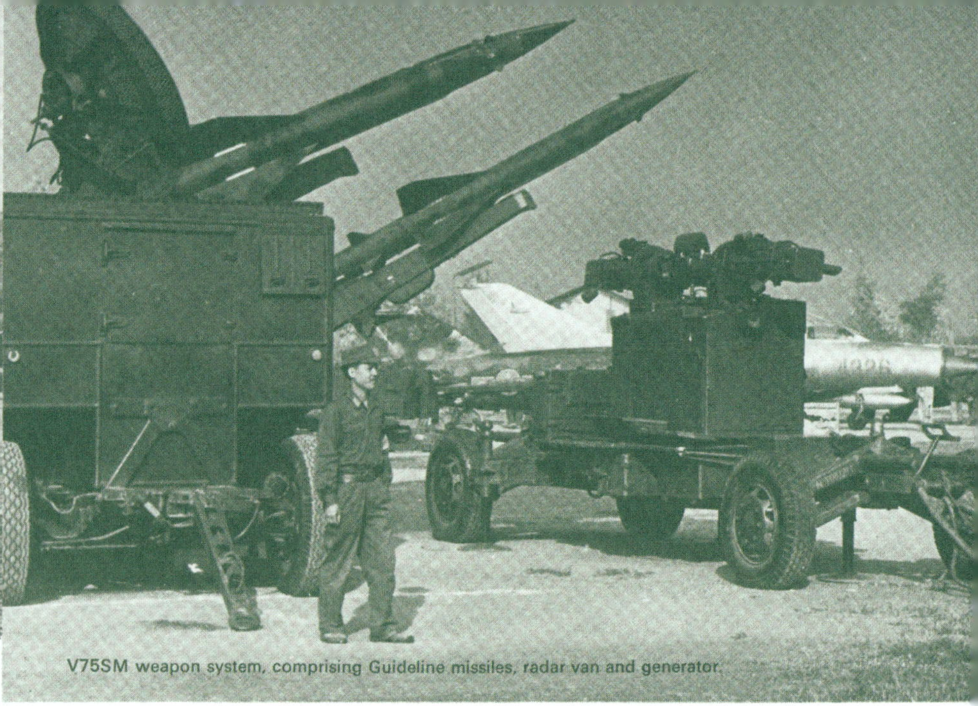

V75SM weapon system, comprising Guideline missiles, radar van and generator.

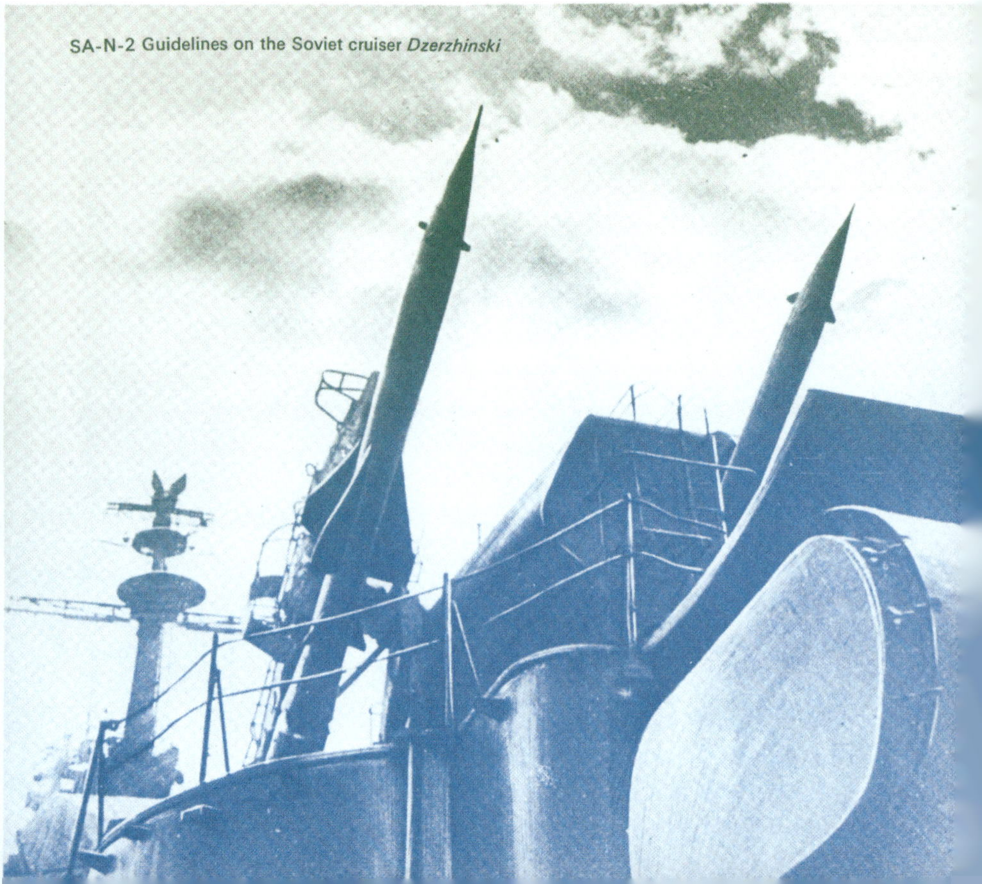

SA-N-2 Guidelines on the Soviet cruiser *Dzerzhinski*

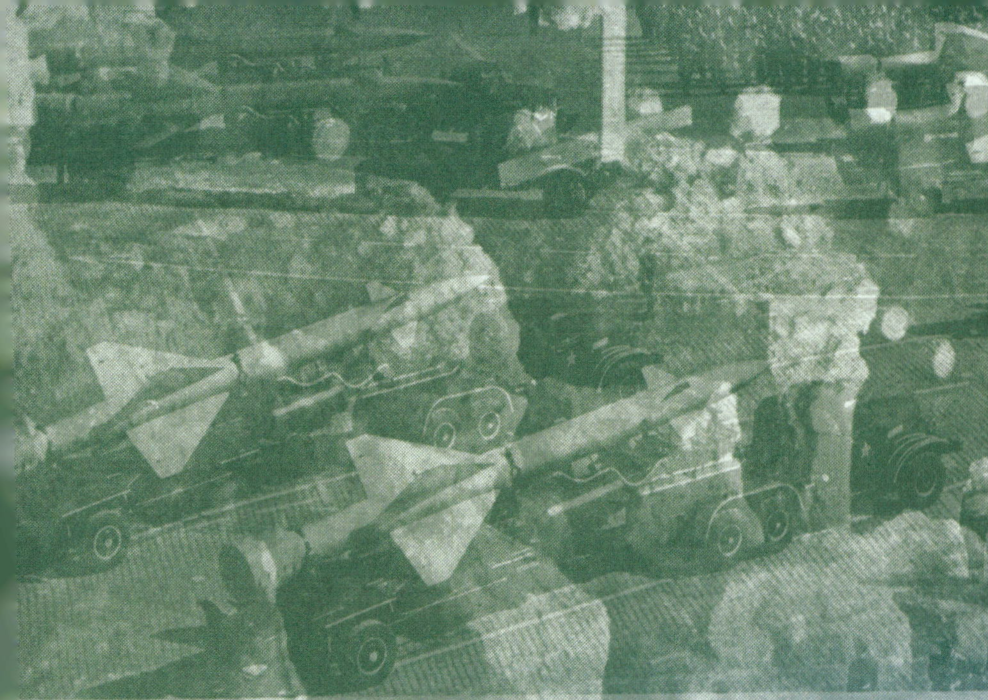

Guild

USSR

Surface-to-air missile. In service.

Powered by: Solid-propellant rocket motor.
Airframe: Cylindrical body, with pointed ogival
nose. Cruciform cropped-delta wings, each with
trailing-edge control surface. Cruciform foreplane
control surfaces indexed in line with wings.
Guidance and Control: Control by foreplanes
and wing trailing-edge surfaces.
Warhead: High-explosive.
Length: 39ft 0in (12.0m).

Development and Service
'Guild' was the second type of Soviet surface-
to-air missile displayed in a Moscow parade,
on November 7, 1960. Unlike 'Guideline' it
has no separate booster, which may imply
the use of a dual-thrust solid-propellant
motor. Although there is good reason to
believe that 'Guild' is a standard defensive
weapon in the USSR, there is no evidence
to suggest that it has been exported.

Hardsite

USA

**Anti-ballistic missile defence system.
Under development.**

Development and Service
The US Army began advanced development
of prototype Hardsite Defense (HSD) com-
ponents in the 1971 Fiscal Year. No details
may yet be published; but HSD is envisaged
as an 'add-on' to the Safeguard ABM system
(see page 104), enabling it to cope with new
Soviet submarine-launched ballistic missiles
and land-based ICBMs fitted with multiple
independently-targeted re-entry vehicles
(MIRV). Elements of HSD include a new
computer radar and a new high-acceleration
short-range missile to supplement Sprint.

HARM

High-velocity air-to-surface anti-radar missile. Under development.

Prime contractor: Naval Weapons Center, China Lake, California.

Development and Service
Little information on this new missile is yet available. Its development was prompted by experience in Vietnam, where Soviet-bu radars were often able to detect oncomi first-generation anti-radiation weapons su as Shrike and shut down before the miss could home on their emissions. HAR (High-velocity Anti-Radiation Missile) is i tended to have such a high performan that it would home on any radar before t operators had time to switch off.

Harpon

Anti-tank missile. In production.

Prime contractor: Nord-Aviation/Aérospatiale, Division Engins Tactiques.
Guidance and Control: Wire-guidance, using TCA optical aiming/infra-red tracking system.

Development and Service.
Harpon is externally similar to the SS.11 B.1 anti-tank missile (see page 145), with similar performance and alternative war-heads, but utilises the TCA type of auto-matic guidance described under the AS.30 entry (page 13). It was, in fact, the first of a long series of weapons which Nord-Aviati (now Aérospatiale) adapted or designed use this guidance system. Harpon has prov able to operate effectively over ranges small as 1,200ft (400m) as no time is lost the operator having to acquire the miss after launch. It is normally deployed on launcher turret carried by light armou vehicles, and is claimed to offer a defe against head-on attack by low-flying fix wing aircraft or helicopters in a surface-to-role.

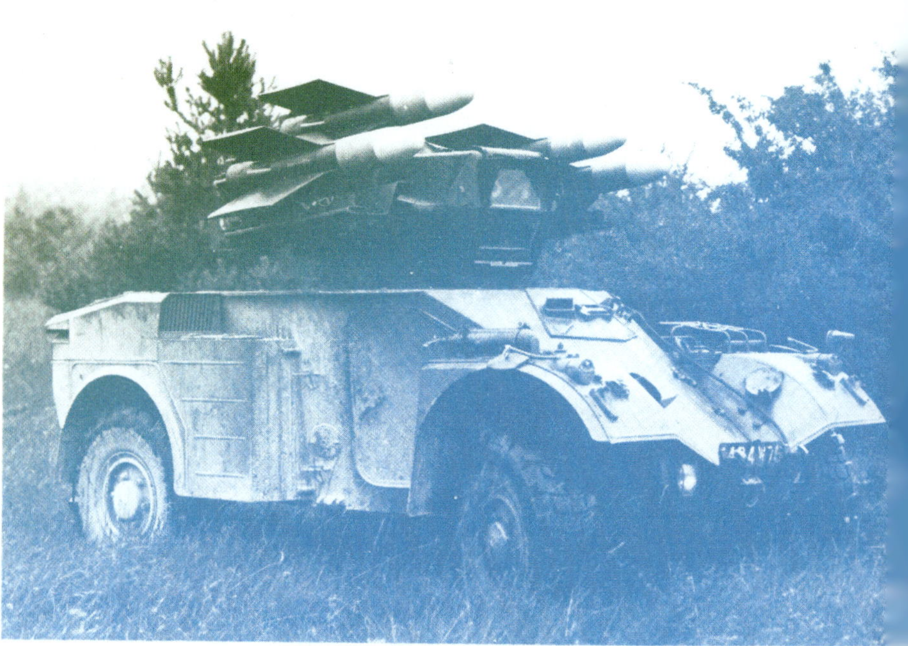

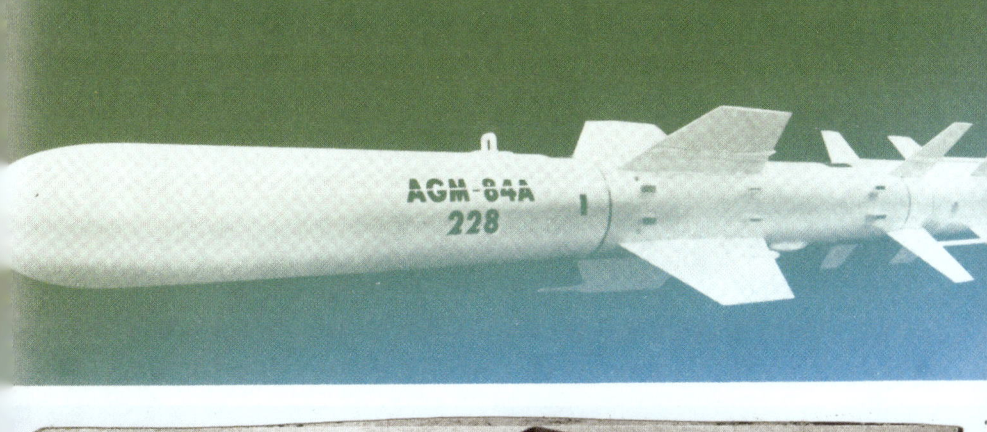

Harpoon in surface-launched form, with solid-propellant booster attached in tandem

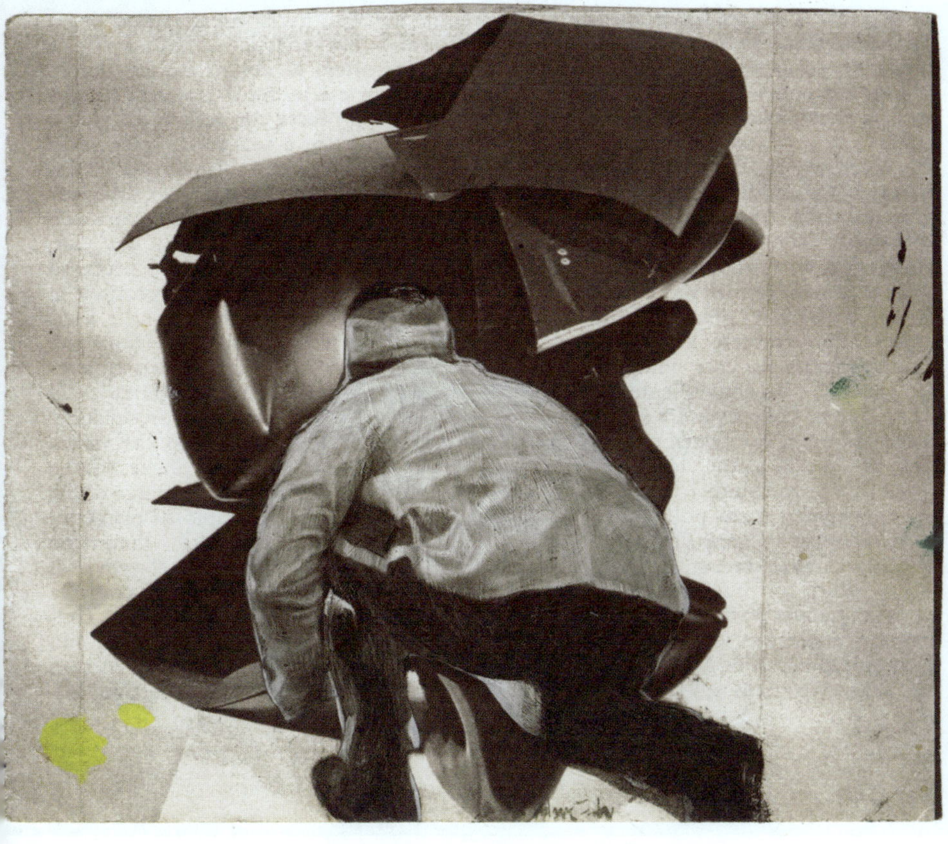

Hawk (MIM-23A)

Surface-to-air close-range missile. In production and service.

Data apply to Basic Hawk.
Prime contractor: Raytheon Company.
Powered by: Aerojet-General M22 E8 dual-thrust solid-propellant motor.
Airframe: Cylindrical metal body with pointed ogival nose. Long-chord cruciform wings, each with trailing-edge elevon.
Guidance and Control: Continuous-wave semi-active radar homing system by Raytheon.
Warhead: High-explosive.
Length: 16ft 6in (5.03m).
Body diameter: 1ft 2in (0.36m).
Wing span: 3ft 11.4 in(1.20m).
Launch weight: 1,295lb (587kg).
Max speed: Mach 2.5.
Max range: 22 miles (35km).
Ceiling: over 38,000ft (11,600m).

Development and Service

Manufactured in thousands, in Europe and Japan as well as by Raytheon in America, Hawk (Homing-All-the-Way Killer) is the low/medium-altitude anti-aircraft weapon which set the pace in this difficult role. As early as January 1960 a Hawk intercepted and destroyed an Honest John supersonic

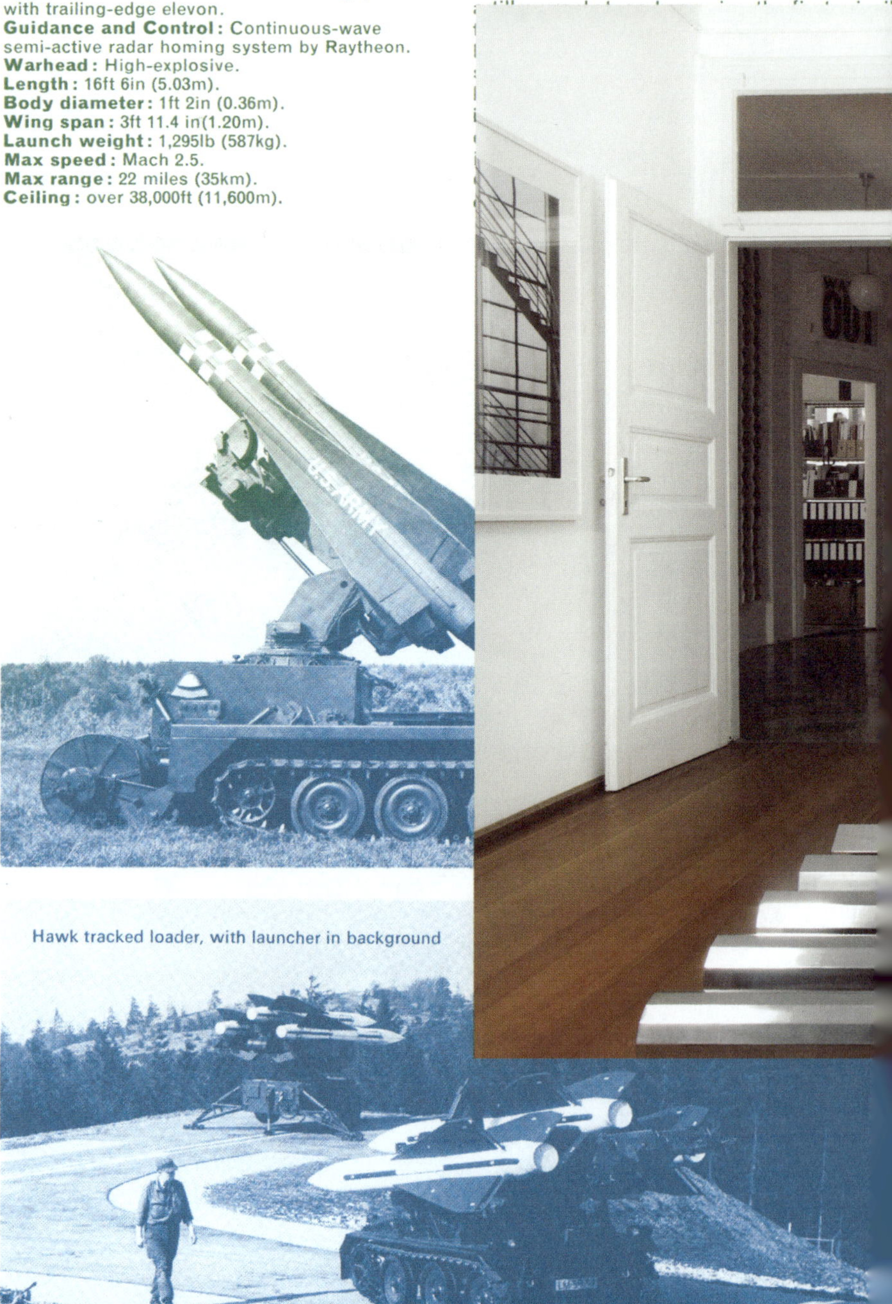

Hawk tracked loader, with launcher in background

France, Israel, Italy, Japan, Korea, Netherlands, Saudi Arabia, Spain, Sweden, Taiwan and West Germany.

The complete Hawk weapon system is transportable by fixed-wing aircraft and helicopters. A typical battery consists of six three-round launchers, a tracked loader which collects three missiles at a time for delivery to the launchers, a pulse acquisition radar, a CW acquisition radar, a range-only radar, two target illumination radars and a

launcher able to tow an item of ground support equipment. The effectiveness of Hawk, down to treetop level, results from the fact that its radars can pick out reflected signals from a moving target at low altitude from the mass of signals reflected by objects on the ground.

In 1964, Raytheon began development of Improved Hawk, a completely redesigned missile with solid-state guidance package, larger warhead and improved Aerojet-

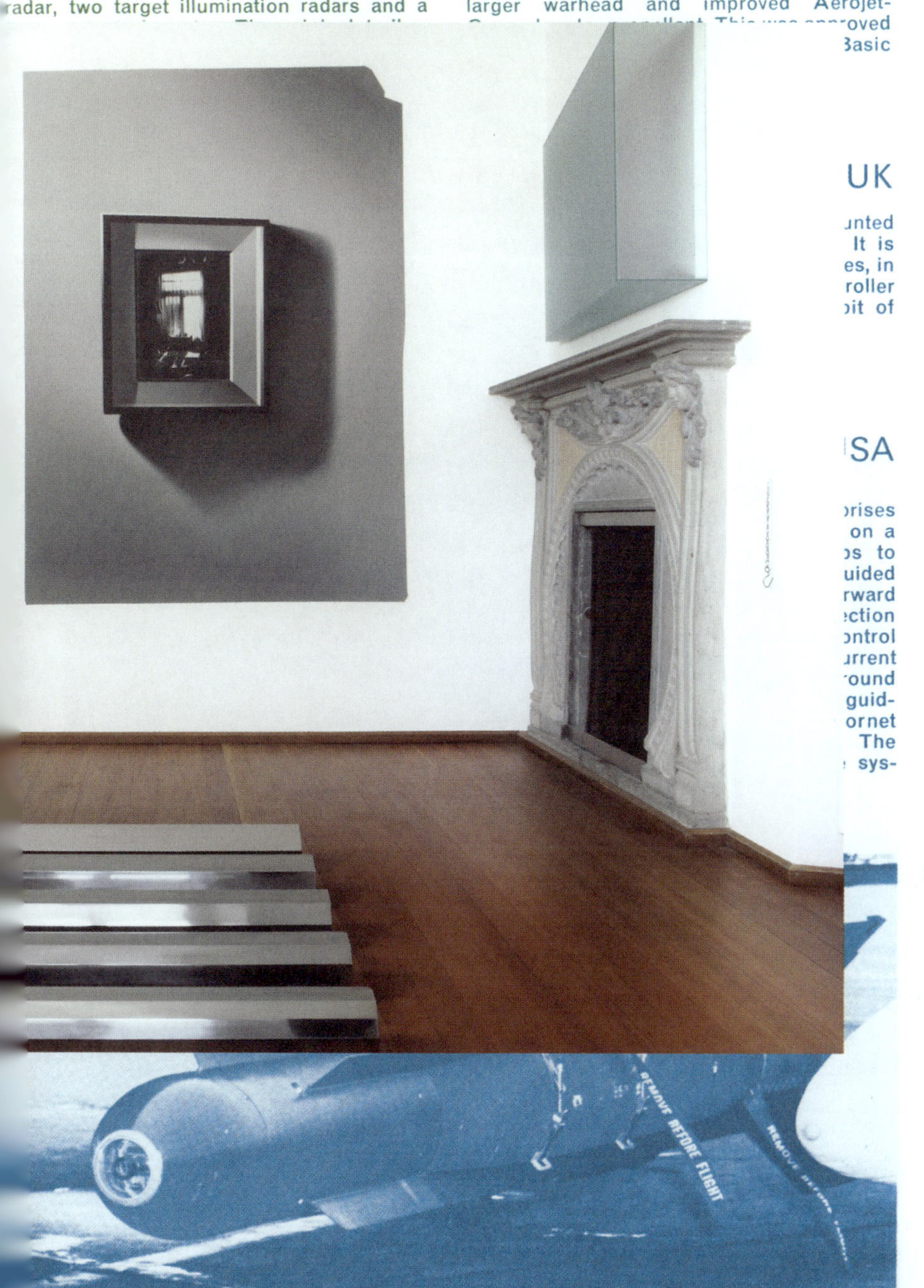

UK

...unted ... It is ...es, in ...roller ...it of

USA

...rises ... on a ...s to ...uided ...rward ...ction ...ntrol ...rrent ...ound ...guid-...ornet ... The ... sys-

Honest

**Surface-to-s[urface]
missile. In se[...]**

Data apply to M[...]
Prime contrac[t...]
(USAMICOM). [...]
Powered by: H[...]
solid-propellant [...]
Airframe: Cylir[...]
ogival nose-con[...]
Guidance and [...]
initial spin impa[...]
warhead and ma[...]
canted tail-fins. [...]
Warhead: Alte[...]
weighing about [...]
Length: 24ft 9½i[n...]
Body diameter [...]
Fin span: 4ft 6i[n...]
Launch weight [...]
Max speed: Ma[...]
Range limits: [...]

Development [...]
Although ung[...]

US[...]

[...]port [...]
[...]ecade[...]
[...]ougla[...]
the [...]
[...]ries [...]
g te[...]
ceipt [...]
[M]GR-1[...]
[man]factur[...]
by bo[...]

[M]GR-1[...]
(0.76[...]
versi[...]
is s[...]
pe a[...]
such [...]
The [...]
t Jo[...]
en [...]
ome [...]

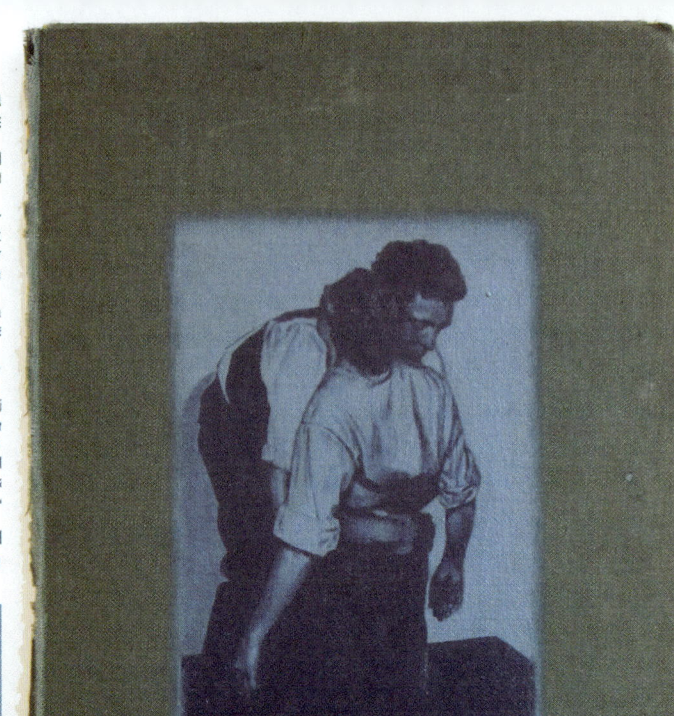

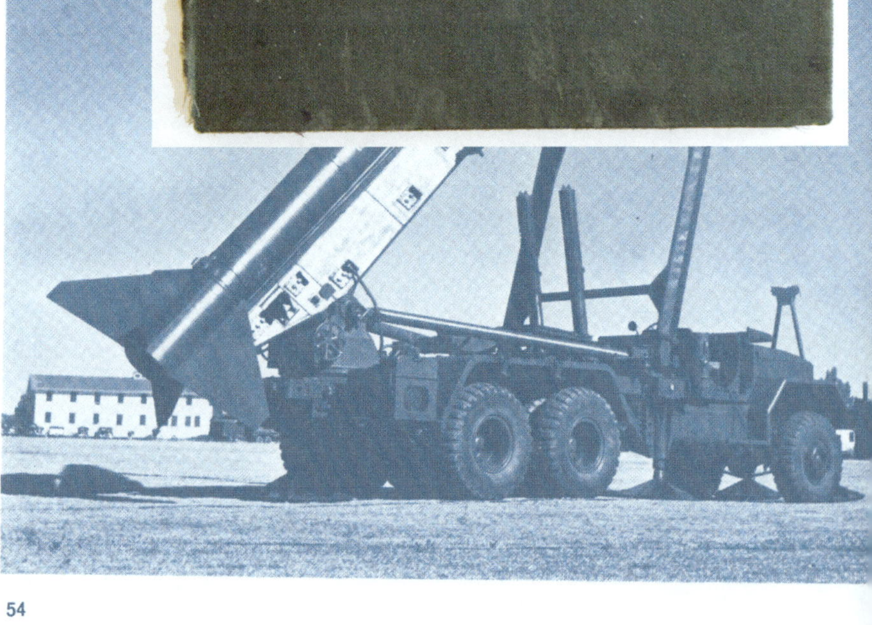

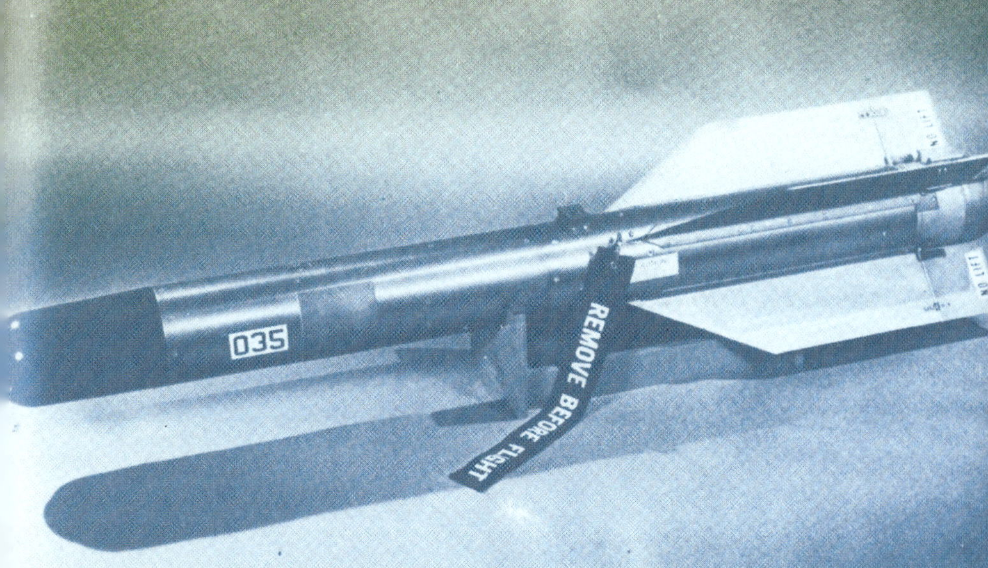

Hornet (ZAGM-64A) USA

Air-to-surface and surface-to-surface anti-tank missile. Under development.

Prime contractor: North American Rockwell Corporation.
Powered by: Dual-thrust solid-propellant rocket motor.
Airframe: Cylindrical body; rear-mounted cruciform wings, each with a trailing-edge flap control surface. TV homing version has hemispherical glass nose.
Guidance and Control: Variety of alternative guidance systems. Version illustrated uses TV guidance. Control by flaps on wings.
Warhead: None at present stage of development.
Range: more than 2.3 miles (3.7km).

Development and Service
North American Rockwell's Columbus Division developed Hornet originally under a USAF contract, in 1965-66, to demonstrate the feasibility of TV homing guidance for an air-to-surface anti-tank missile. Launches from an F-100 resulted in five direct hits on stationary and moving targets, but Hornet was not developed further. Instead, the USAF adapted the Hornet guidance system for the HOBOS guided bomb (page 53).

In 1970, the US Army decided to utilise a new version of Hornet to test a variety of laser and TV seekers that were projected for the next generation of close-support missiles. A larger rocket motor was fitted for ground launching, and the control system was modified to use improved cold-gas actuators; otherwise the current version—known as a Terminal Homing Flight Test Vehicle—is little changed. When using the TV version, the operator has only to lock the missile's stabilised vidicon camera on to the target before launch, by means of a TV monitor. The missile then homes automatically on the target after launch, without further action by the operator.

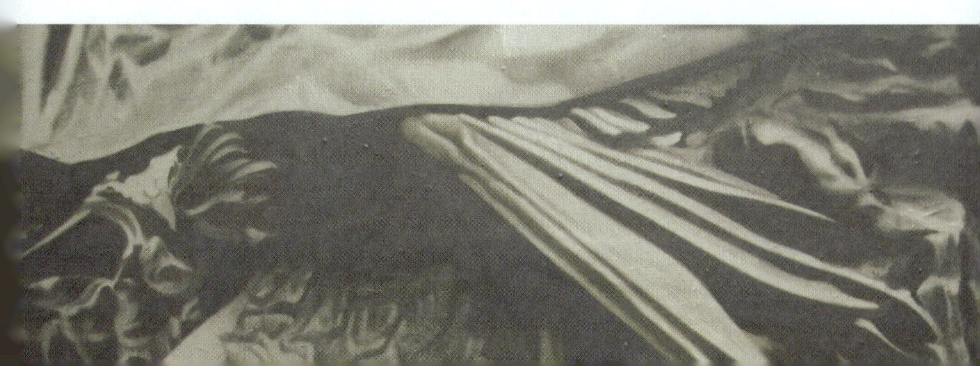

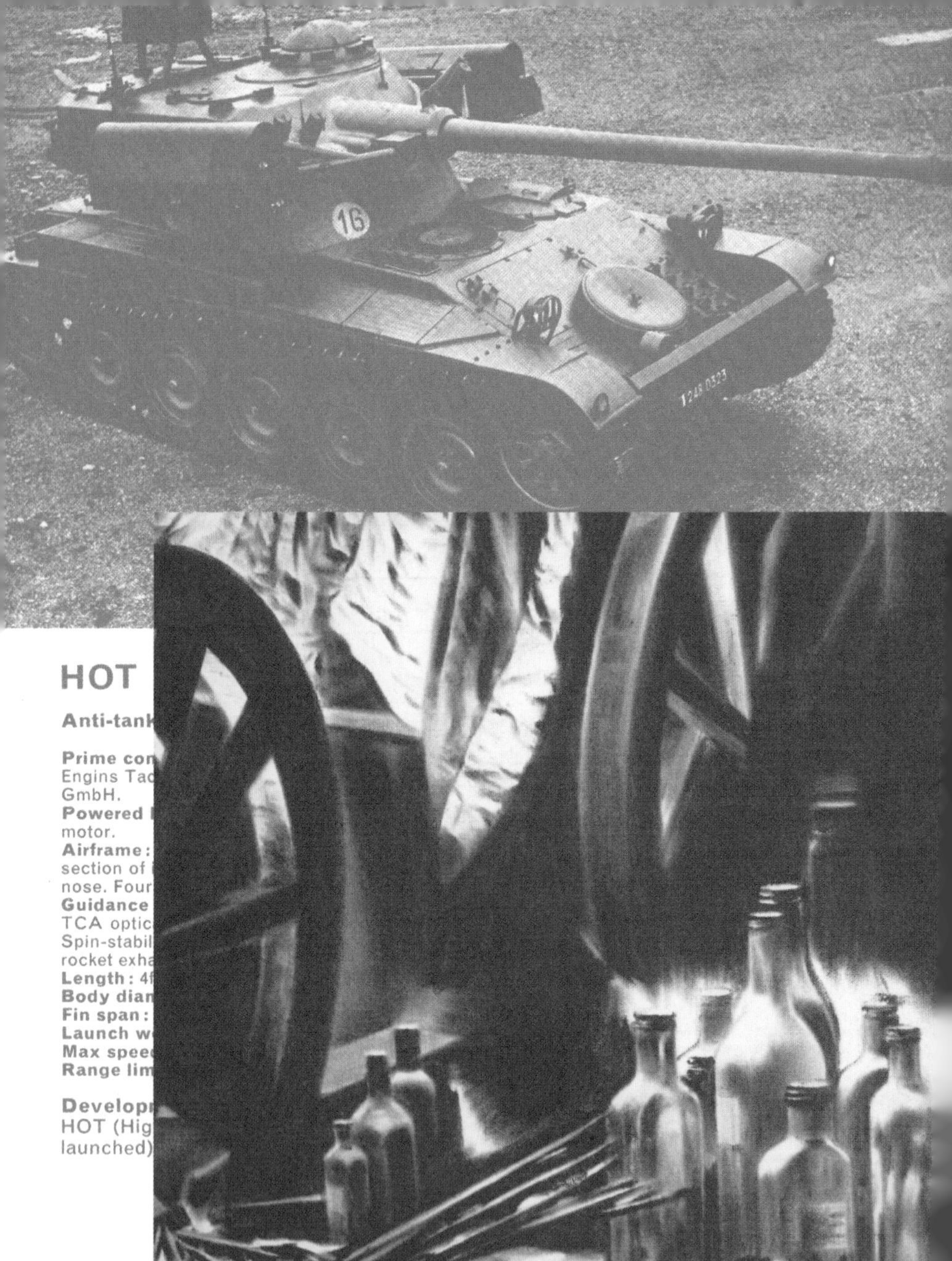

HOT

Anti-tank

Prime con
Engins Ta
GmbH.
Powered
motor.
Airframe:
section of
nose. Four
Guidance
TCA optic
Spin-stabil
rocket exha
Length: 4f
Body dian
Fin span:
Launch w
Max spee
Range lim

Developr
HOT (Hig
launched)

Hound Dog (AGM-28)

Air-to-surface strategic stand-off missile. In service.

Prime contractor: North American Aviation Inc.
Powered by: Pratt & Whitney J52-P-3 turbojet, rated at 7,500lb (3,400kg) st.
Airframe: Cylindrical body, with movable delta foreplanes on long pointed ogival nose. Rear-mounted delta wings, with ailerons, and vertical tail-fin and rudder. Engine pod-mounted beneath rear of body, on a short pylon.
Guidance and Control: Inertial guidance system by North American Autonetics, supplemented by a star-tracking system supplied by Kollsman Instrument Company. Control by aerodynamic surfaces.
Warhead: Thermonuclear, reported yield 4 megatons.
Length: 42ft 6in (12.95m).
Body diameter: 2ft 4½in (0.72m).
Wing span: 12ft 2in (3.71m).
Launch weight: 9,600lb (4,350kg).
Cruising speed: Mach 2.

carries two Hound Dogs on underwing pylons. The weapon system entered service on the 'G' in December 1959. Earlier versions of the B-52 were subsequently adapted to carry and launch Hound Dog, and it was deployed with 29 Strategic Air Command wings by August 1963. Several hundred missiles remained operational in the early 'seventies, with regular refurbishing to maintain their capability. Most are of the AGM-28B (formerly GAM-77A) version, with modifications to improve navigational accuracy.

Hound Dog is stored and mounted on its launch aircraft with its wing pylon in place. This pylon contains the astro-tracking system, which supplements data fed into Hound Dog's inertial navigation system from the B-52's navigation system before launch. The missiles' engines can be run during take-off of the heavily-laden launch-aircraft, to shorten its run. This does not shorten the missiles' range, as their tanks can be topped up in flight from those of the bomber. The aircrew can also make changes of target and missile flight profile whilst airborne, before the missiles are launched. Ceiling of the Hound Dog is given as above 52,000ft (15,850m).

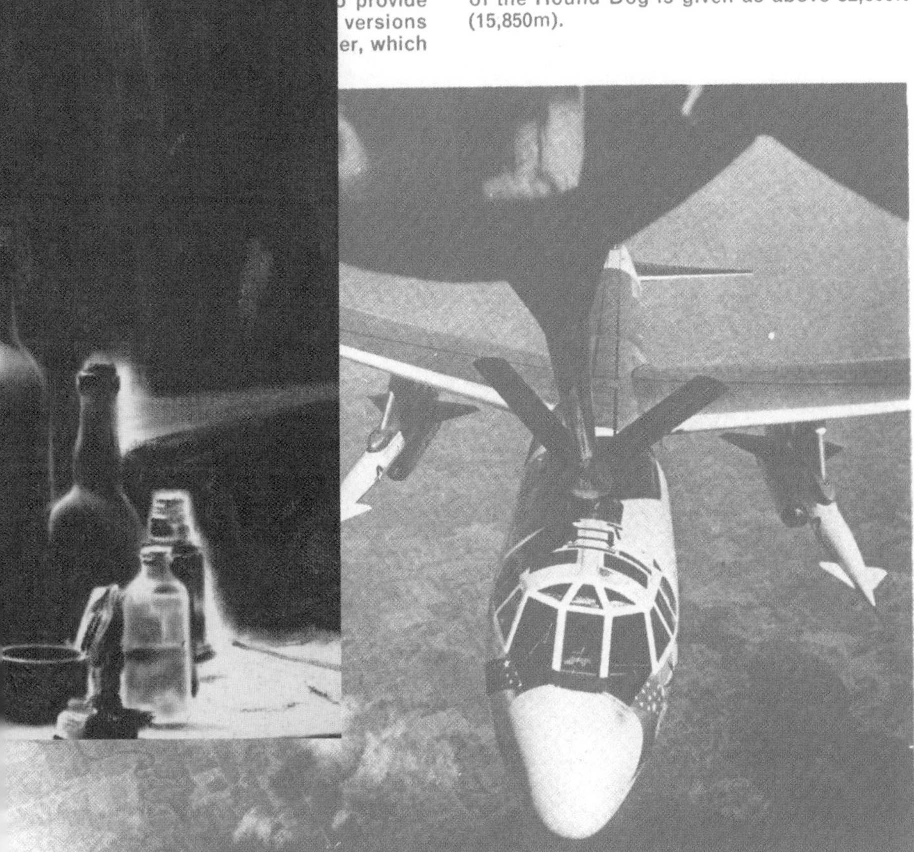

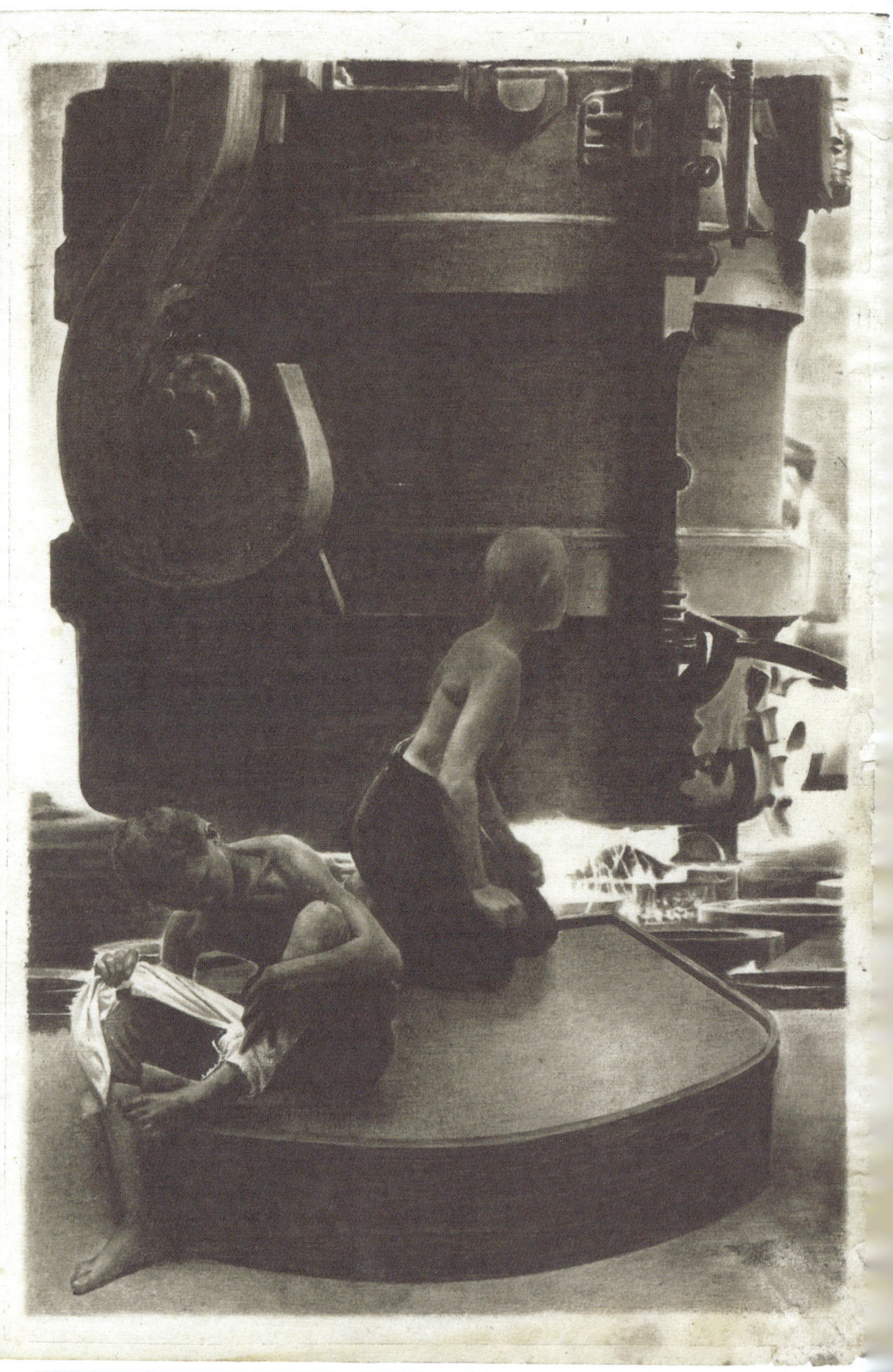

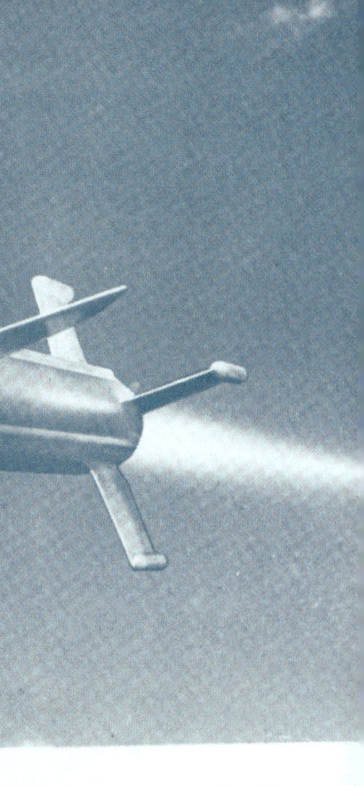

Indigo

Italy

Surface-to-air short-range missile. Under development.

Prime contractor: Sistel—Sistemi Elettronici SpA.
Powered by: Solid-propellant rocket motor of 7,055lb (3,200kg) st.
Airframe: Cylindrical light alloy body with pointed ogival nose. Movable cruciform wings mid-way along body, indexed in line with fixed cruciform tail-fins.
Guidance and Control: Beam-riding/radio command guidance. Control by movable cruciform wings.
Warhead: High-explosive warhead of fragmentation type, with Hawker Siddeley Dynamics infra-red proximity fuse.
Length: 10ft 6in (3.20m).
Body diameter: 7.5in (19cm).
Wing span: 2ft 7in (0.79m).
Launch weight: 214lb (97kg).
Max speed: Mach 2.5.
Range limits: 0.6-6.2 miles (1-10km).

Development and Service
Following successful firing trials at the Italian range in Sardinia, Indigo is being evaluated by the Italian Army. Contraves Italiana, one of the parent companies of Sistel, has developed an integration kit enabling the missile to be operated by anti-aircraft gun batteries equipped with either the Super Fledermaus fire control system designed by Contraves AG of Switzerland or the CT40-G system of its own design. Beam-riding guidance is standard, with stand-by radio command and infra-red tracking to counter enemy jamming or ECM.

KAM-3D (Type 64 ATM-1) Japan

Anti-tank missile. In production and service.

Prime contractor: Kawasaki Jukogyo Kabushiki Kaisha.
Powered by: Dual-thrust solid-propellant rocket motor, first stage rated at 286lb (130kg) st and second stage at 33lb (15kg) st.
Airframe: Cylindrical steel body, with a blunt-top conical centre-body on the rounded nose. Large rear-mounted cruciform wings, of all-metal construction, each with full-span trailing-edge spoiler.
Guidance and Control: Wire guidance, with gyro-stabilisation. Control by spoilers on wings.
Warhead: High-explosive.
Length: 3ft 4in (1.02m).
Body diameter: 4.7in (12cm).
Wing span: 1ft 11½in (0.60m).
Launch weight: 34.6lb (15.7kg).
Cruising speed: 190mph (306km/h).
Range limits: 1,150–5,900ft (350–1,800m).

Development and Service
Kawasaki started development of this missile in 1957, under contract to the Technical Research and Development Institute of the Japan Defence Agency. Seven years later, after several hundred rounds had been test fired, production was authorised for the Japan Ground Self-Defence Force, under the official designation Type 64 ATM. Experience has shown that the KAM-3D's velocity control system is so effective that three out of four unskilled operators can hit the target with their first round after simulator training. Skilled operators can achieve a 95 per cent success rate. A two-man firing team is standard, using a push-button control box. The KAM-3D can be fired by infantry as single rounds or from multiple-round emplacements. It is also carried on jeeps and helicopters. Optical tracking is aided by a flare in daytime; at night the rocket exhaust provides adequate visual reference.

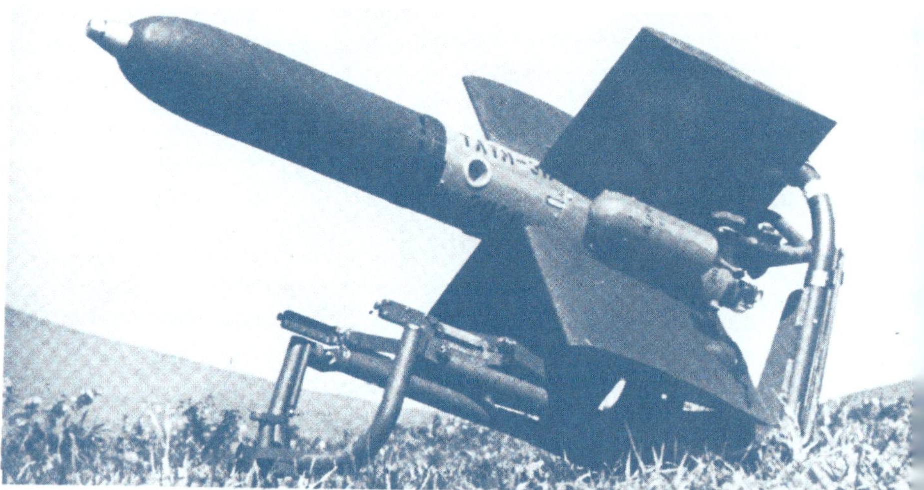

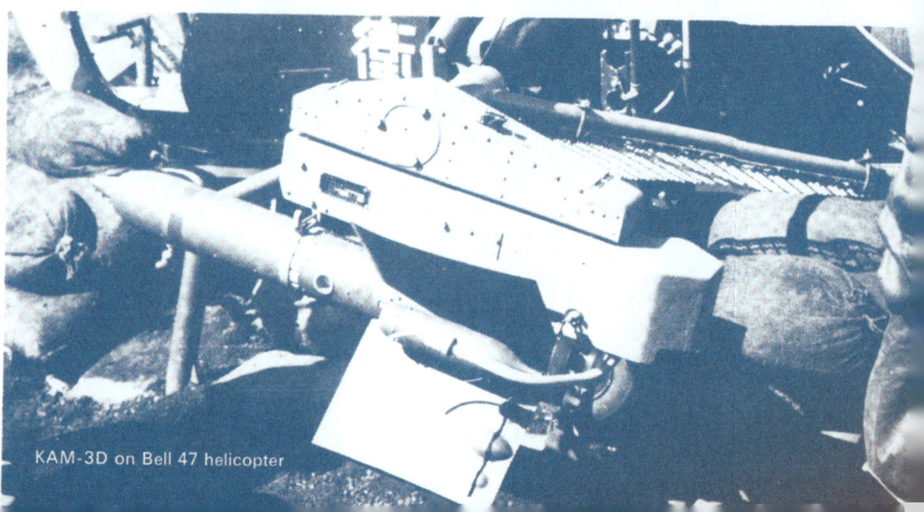

KAM-3D on Bell 47 helicopter

KAM-9 (TAN-SSM) — Japan

Anti-tank missile. Under development.

Prime contractor: Kawasaki Jukogyo Kabushiki Kaisha.
Powered by: Daicel dual-thrust solid-propellant sustainer. Nippon Oils and Fats Co solid-propellant rocket booster.
Guidance and Control: Nippon Electric Co wire-guidance system, with optical aiming and automatic tracking.
Warhead: Armour-piercing type.
Length: 4ft 11in (1.50m).
Body diameter: 5.9in (15cm).
Wing span: 1ft 1in (0.33m).

Development and Service

Under development since 1966, this missile is described as a higher-performance, extended-range version of the KAM-3D, suitable for use against armoured vehicles on both land and water. It differs from the earlier missile in several important respects. It is, for example, launched from the tubular container in which it is transported and stored. In action, the container is placed on a launch and tracking unit, incorporating the firing mechanism, optical sight and missile check-out device. A booster fires briefly to eject the KAM-9 from the launch-tube. Then, at a safe distance, the sustainer fires to accelerate the missile to cruising speed. The operator has only to keep his optical sight aligned on the target. Deviations from the line-of-sight track to the target are sensed automatically and corrective signals are fed from a computer to the missile via the wire-guidance system. Pre-series production of the KAM-9 was started in 1970.

Kangaroo (AS-3) — USSR

Air-to-surface strategic missile. In service.

Powered by: Unidentified turbojet engine.
Airframe: Aeroplane configuration. Sweptback wings and tail unit, with vertical surfaces of rhomboid form. Nose air-intake.
Guidance and Control: Aerodynamic control surfaces.
Length: 48ft 11in (14.9m).
Max range: 400 miles (650km).

Development and Service

'Kangaroo' is similar in size and configuration to a single-seat, single-engined swept-wing fighter aircraft. It was first displayed, clamped under the cutaway bomb-bay of its Tupolev Tu-95 mother-plane, during the fly-past at the 1961 Soviet Aviation Day display at Tushino Airport, Moscow. Further details became available subsequently when a Soviet film showed a 'Kangaroo' being released from a Tu-95 in flight. In particular, the film showed the shape of the vertical tail surfaces for the first time, and confirmed that the ram air-intake of 'Kangaroo' is blanked off by a duct fairing under the Tu-95's belly in flight. This may convey compressed air from an auxiliary power unit to start the missile's engine before launch. A large, radar scanner in the Tu-95's nose is probably used to compute the course to target, so that 'Kangaroo' can be directed initially on the correct compass bearing.

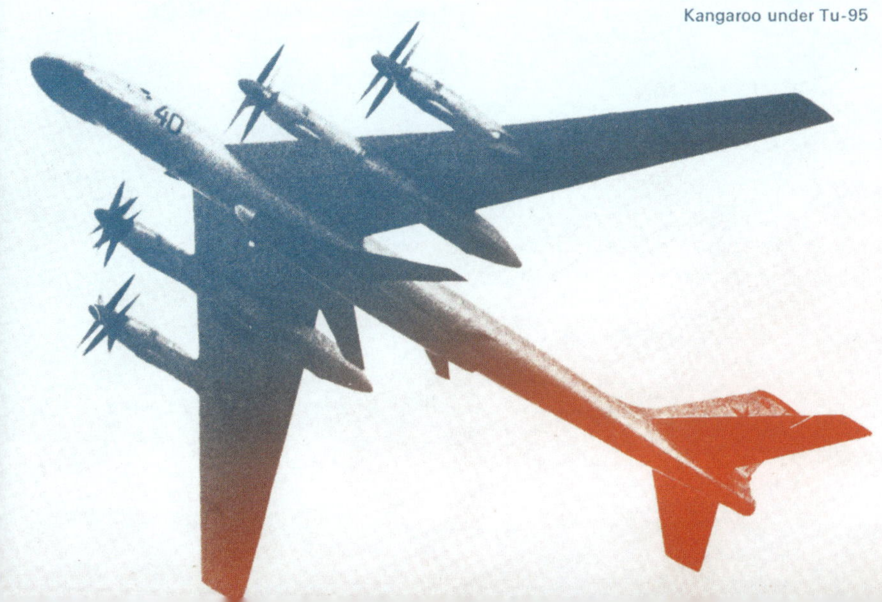

Kangaroo under Tu-95

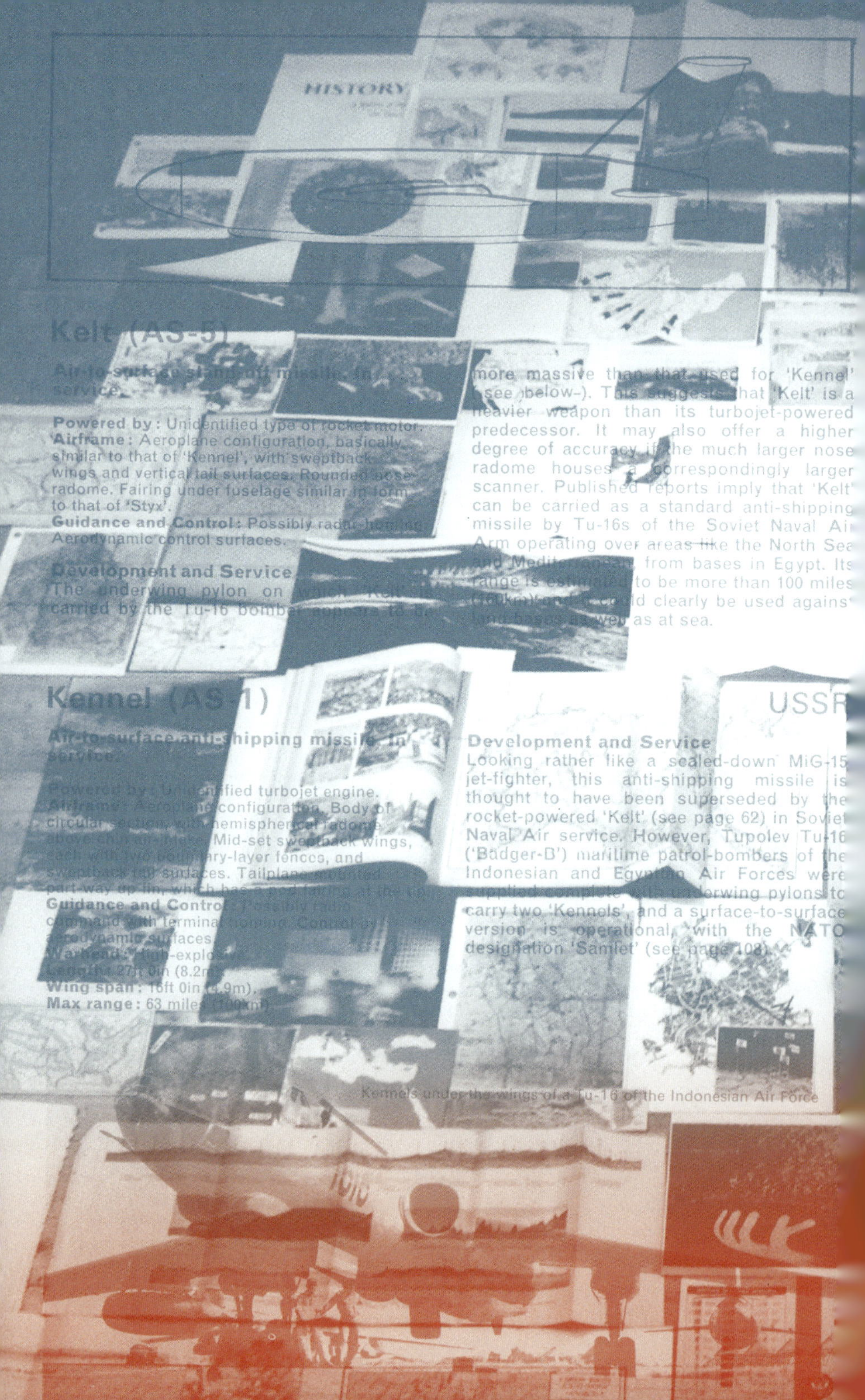

Kelt (AS-5)

Air-to-surface stand-off missile. In service.

Powered by: Unidentified type of rocket motor.
Airframe: Aeroplane configuration, basically similar to that of 'Kennel', with sweptback wings and vertical tail surfaces. Rounded nose-radome. Fairing under fuselage similar in form to that of 'Styx'.
Guidance and Control: Possibly radar-homing. Aerodynamic control surfaces.

Development and Service
The underwing pylon on which 'Kelt' is carried by the Tu-16 bomber appears to be more massive than that used for 'Kennel' (see below). This suggests that 'Kelt' is a heavier weapon than its turbojet-powered predecessor. It may also offer a higher degree of accuracy if the much larger nose radome houses a correspondingly larger scanner. Published reports imply that 'Kelt' can be carried as a standard anti-shipping missile by Tu-16s of the Soviet Naval Air Arm operating over areas like the North Sea and Mediterranean from bases in Egypt. Its range is estimated to be more than 100 miles (160km) and it could clearly be used against land bases as well as at sea.

Kennel (AS-1)

Air-to-surface anti-shipping missile. In service.

Powered by: Unidentified turbojet engine.
Airframe: Aeroplane configuration. Body of circular section, with hemispherical radome above chin air intake. Mid-set sweptback wings, each with two boundary-layer fences, and sweptback tail surfaces. Tailplane mounted part-way up fin, which has a small fairing at the top.
Guidance and Control: Possibly radio command with terminal homing. Control by aerodynamic surfaces.
Warhead: High-explosive.
Length: 27ft 0in (8.2m).
Wing span: 16ft 0in (4.9m).
Max range: 63 miles (100km).

Development and Service
Looking rather like a scaled-down MiG-15 jet-fighter, this anti-shipping missile is thought to have been superseded by the rocket-powered 'Kelt' (see page 62) in Soviet Naval Air service. However, Tupolev Tu-16 ('Badger-B') maritime patrol-bombers of the Indonesian and Egyptian Air Forces were supplied complete with underwing pylons to carry two 'Kennels', and a surface-to-surface version is operational, with the NATO designation 'Samlet' (see page 108).

USSR

Kennels under the wings of a Tu-16 of the Indonesian Air Force

Kipper (AS-2) USSR

Air-to-surface stand-off missile. In service.

Powered by: Unidentified turbojet engine.
Airframe: Aeroplane configuration, with cylindrical body, ogival nose-cone, mid-set sweptback wings and conventional sweptback tail surfaces. Engine slung under rear fuselage in pod.
Length: 31ft 0in (9.5m).
Max range: 132 miles (213km).

Development and Service
Like 'Kangaroo' and 'Kitchen', this anti-shipping missile put in a surprise first appearance in the 1961 Soviet Aviation Day display at Tushino Airport, Moscow. It was seen to be similar in general configuration to the American Hound Dog, but smaller and of less refined form. 'Kipper' is carried by Tu-16 twin-jet bombers of the Soviet Naval Air Arm, clasped under the modified bomb-bay. This version of the Tu-16 is known to NATO as 'Badger-C'. It differs from the 'Kennel'-armed 'Badger-B' in having radar in a wide nose radome, presumably for detecting and fixing the position of the target before 'Kipper' is launched.

'Badger-Cs' have been reported over the North Sea and over the Mediterranean, the latter from bases in Egypt. It also could clearly be used against targets on land as well as at sea.

Kitchen (AS-4) USSR

Air-to-surface strategic missile. In service.

Airframe: Aeroplane configuration. Basically-cylindrical body, with short-span delta wings and cruciform tail surfaces.
Length: 37ft 0in (11.3m).
Max range: 460 miles (740km).

Development and Service
Although this weapon was first identified more than a decade ago, at the 1961 Soviet Aviation Day display, little is known about it. The commentator at Tushino Airport then referred to the Tu-22 carrying 'Kitchen' as the spearhead of the Soviet strategic rocket force, and most of the 22 Tu-22s which took part in the 1967 display at Domodedovo were armed with this missile. There is, however, reason to believe that the Tu-22 failed to fulfil Soviet requirements as a supersonic strategic bomber and has been switched largely to a maritime reconnaissance role. It remains to be seen whether 'Kitchen', or a development of it, will be carried by the Tupolev swing-wing bomber ('Backfire') which is intended to replace the Tu-22 in the Soviet Air Force. Meanwhile, 'Kitchen' remains the most advanced Soviet air-to-surface missile yet known.

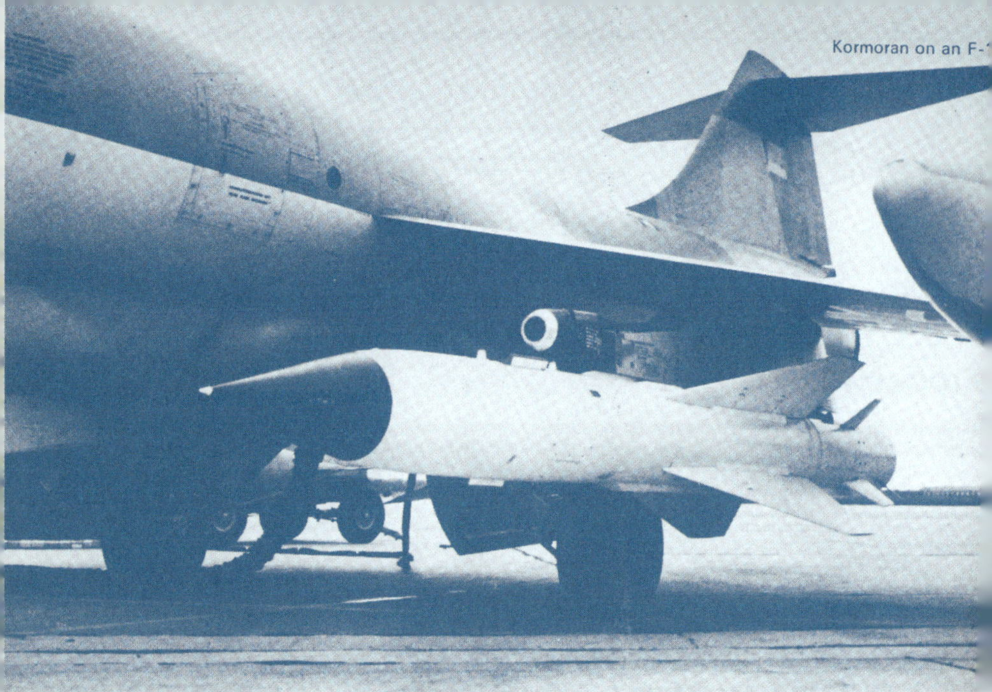

Kormoran

German

**Air-to-surface anti-shipping missile.
Under development.**

Prime contractor: Messerschmitt-Bölkow-
Blohm GmbH.
Powered by: Solid-propellant rocket motor,
with boost and sustainer stages.
Airframe: Cylindrical body with pointed
nose-cone. Cruciform sweptback wings,
indexed in line with cruciform tail control
surfaces.
Guidance and Control: Inertial guidance
system, with active or passive terminal homing
by CSF RE576 radar homing head. Control via
tail surfaces.
Warhead: High-explosive.
Length: 14ft 5in (4.40m).
Wing span: 3ft 3½in (1.00m).
Body diameter: 1ft 1½in (34.2cm).
Launch weight: 1,280lb (580kg).
Max speed: Mach 0.95.
Max range: 23 miles (37km).

Development and Service
Largest post-war missile project undertake
in West Germany, Kormoran is being dev
loped to equip F-104G Starfighters of t
German Naval Air Service. Work on t
weapon was started in 1964, initially as
collaborative programme by MBB and Nor
Aviation of France, who allocated the desi
nation AS.34 to the missile. Nord subs
quently withdrew, and MBB have continu
the development and testing of Kormoran
themselves. The first air launch from
F-104G was made successfully on March
1970. Tests of fully-equipped but inert m
siles against targets many miles away fro
the launch aircraft began with equal succe
in early 1971. Normally, Kormoran is launch
at low level and travels towards the target
an altitude which puts it below shipboa
radar cover. At a predetermined distan
from the target, it enters a climb to ena
its homing radar to 'see' and lock on to
target.

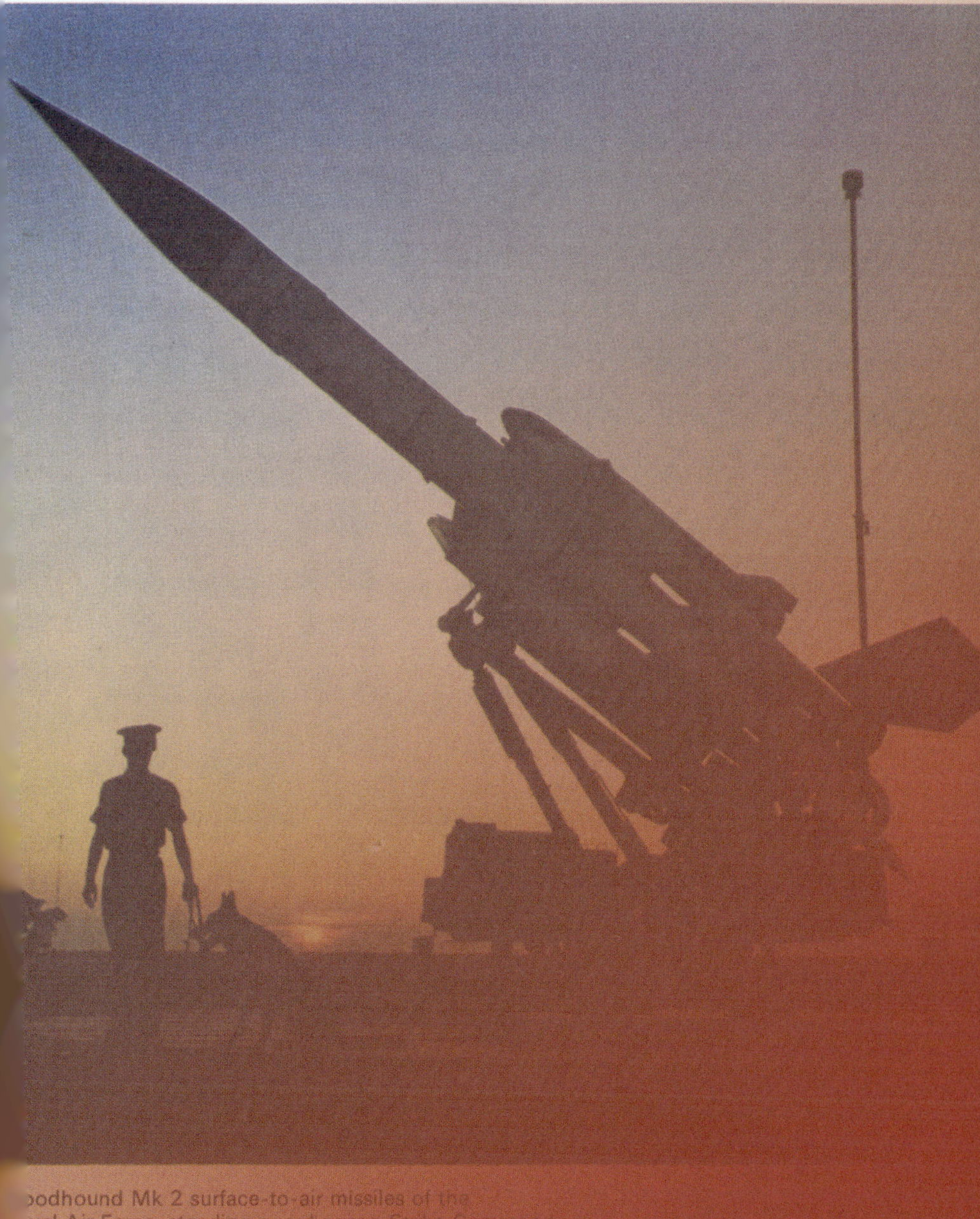

Bloodhound Mk 2 surface-to-air missiles of the Royal Air Force, standing guard near a Strike Command base in Britain

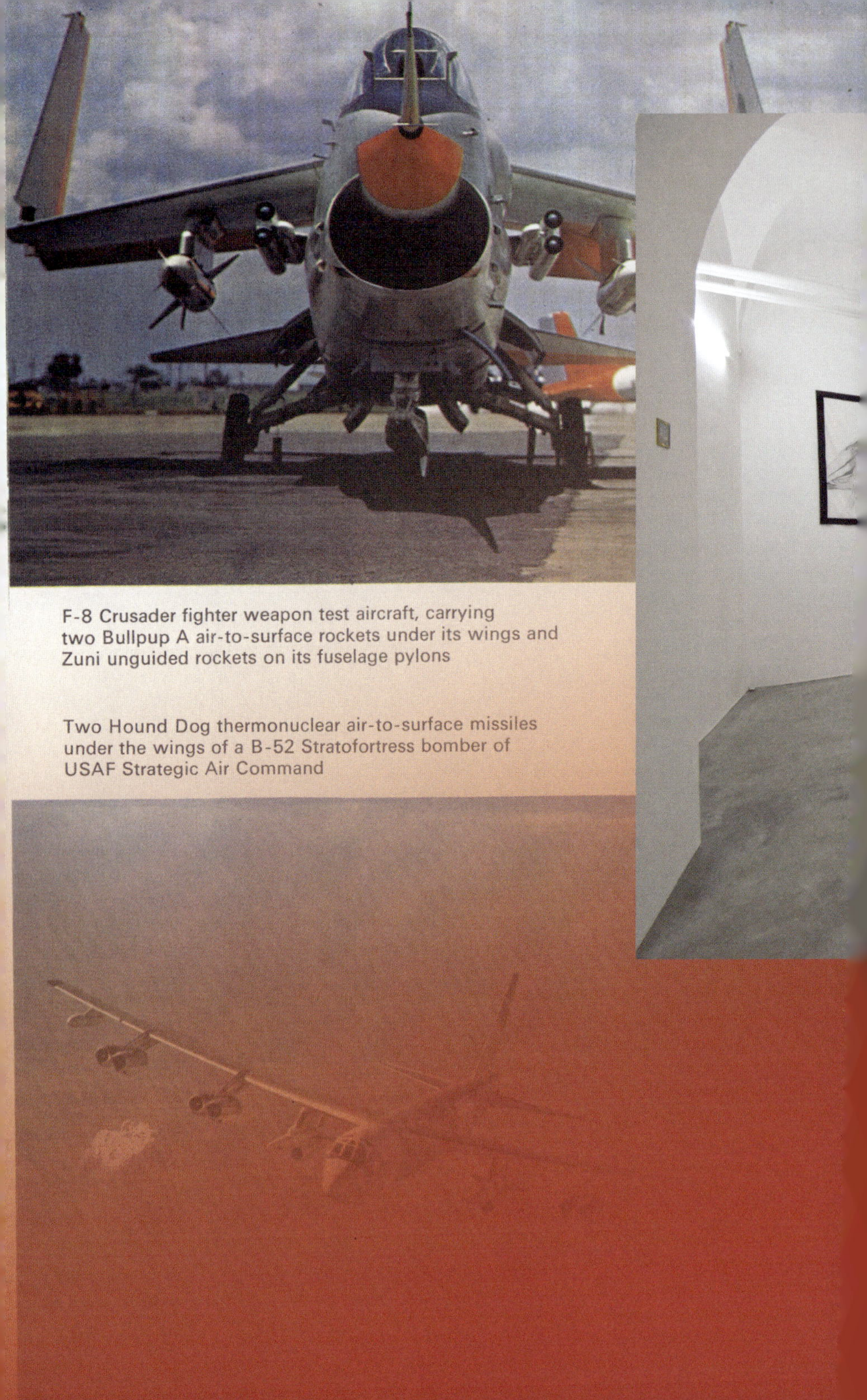

F-8 Crusader fighter weapon test aircraft, carrying
two Bullpup A air-to-surface rockets under its wings and
Zuni unguided rockets on its fuselage pylons

Two Hound Dog thermonuclear air-to-surface missiles
under the wings of a B-52 Stratofortress bomber of
USAF Strategic Air Command

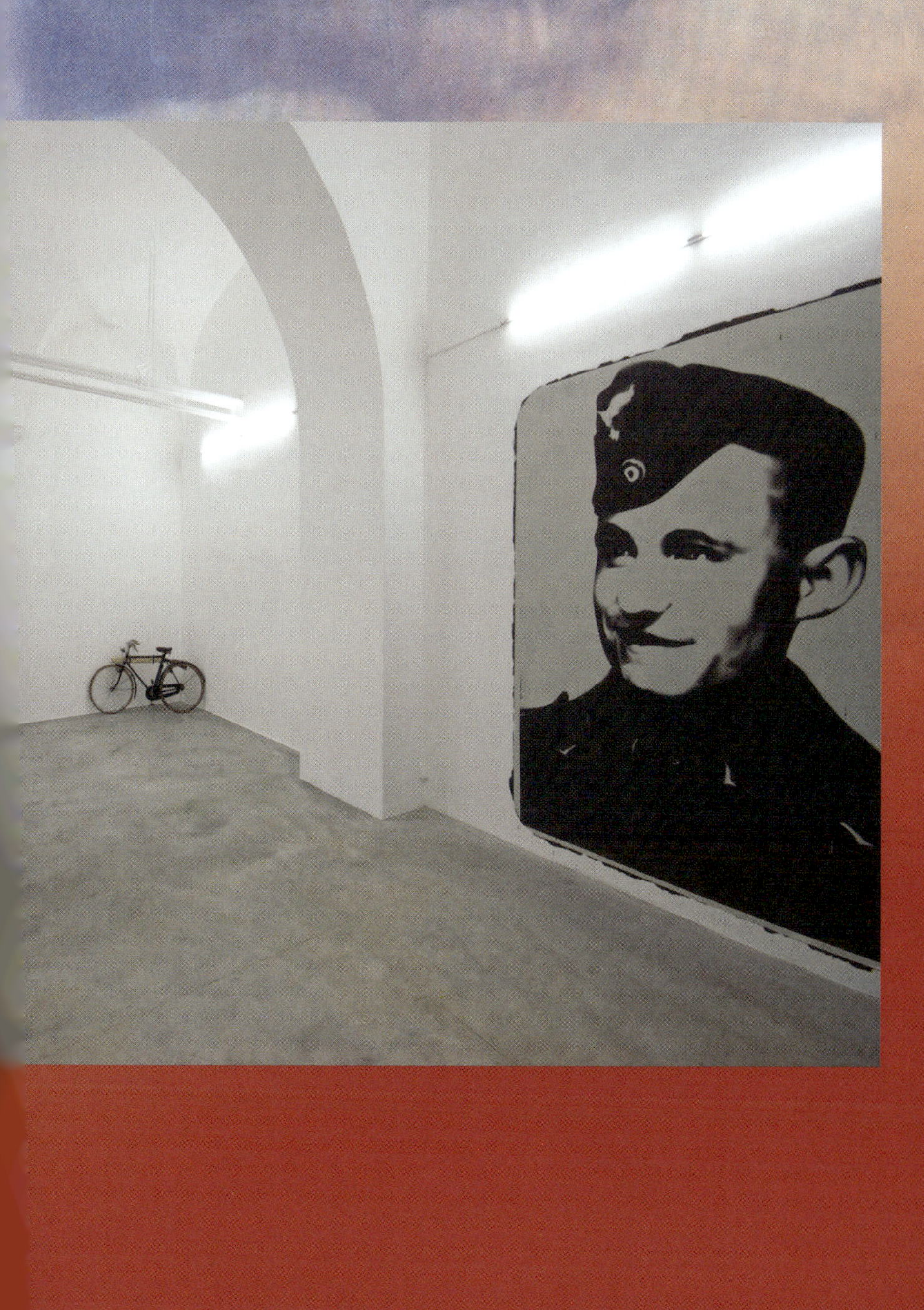

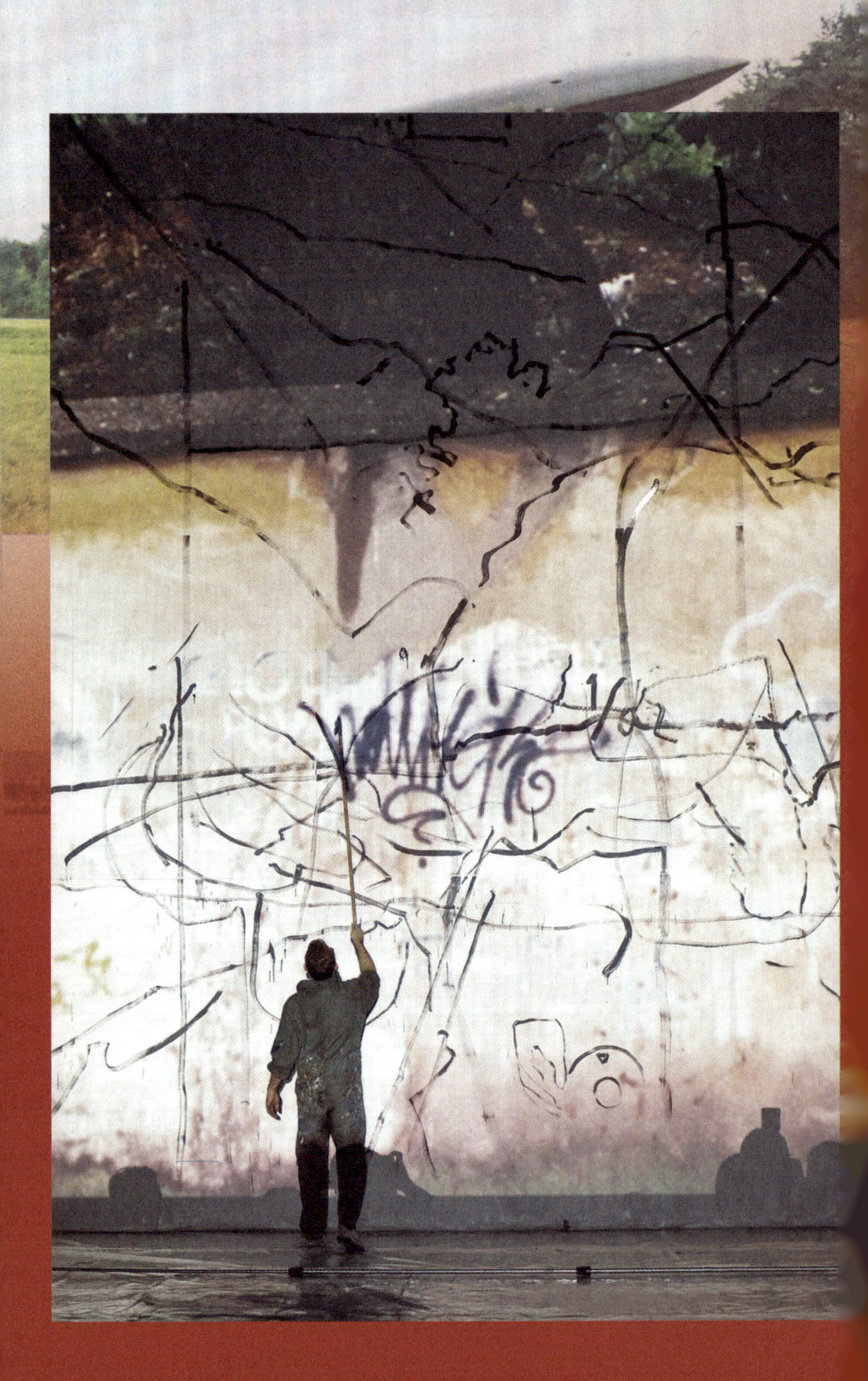

CHINA
LAKE
7680
NAVY

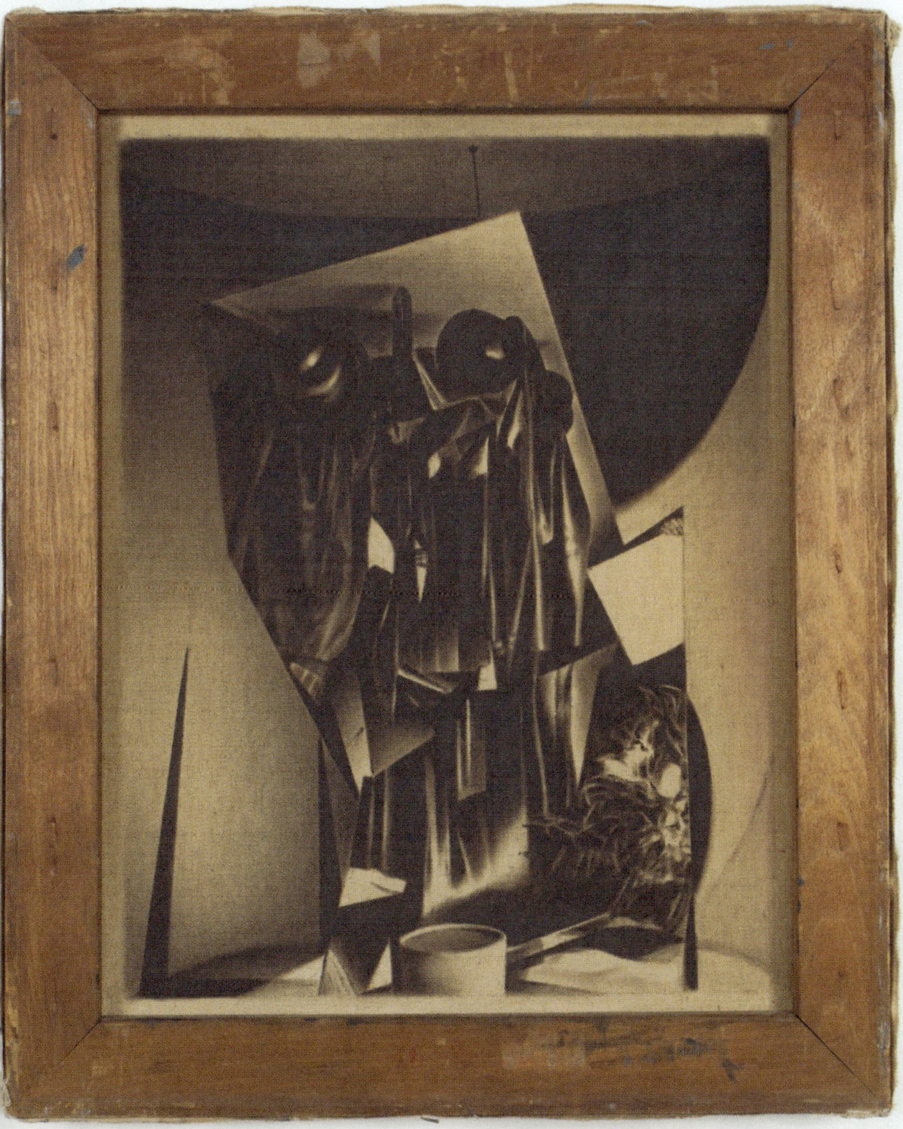

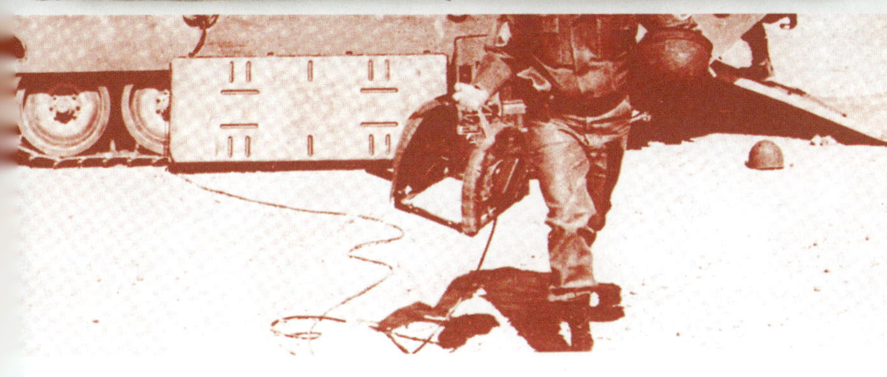

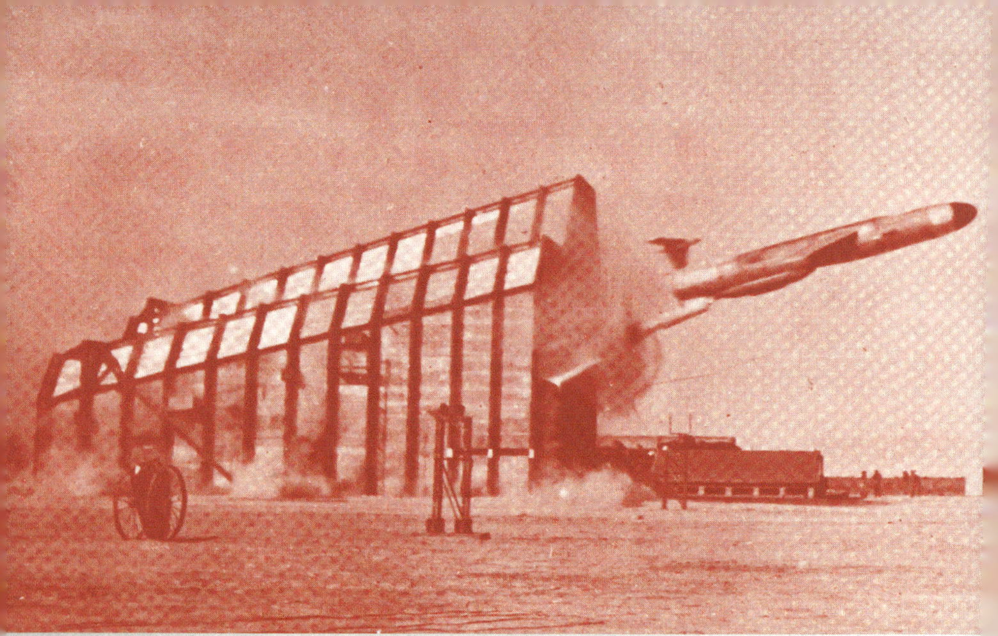

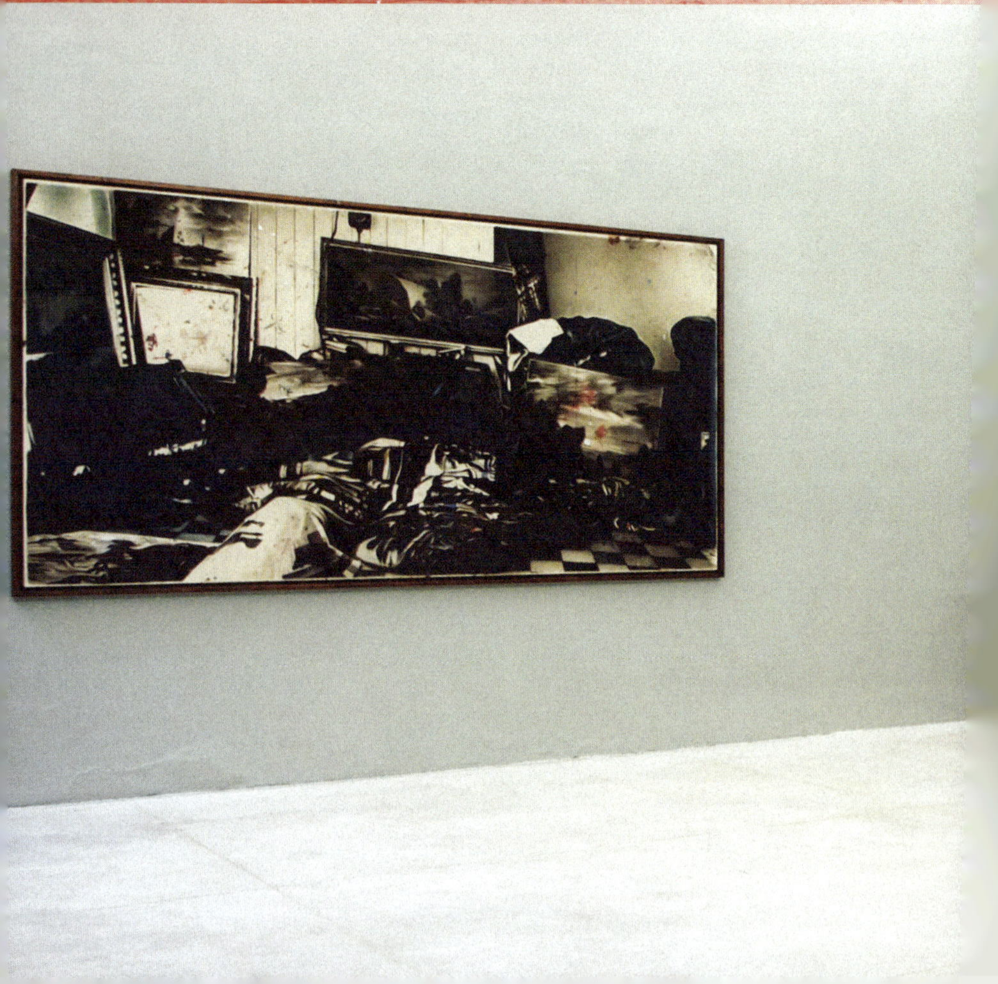

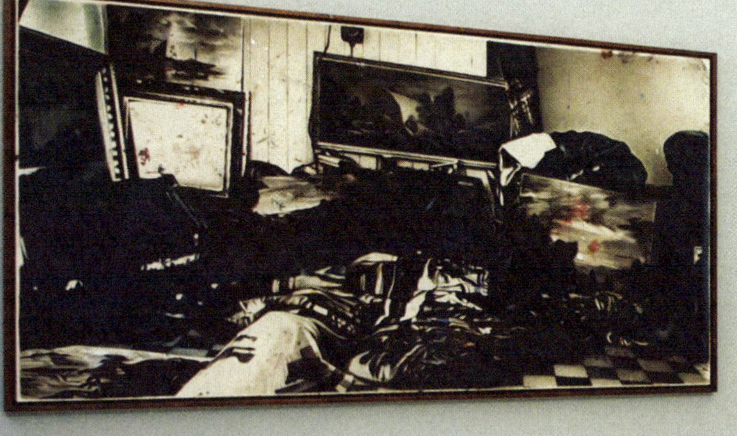

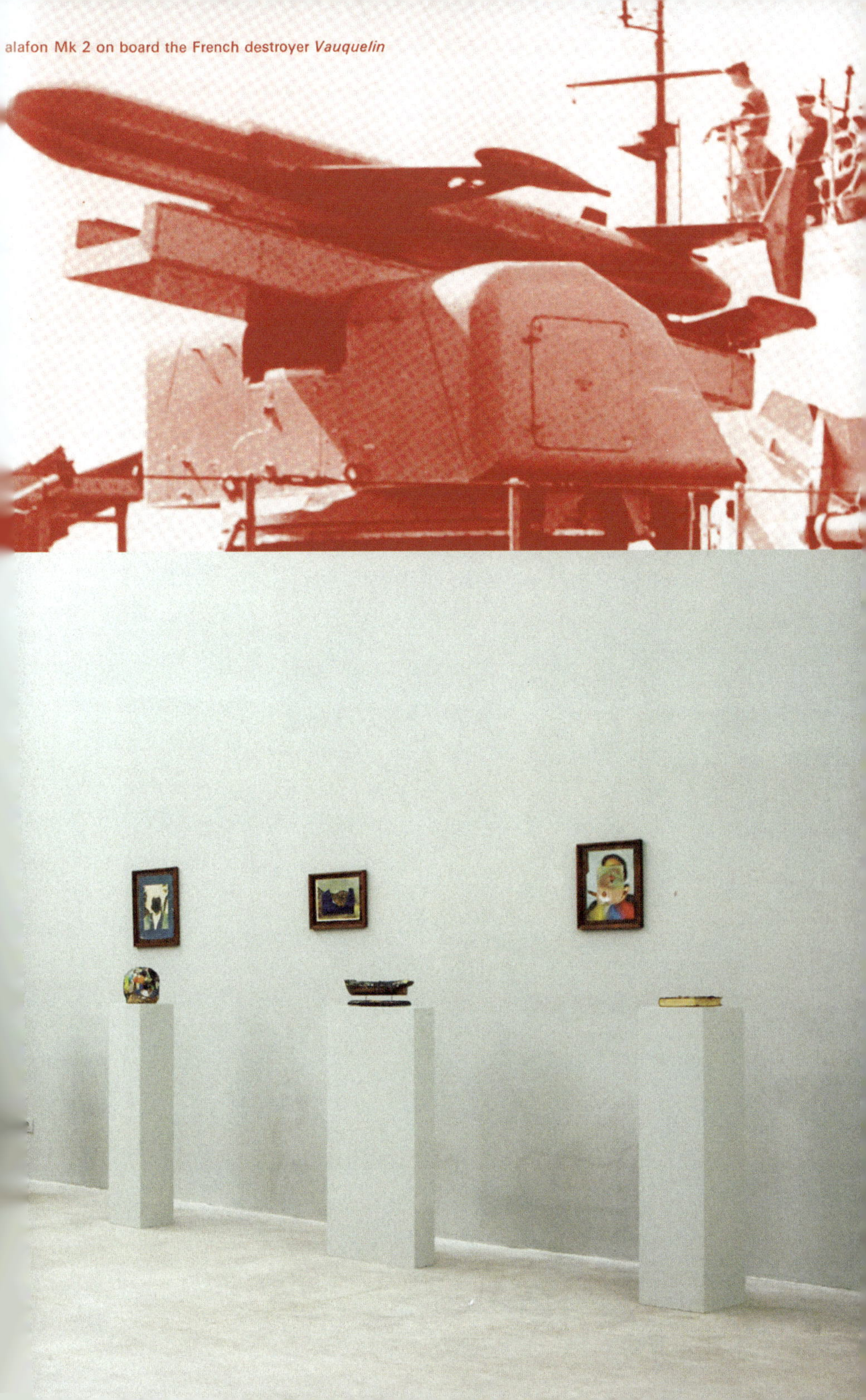
alafon Mk 2 on board the French destroyer *Vauquelin*

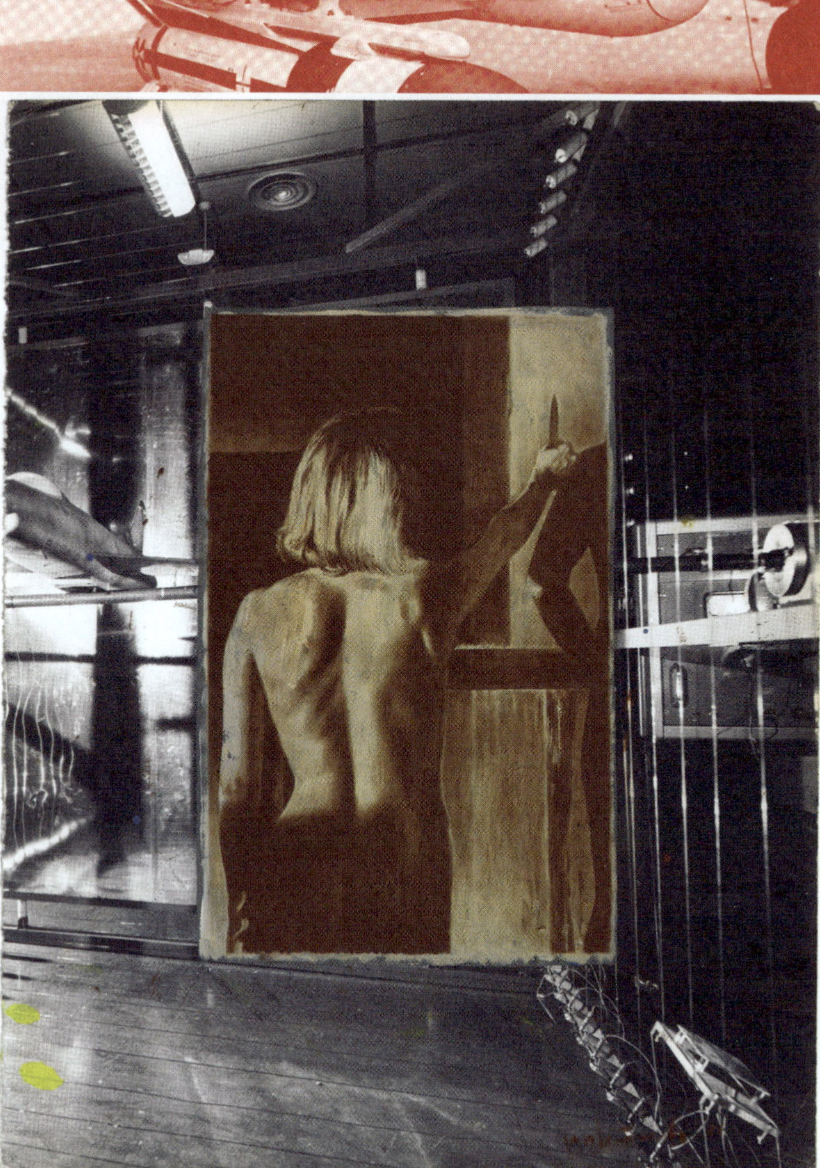

East, it is hardly surprising that no details have come officially from Israeli sources to confirm reports of the existence of this mobile, ramp-launched weapon. The availability of a rocket able to hit major targets throughout the Arab world from inside

This may be linked with reports of a Dassa surface-to-surface weapon named Jeric some years ago, and the knowledge t firing trials of such a missile were be conducted in the Mediterranean, off Toul in the Spring of 1968.

Minuteman (LGM-30)　　　　　　USA

Intercontinental ballistic missile. In production and service.

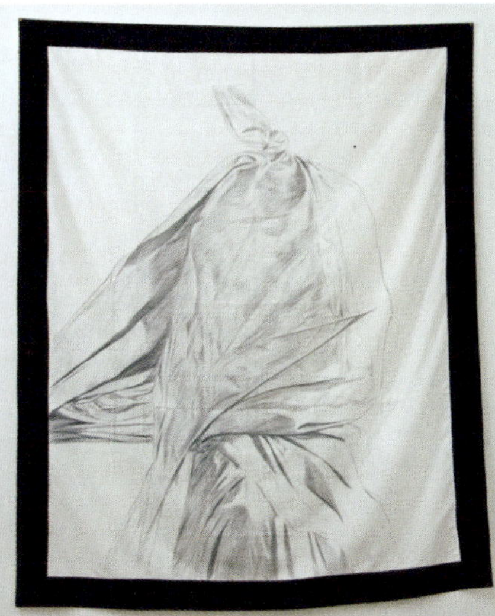

Although much smaller and lighter in weight than the first-generation weapons, its range is similar. The warhead is smaller, but the use of MIRV warheads on Minuteman III increases enormously the possibility of pene-trating enemy defence systems.

Three versions of Minuteman are currently operational. Wing II at Ellsworth AFB, S Dakota, and Wing V at Warren AFB, Wyoming, have a total of 350 LGM-30B Minuteman Is. These are 55ft 11in (16.99m) long, with weight of 65,000lb (29,500kg) and range of 6,300 miles (10,130km). Each successive stage is smaller than the one before, with a still-smaller cylindrical warhead of more than one megaton in an Avco Mk 11 re-entry vehicle. Wings I at Malmstrom AFB, Montana, III at Minot AFB, N Dakota, IV at Whiteman AFB, Missouri, and VI at Grand Forks, Utah, have LGM-30F Minuteman IIs, of similar configuration to the LGM-30B but 59 ft 10in (18.20m) long, with a weight of 70,000lb (31,750kg), range of 7,000 miles (11,265km) and warhead of over two megatons in a General Electric Mk 12 re-entry vehicle. The first Minuteman III squadron (data above) was installed at Minot in December 1970. Eventually, the force will comprise 490 LGM-30Fs and 510 LGM-30Gs.

The 200 silo launchers of Wing I are dispersed over an area of 18,000 sq miles (46,600km²). Each silo is 80ft (24.4m) deep. Two Strategic Air Command officers control each flight of 10 missiles from an underground launch centre. Airborne control can be exercised from KC-135 command post aircraft.

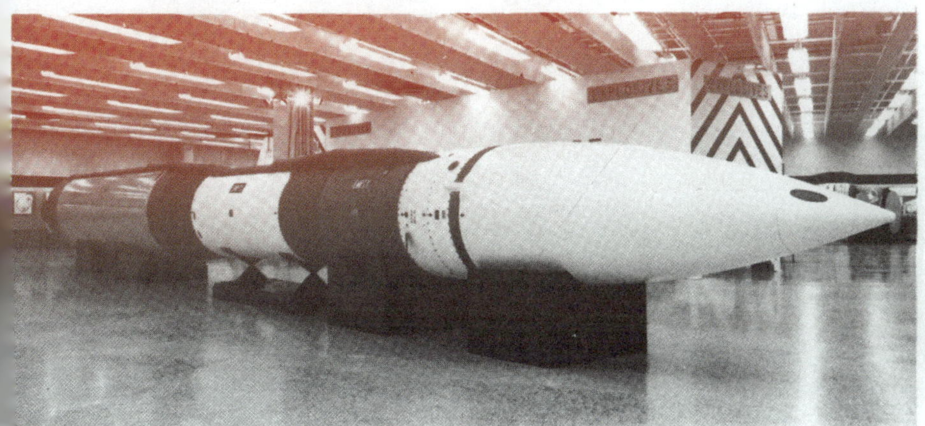

Minuteman III

"

Mosquito Switzerland/Italy

Lightweight anti-tank missile. In service.

Prime contractor: Contraves Italiana SpA.
Powered by: Two-stage solid-propellant rocket motor.
Airframe: Cylindrical glass-fibre body with pointed conical nose. Folding cruciform wings of sandwich construction, each with trailing-edge vibrating spoiler.
Guidance and Control: Wire guidance, with roll-stabilisation by powder-driven gyro. Control by vibrating spoilers on wings.
Warhead: Hollow charge, weighing 9lb (4kg) and able to penetrate more than 26in (660mm) of armour, or fragmentation type.
Length: 3ft 7.7in (1.11m).
Body diameter: 4.72in (12cm).
Wing span: 1ft 11.6in (0.60m).
Launch weight: 31lb (14.1kg).
Cruising speed: 205mph (330km/h).
Range limits: 1,200-7,800ft (360-2,375m).

Development and Service
This simple, one-man, infantry anti-tank weapon was developed by Contraves-Oerlikon of Switzerland but manufactured until 1971 by Contraves Italiana. It is standard equipment in the Swiss and Italian Armies, who use also a version fitted with a parachute recovery system, instead of a warhead, for training. Six Mosquitos can be carried in their container-launchers, ready for firing, by the Puch-Haflinger light cross-country vehicle. Mosquitos have also been fired successfully from Agusta-Bell 47 helicopters.

In conventional infantry use, the Mosquito is controlled and fired by means of a small control box carrying a joystick and optical sight. The container-launcher houses the missile with its warhead detached, and weighs 48.5lb (22.0kg).

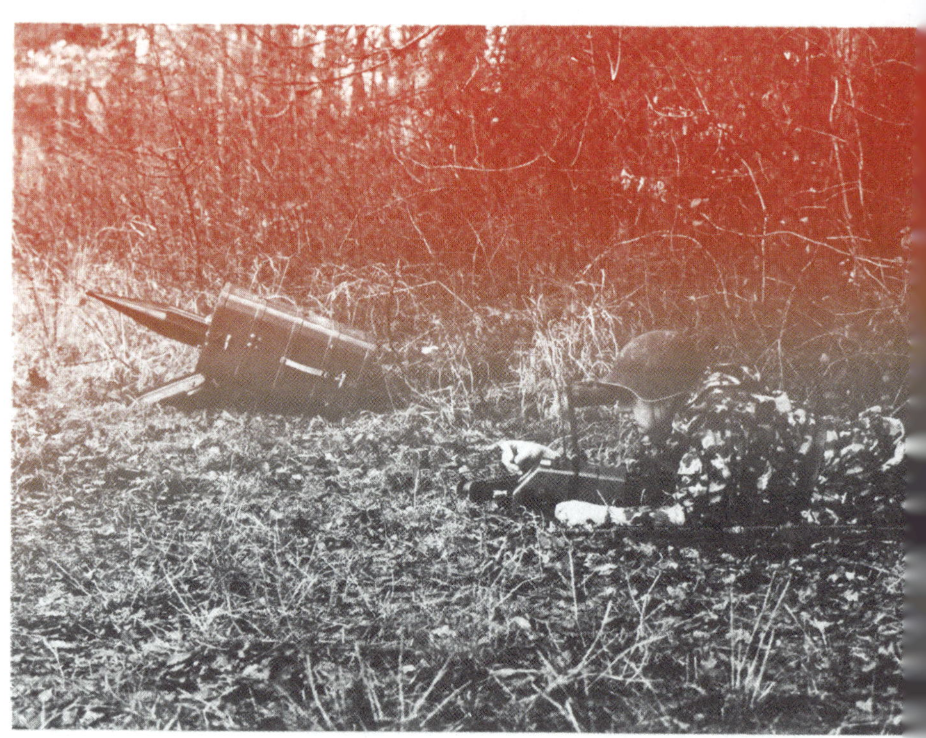

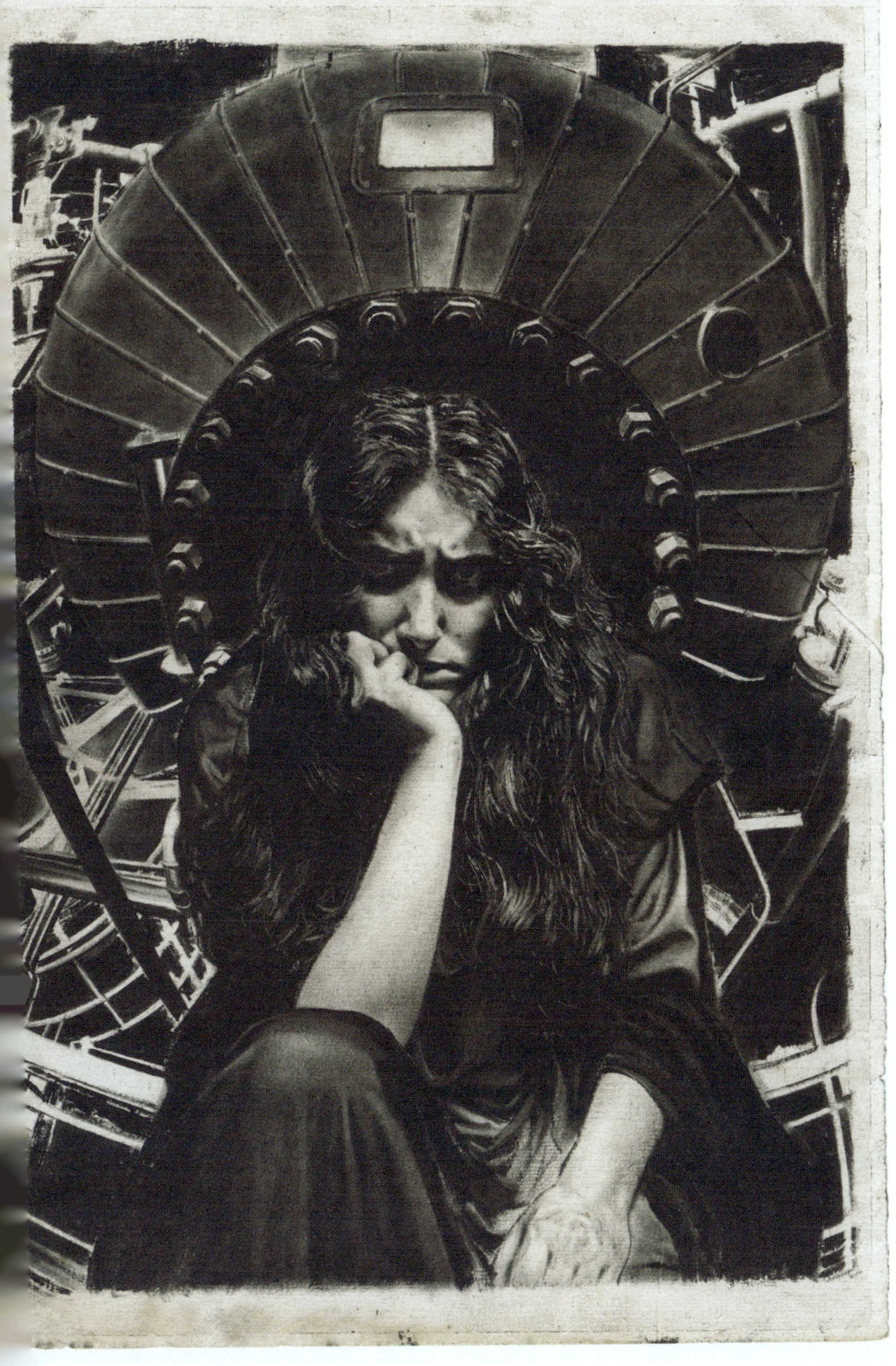

Murene

France

Ship-based surface-to-air close-range weapon system. Under development.

Prime contractor: Thomson-CSF.

Development and Service
Matra's Crotale all-weather surface-to-air weapon system (see page 46) offers such promise that Thomson-CSF decided to develop a ship-based version as a private venture. The result is Murene, which comprises one or more eight-round turret-launchers, a Triton air and sea surveillance radar with a range of 23 miles (37km), a pulse-Doppler radar providing aerial surveillance and IFF interrogation over an 11.2-mile (18-km) range, Pollux stabilised fire control radar with a range of 10 miles (16km), a digital computer for automatic tracking and a display console. The effectiveness of Murène can be extended by linking it with a Mureca weapon system, which adds a 48-round Catulle rocket-launcher to the Crotale launcher.

Nike Ajax (MIM-3)

USA

Surface-to-air missile. In service.

Prime contractor: Western Electric Company Inc.
Powered by: Tandem Aerojet-General liquid-propellant sustainer of 2,600lb (1,180kg) st and Hercules Inc solid-propellant jettisonable booster, giving 59,000lb (26,760kg) st for 2½ seconds.
Airframe: Two-stage design. Cylindrical missile body, tapering towards long ogival nose, with four small pivoted foreplanes on nose indexed in line with cruciform delta wings at rear. Cylindrical booster with three large stabilising fins.
Guidance and Control: Western Electric Command system. Control by foreplanes.
Warhead: High-explosive, detonated by signal from ground.
Length: 34ft 0in (10.36m).
Body diameter: 1ft 0in (30cm).
Wing span: 4ft 0in (1.22m).
Launch weight: 2,455lb (1,113kg).
Max speed: Mach 2.25.
Max range: 25 miles (40km).

Development and Service
When the first Nike Ajax site became operational in December 1953, it inaugurated America's integrated missile/aircraft air defence system. About 15,000 Nike Ajax missiles were built before the type was superseded in production by the more powerful Nike Hercules; of these 5,500 were fired during development and training. None remain operational in the USA; but Nike Ajax continues in service in a few countries, such as Greece, Italy and Japan, sometimes in a semi-mobile form, although considerable ground equipment is required to support the launchers. The guidance system is similar to that described for Nike Hercules, utilising separate missile and target tracking radars and a computer to work out the necessary command signals to achieve an interception.

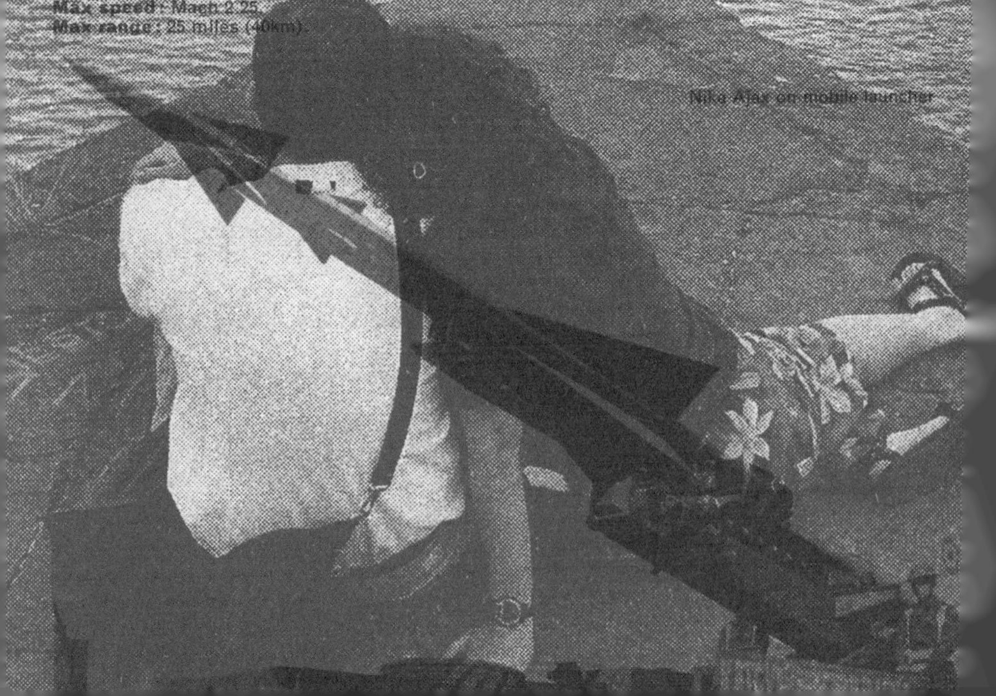

Nike Ajax on mobile launcher

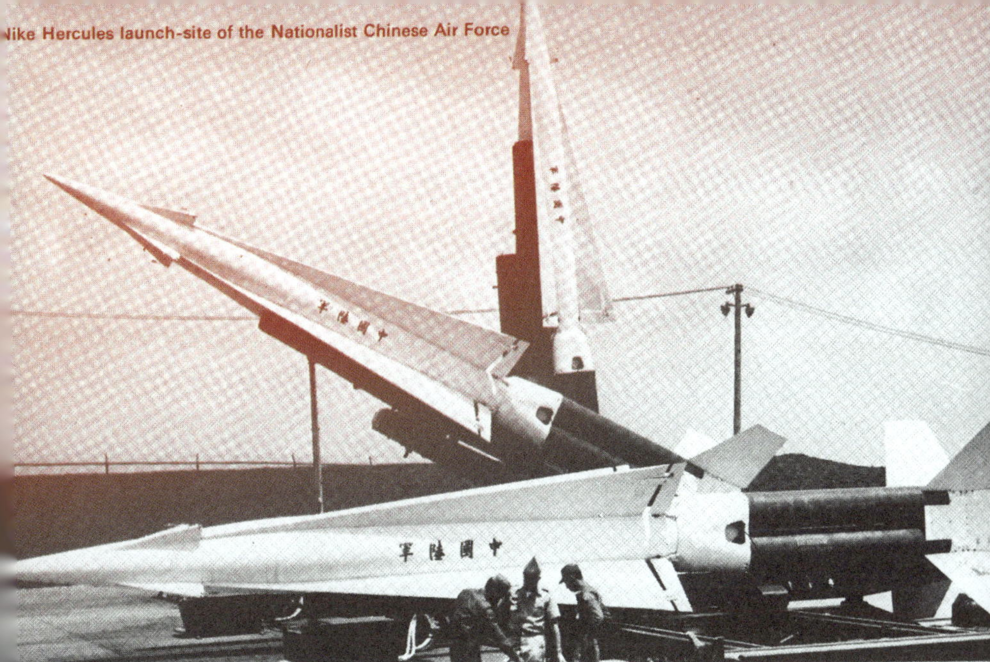

Nike Hercules (MIM-14)   USA

Surface-to-air missile. In production and service.

Prime contractors: Western Electric Company Inc/Mitsubishi Jukogyo Kabushiki Kaisha.
Powered by: Thiokol solid-propellant sustainer. Hercules Inc clustered four-motor solid-propellant jettisonable booster.
Airframe: Tandem two-stage missile. Basically-cylindrical missile body, tapering towards nose which carries small cruciform delta surfaces. Long-chord cruciform delta wings, each with trailing-edge control surface. Booster is made up of four cylindrical motors of the type used singly on Nike Ajax, with cruciform stabilising fins indexed in line with missile wings.
Guidance and Control: Western Electric command system. Control by wing trailing-edge surfaces.
Warhead: Alternative nuclear or high-explosive types.
Length: 41ft 6in (12.65m).
Max body diameter: 2ft 7½in (80cm).
Wing span: 6ft 2in (1.88m).
Launch weight: 10,400lb (4,720kg).
Max speed: Mach 3.65.
Max range: 80 miles (130km).

Development and Service
Although development of Nike Hercules (then known as Nike B) was started in 1953, to replace Nike Ajax, it remains in production by Mitsubishi in Japan. In the USA, where it became operational as the nation's primary anti-aircraft defence weapon in 1958, the number of launch-sites has been reduced progressively. In the early 'seventies, only 13 batteries were still active, with a further 27 manned by the National Guard. These will be re-equipped with SAM-D in due course.

The Nike Hercules missile was developed and produced originally by the Douglas Aircraft Company, and achieved a notable early success when one Nike Hercules intercepted another at a range of 30 miles (48km) from its launch-point, and altitude of about 100,000ft (30,500m) over White Sands Missile Range in September 1960.

In operation, the target is acquired first by acquisition radars, which pass it on to the target tracking radar. When the missile is launched, another tracking radar issues command guidance and detonation instructions under the control of the weapon system's data processing equipment. In the USA, Nike Hercules batteries were integrated into the SAGE defence system, which controlled all air defence fighters and missiles. Nike Hercules is also operational in a mobile role, notably with NATO and SEATO forces, using a HIPAR advanced high-power acquisition radar which greatly increases the mobility and detection capability.

Nuclear Falcon (AIM-26) USA

Air-to-air nuclear armed missile. In service.

Data apply to AIM-26A.
Prime contractor: Hughes Aircraft Company.
Powered by: Thiokol M60 solid-propellant rocket motor.
Airframe: Circular-section body, with maximum diameter at mid-length and tapering towards nose and tail. Rounded nose. Long-chord cruciform delta wings, each with a tail control surface aft of its trailing edge.
Guidance and Control: Hughes semi-active radar homing guidance. Control by tail surfaces.
Warhead: Nuclear, with active proximity fuse.
Length: 7ft 0in (2.13m).
Max body diameter: 11in (28cm).
Wing span: 1ft 8in (0.51m).
Launch weight: 203lb (92kg).
Max speed: Mach 2.
Max range: 5 miles (8km).

Development and Service

The AIM-26A Nuclear Falcon (originally XGAR-11) appeared in 1960, combining the basic control and guidance equipment of the AIM-4A Falcon (page 33) with the vastly-increased destructive power of a nuclear warhead. Radar homing was chosen in preference to infra-red because of its better all-weather capability, longer acquisition range and suitability for attack from any direction, including head-on. Externally, the AIM-26A differed from earlier Falcons in having a more bulbous body, without the nose vanes of AIM-4A/C/D. When the AIM-26A entered service with F-102 Delta Dagger squadrons of USAF Air Defense Command, it was the first nuclear-tipped air-to-air guided missile in the world, just as the AIM-4A had been the USAF's first air-to-air guided weapon of any kind. It was followed into production in 1963 by the AIM-26B (originally GAR-11A) which differs in having a non-nuclear warhead. (See also HM-55, page 34).

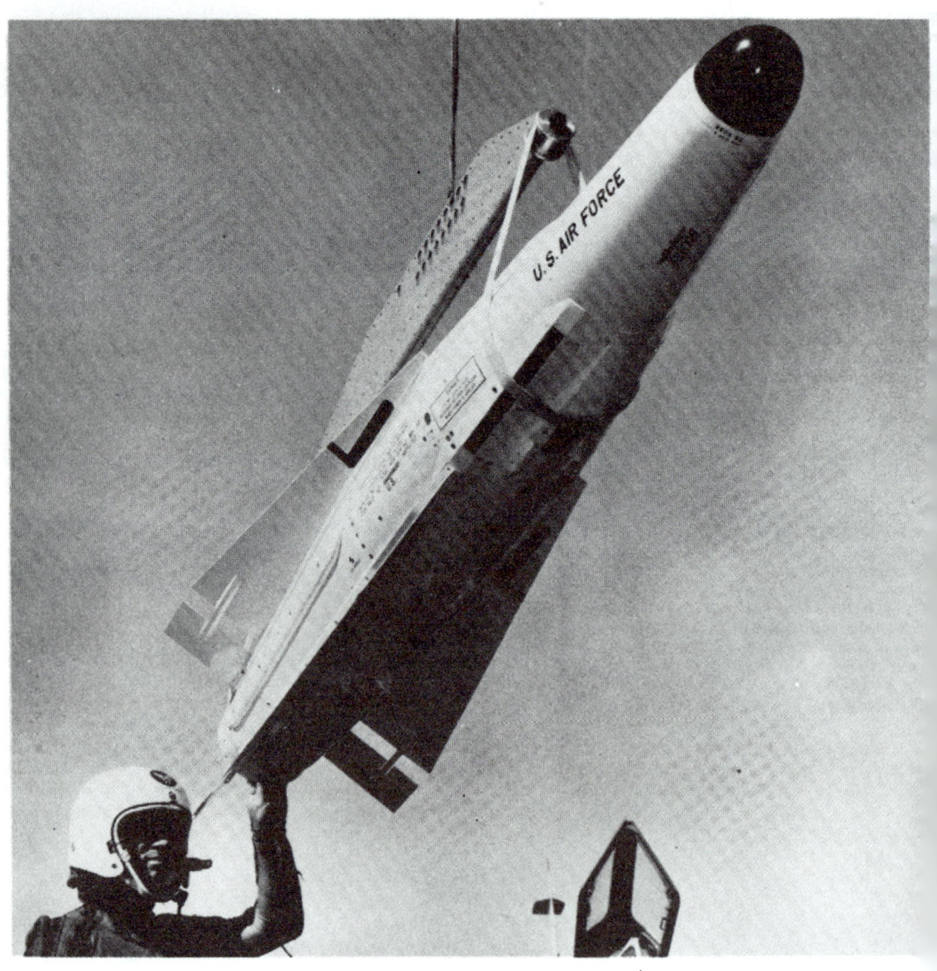

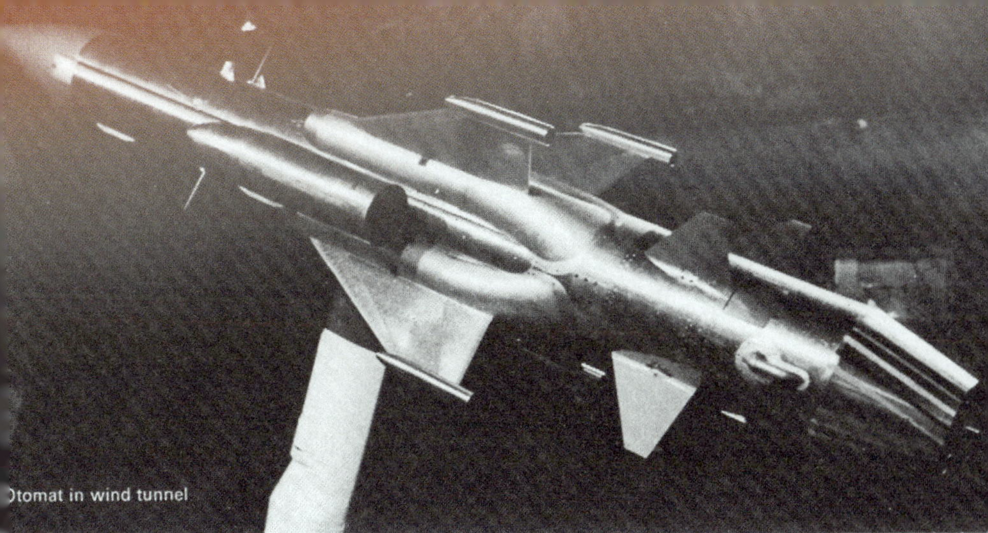

Otomat in wind tunnel

Otomat

France/Italy

Ship-to-ship tactical missile. Under development.

Prime contractors: SA Engins Matra (France) and Oto Melara SpA (Italy).
Powered by: Turboméca Arbizon III turbojet, rated at 882lb (400kg) st. Two side-mounted jettisonable boosters.
Airframe: Cylindrical body. Four semi-circular engine air-intake ducts, each supporting a cropped-delta wing, equi-spaced around body mid-way between nose and tail. Cruciform tail control surfaces indexed in line with wings. Ogival nose-cone and tapered tail fairing.
Guidance and Control: Inertial guidance, with

Exocet, but with a much longer range as a result of its use of a turbojet engine instead of a rocket motor. The warhead is unusually large and its effects are increased by the incendiary effect of any fuel remaining in the missile when it strikes the target.

Otomat does not require a swivelling launcher. It can be mounted in a fixed position on the launching craft, inside its delivery container which doubles as launcher. Firing is possible in all weathers, by day or night, and the missile is able to change direction up to 180 degrees, to port or starboard, to align itself on the target, which can therefore

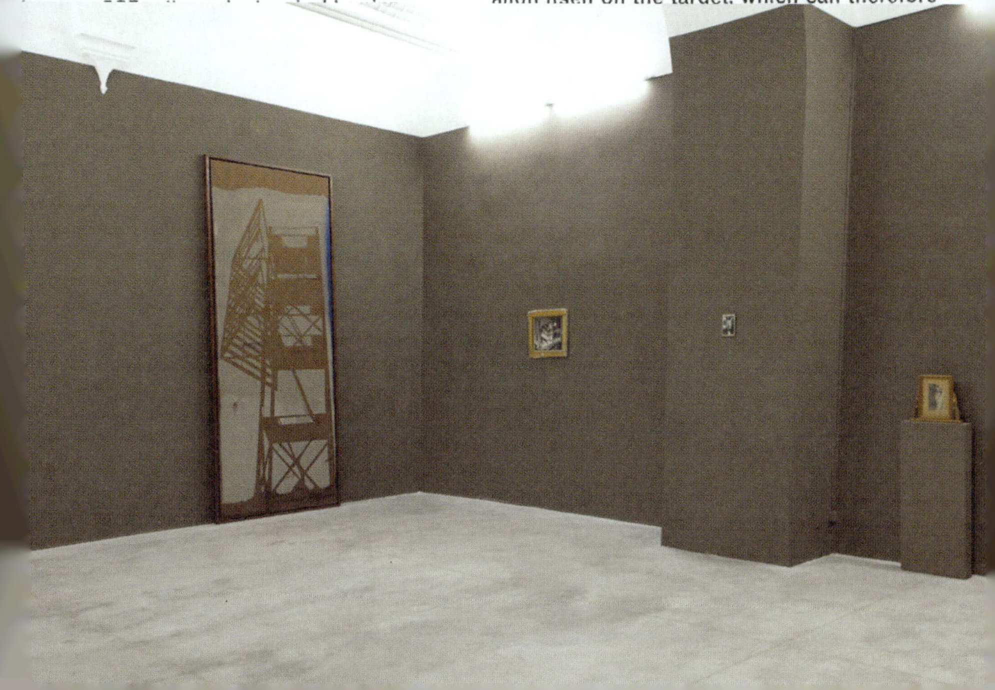

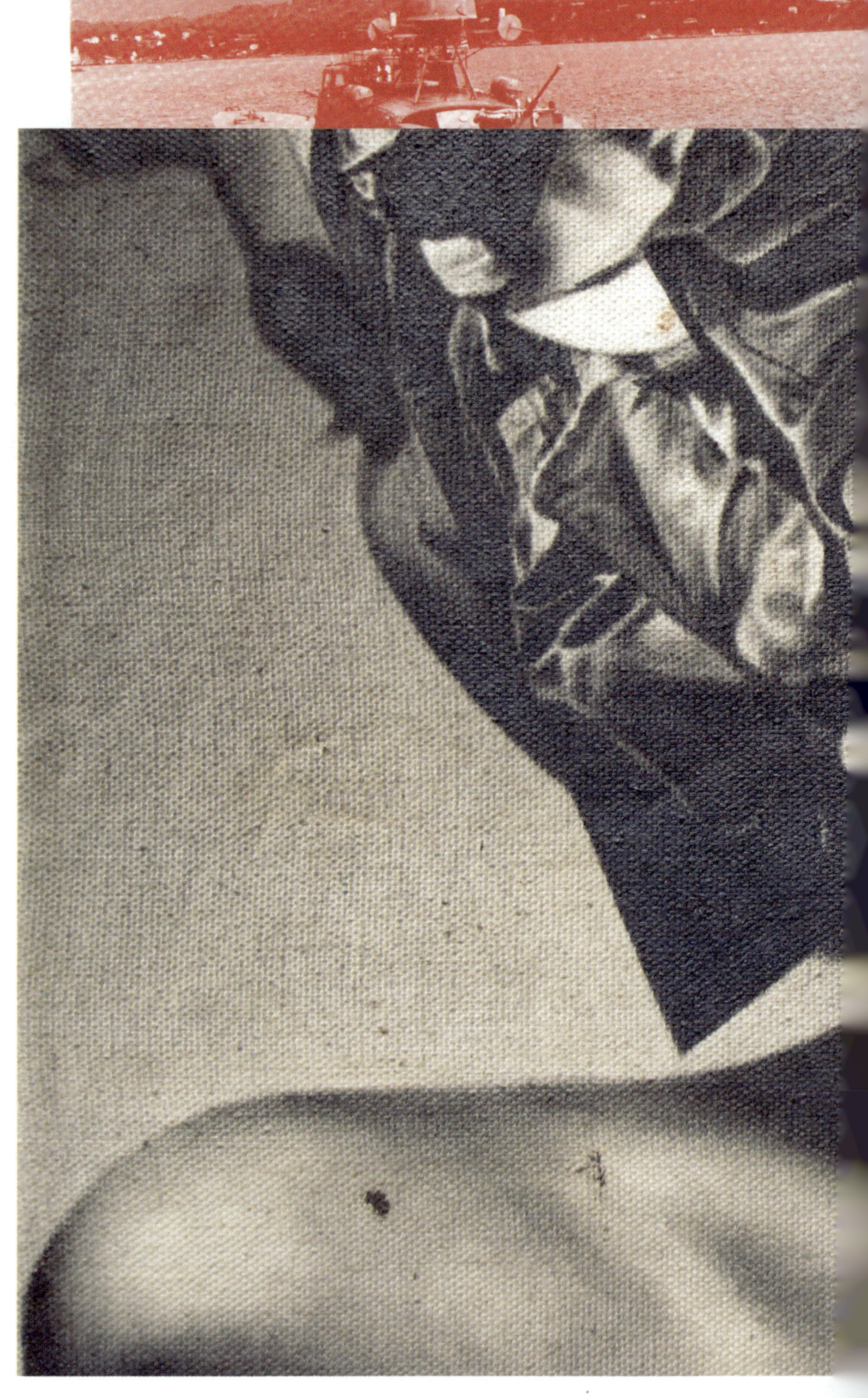

ment programme, these were replaced by four wheeled vehicles based on the Ford M656 five-ton truck, carrying new support equipment to increase rate of fire and improve system reliability. The Pershing 1-A vehicles comprise the improved erector-

try; a transporter for the improved programmer/test station and power station; the firing battery control centre truck; and the radio terminal set vehicle with an inflatable antenna. The MGM-31A (originally M-14) operational missile is unchanged by this [...] aining version [...] tion MTM-31B

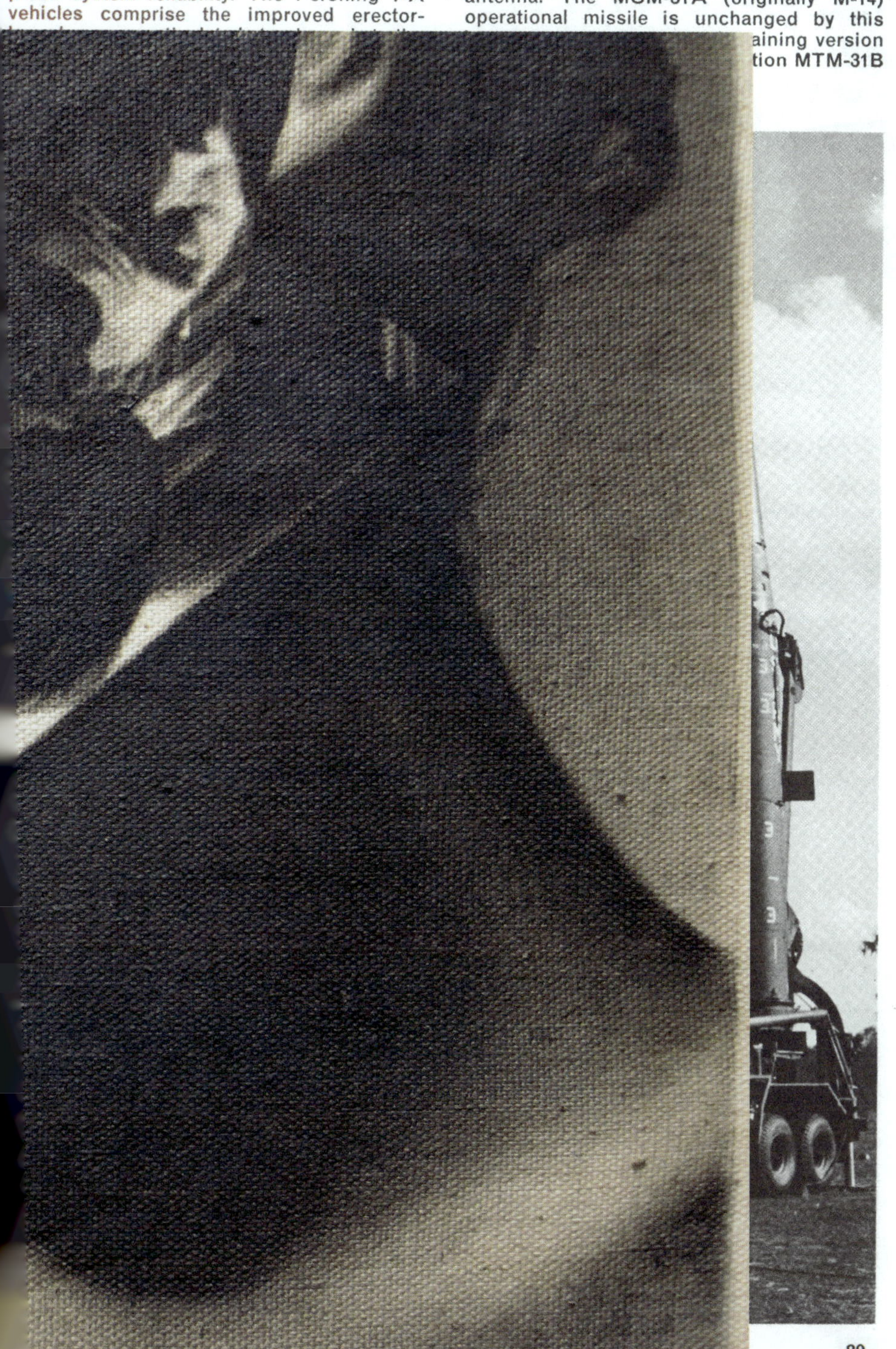

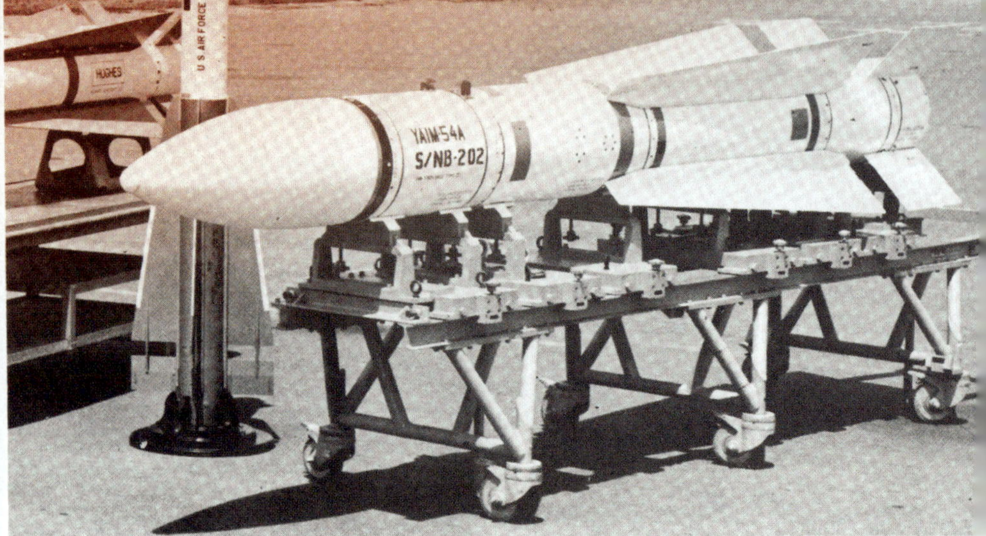

Phoenix (AIM-54A)

Long-range air-to-air missile. In production.

Prime contractor: Hughes Aircraft Company.
Powered by: Rocketdyne Mk 47 Mod 0 solid-propellant rocket motor.
Airframe: Cylindrical body with ogival nose. Long-chord cruciform wings and cruciform tail control surfaces.
Guidance and Control: Hughes radar-homing guidance system. Control by tail surfaces.
Warhead: High-explosive, with proximity fuse.
Length: 13ft 0in (3.96m).
Body diameter: 1ft 3in (38cm).
Wing span: 3ft 0in (0.91m).
Launch weight: 838lb (380kg).
Estimated range: 70-100 miles (110-160km).

Development and Service

Intended originally for the now-abandoned swing-wing F-111B tactical fighter, Phoenix offers such a great increase over the capability of current missiles that it was resurrected as primary armament of the US Navy's Grumman F-14 Tomcat. Maintenance and reliability are improved by the fact that the missile is made up of a number of self-contained sections, so that it can be handled as a complete unit or broken down for easy shipboard check-out and handling. In action, the target is located by the aircraft's Hughes AN/AWG-9 weapon control system, which can lock on to the enemy in any kind of weather and launch Phoenix at optimum range. The pulse-Doppler radar of the AN/AWG-9 enables it to 'look-down' and sort out a moving target from the ground clutter that obscures such targets in other systems. Its track-while-scan mode also enables the fire control system to keep up to six missiles at a time on course while searching for further targets. Terminal homing is by an active radar system in the missile.

Inert Phoenix missiles were first launched from an A-3A Skywarrior test aircraft in 1965. By March 1969, it was possible to intercept two Firebee target drones simultaneously with two missiles, while the targets were flying several miles apart. In August 1970, the 'look-down' and track-while-scan features of the AN/AWG-9 were tested in a launch against a Cougar jet fighter/drone flying many miles away and at lower altitude than the F-111B launch aircraft; the Cougar was destroyed. The first Phoenix production contract was placed by the US Navy in December 1970. The missile is expected to become operational on the F-14 in 1973-74.

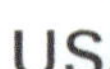

Pluton

France

Tactical nuclear surface-to-surface missile. In production.

Prime contractor: Aérospatiale, Division Engins Tactiques.
Powered by: SEP Styx dual-thrust solid-propellant rocket motor.
Airframe: Cylindrical body, with pointed ogival nose-cone and tail control surfaces.
Guidance and Control: Simplified inertial guidance system, with SAGEM inertial platform linked to a computer. Control by electrically-actuated tail surfaces.
Warhead: Nuclear, approx 10/15-kiloton yield.
Length: 24ft 10¾in (7.59m).
Body diameter: 2ft 1½in (0.65m).
Fin span: 4ft 8in (1.42m).
Launch weight: 5,335lb (2,420kg).
Max range: 62 miles (100km).

Development and Service

This mobile tactical weapon system is being developed and produced to replace the Honest John bombardment missiles which currently equip five battalions of the French Army. Firing trials of full-scale Pluton test vehicles have been underway since 1969. The versions launched since the Summer of 1970 have been fully representative of the operational missile, complete with guidance system but without a warhead. Meanwhile, development of the nuclear charge has been progressing as part of the French programme of atomic tests in the Pacific, and it is hoped to have Pluton in first-line service by 1973.

Aérospatiale is responsible for the missile and its launching equipment, under the direction of the French Army's Division des Engins Tactiques. The missile and its warhead will be supplied to operational units as two separate packages, with the missile container so designed that it will serve also as the launch-tube when mounted on the tracked transporter-launcher. The latter is based on the AMX-30 tank chassis.

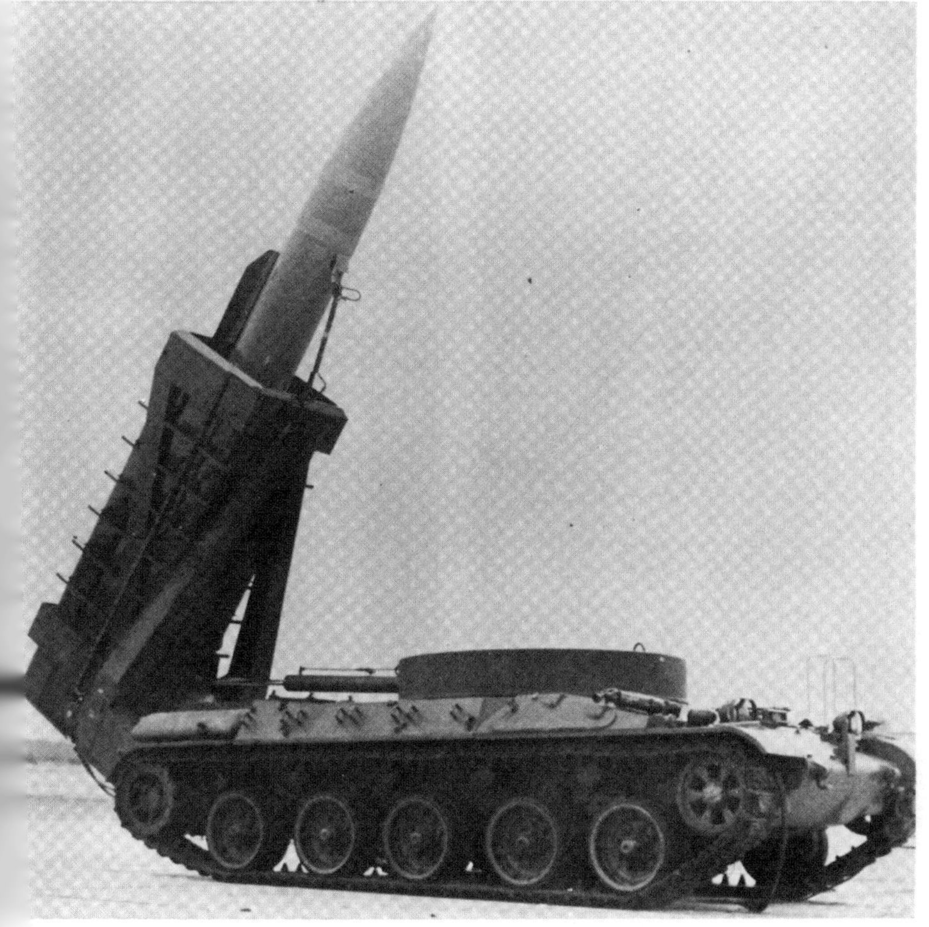

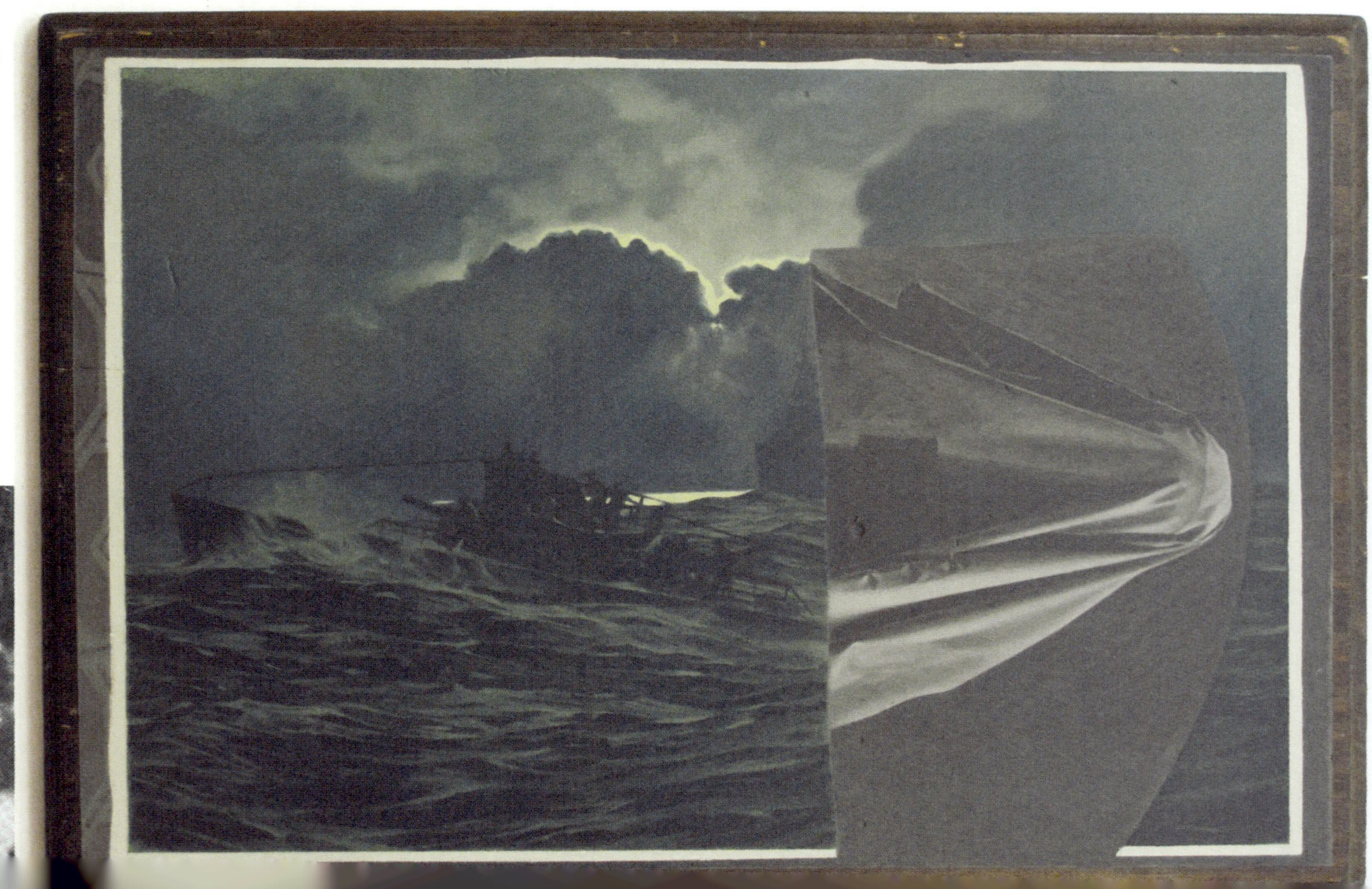

Poseidon (UGM-73)

**Underwater-to-surface or
surface-to-surface ballistic missile.
In production and service.**

Data and photograph: UGM-73A Poseidon C3.
Prime Contractor: Lockheed Missiles and
Space Company.
Powered by: First stage: Hercules or Thiokol
solid-propellant motor. Second stage: Hercules
solid-propellant motor.
Airframe: Two-stage missile. Cylindrical body
with ogival nose-cone. First- and second-stage
casings of glass-fibre. No fins or wings.
Guidance and Control: Inertial guidance
system developed under responsibility of
Massachusetts Institute of Technology and
manufactured by General Electric and Raytheon.
Thrust-vector control by one movable nozzle on
each stage, actuated by gas generator.
Warhead: Thermonuclear, in multiple
independently-targetable re-entry vehicles
developed by LMSC and Atomic Energy
Commission.
Length: 34ft 0in (10.35m).
Max body diameter: 6ft 2in (1.88m).
Launch weight: approx 65,000lb (12,500kg).
Max range: 2,875 miles (4,630km).

Development and Service

Having established the value of a submarine-
launched strategic missile system with
Polaris, the US Navy decided in 1965 to evolve
the more formidable Poseidon to take advan-
tage of new developments in missile technology. It was possible to pack larger missiles
on board existing Polaris A3 submarines
with only minor modification to the launch-
tubes. This enabled Lockheed Missiles and
Space Company (LMSC) to utilise larger
motors and improved equipment and so offer
double the payload and twice the accuracy
of Polaris. When added to the advantages
that come from use of an MIRV warhead,
these advances make Poseidon far more
formidable than its predecessor and it will
eventually replace Polaris on 31 of the US
Navy's 41 Fleet Ballistic Missile submarines.

Firing trials with Poseidon test rounds
began on August 16, 1968. By June 1970 the
initial batch of 20 missiles had all been
launched, 17 of them from pads ashore and
three from tubes on the surface ship USS
Observation Island. Underwater launch trials
began on August 3, 1970, when a Poseidon
was fired from the USS *James Madison,* the
first submarine that had been fitted with
modified launch-tubes and improved navigation and fire control systems for the new
weapon. Subsequent development was so
rapid that the *James Madison* was declared
operational in March 1971.

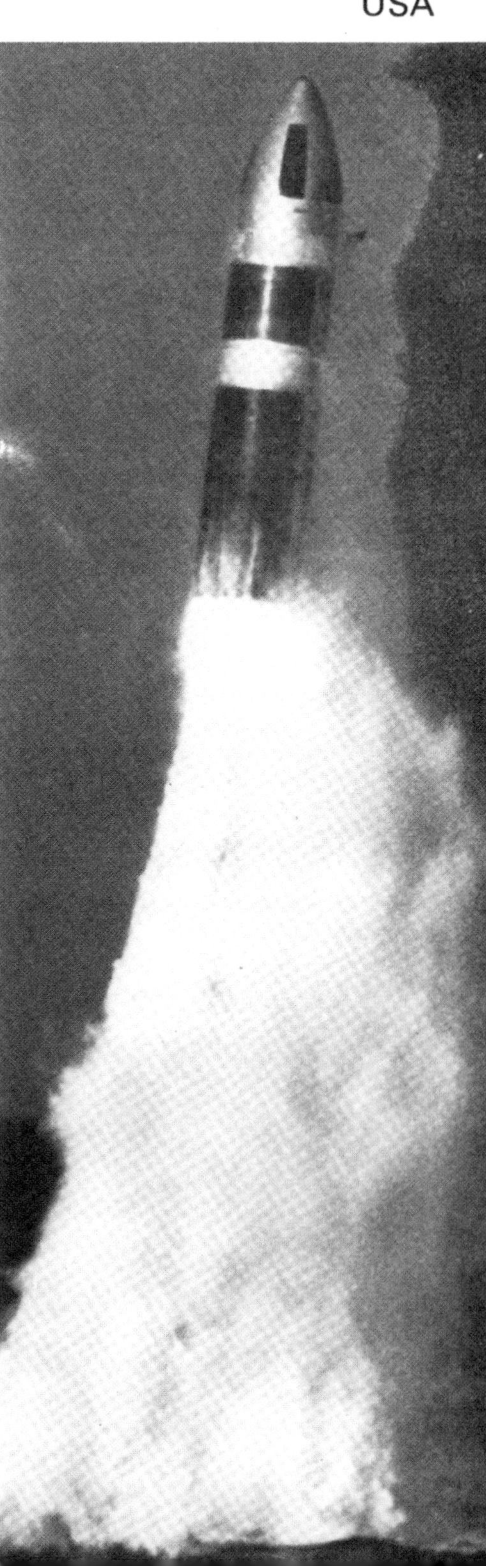

Quail (ADM-20C)

Air-launched decoy missile. In service.

Prime Contractor: McDonnell Aircraft
Corporation.
Powered by: General Electric J85-GE-7
turbojet of 2,450lb (1,112kg) st.
Airframe: Aeroplane configuration. Rectangular
body, with rounded nose. Short, high-set,
folding cropped-delta wings at rear, each with a
vertical tail-fin at mid-span and another
projecting downward from the wingtip. Ram
air-intake on each side of body.
Guidance and Control: McDonnell autopilot.
Warhead: None, but self-destruct device is
fitted to prevent missile being recovered by
enemy.
Length: 12ft 10in (3.91m).
Launch weight: 1,200lb (545kg).
Cruising speed: Mach 0.9.
Range: over 250 miles (400km).

Development and Service

Until SCAD is ready for service, Quail will
remain quite unique in the missile world. Its
sole task is to fly pre-planned 'patterns' in
enemy airspace, so that it will be picked up
on early warning, missile and interceptor
fighter radars and confuse the defences.
This is made possible by one of several
electronic devices packed into Quail's glass-
fibre body, which ensures that the tiny decoy
produces the same 'blip' on a radar screen
as the huge B-52 Stratofortress bomber from
which it is air-launched.

McDonnell began developing Quail, as the
XGAM-72, in 1955. By June 1960, a B-52 was
able to drop three Quails simultaneously
in an operational-type pattern over Eglin
AFB. Before the end of that year, the first of
the improved production-type ADM-20C
Quails showed its paces with a pre-pro-
grammed flight of several hundred miles,
and deployment to Strategic Air Command
bases was completed between March 1961
and January 1962.

Four Quails can be packed into a small
launch package, with their wing and tail
surfaces folded for stowage in the bomb-bay
of th[e]
is st[ill]
The [
ADM[

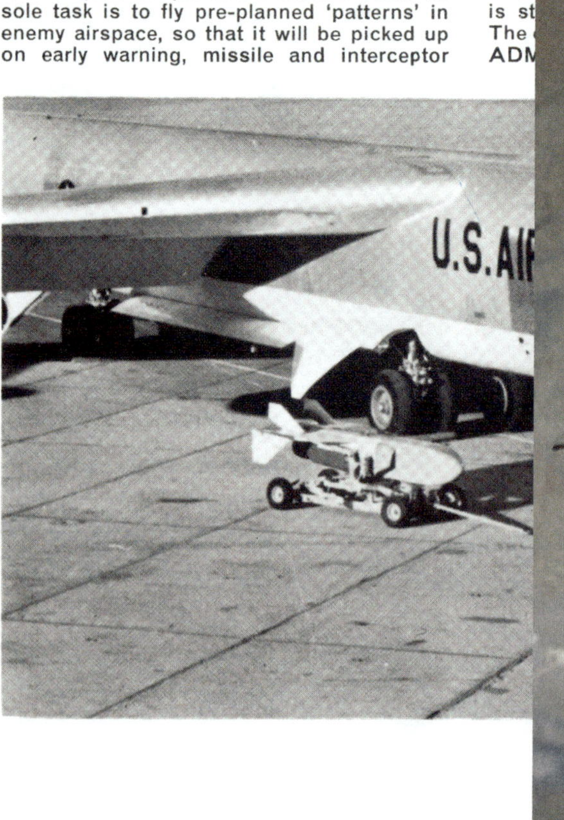

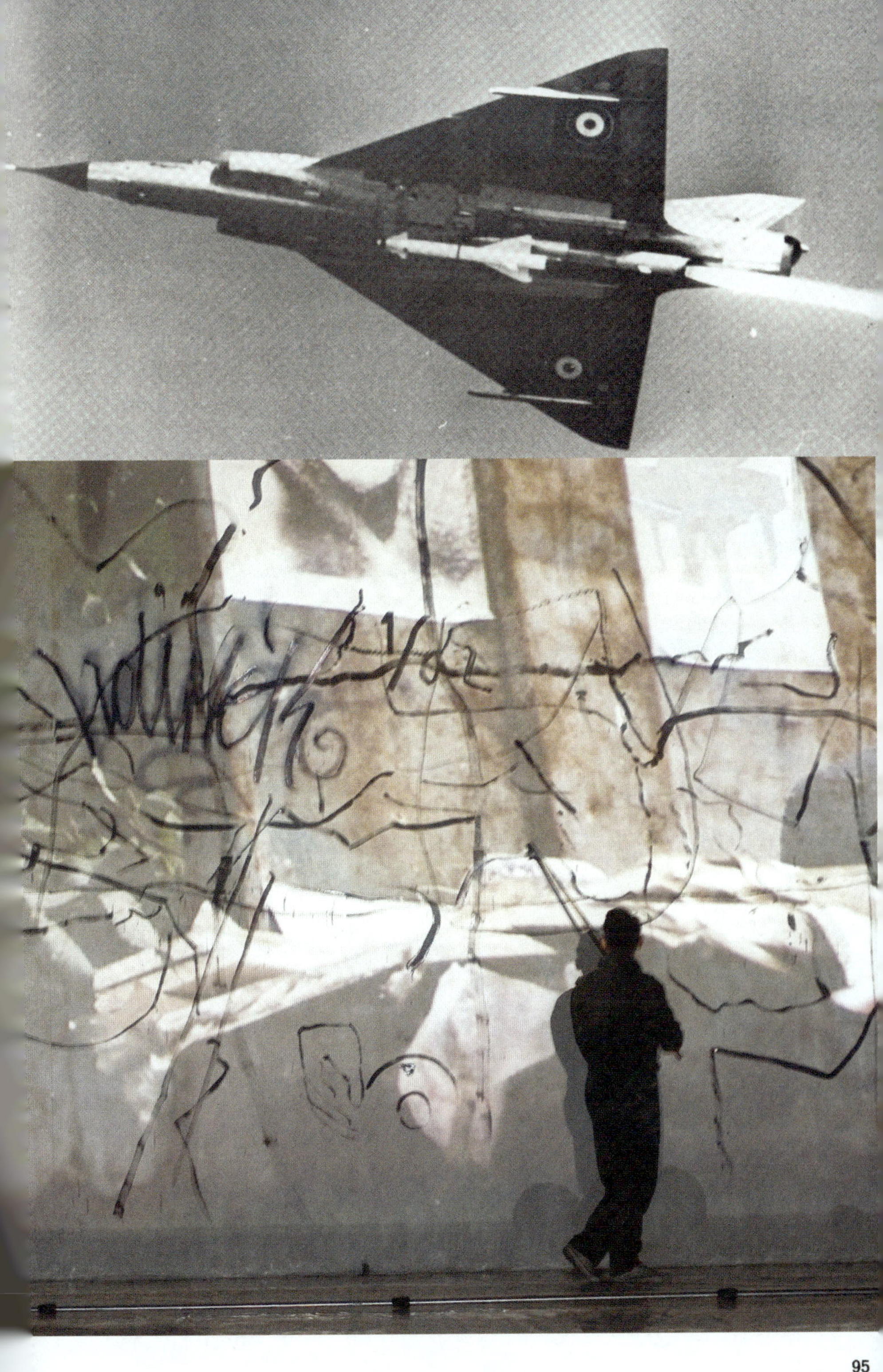

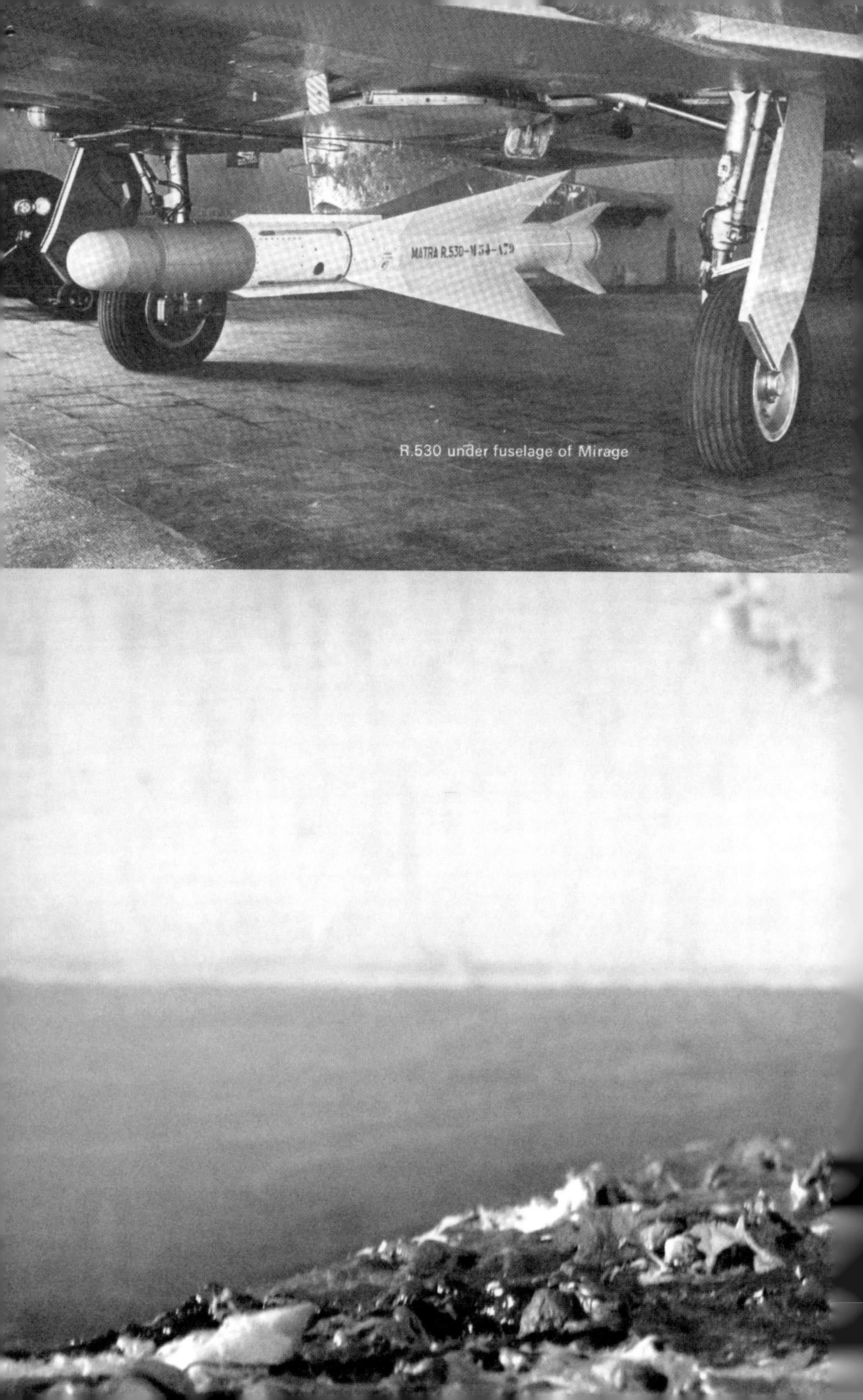

R.530 under fuselage of Mirage

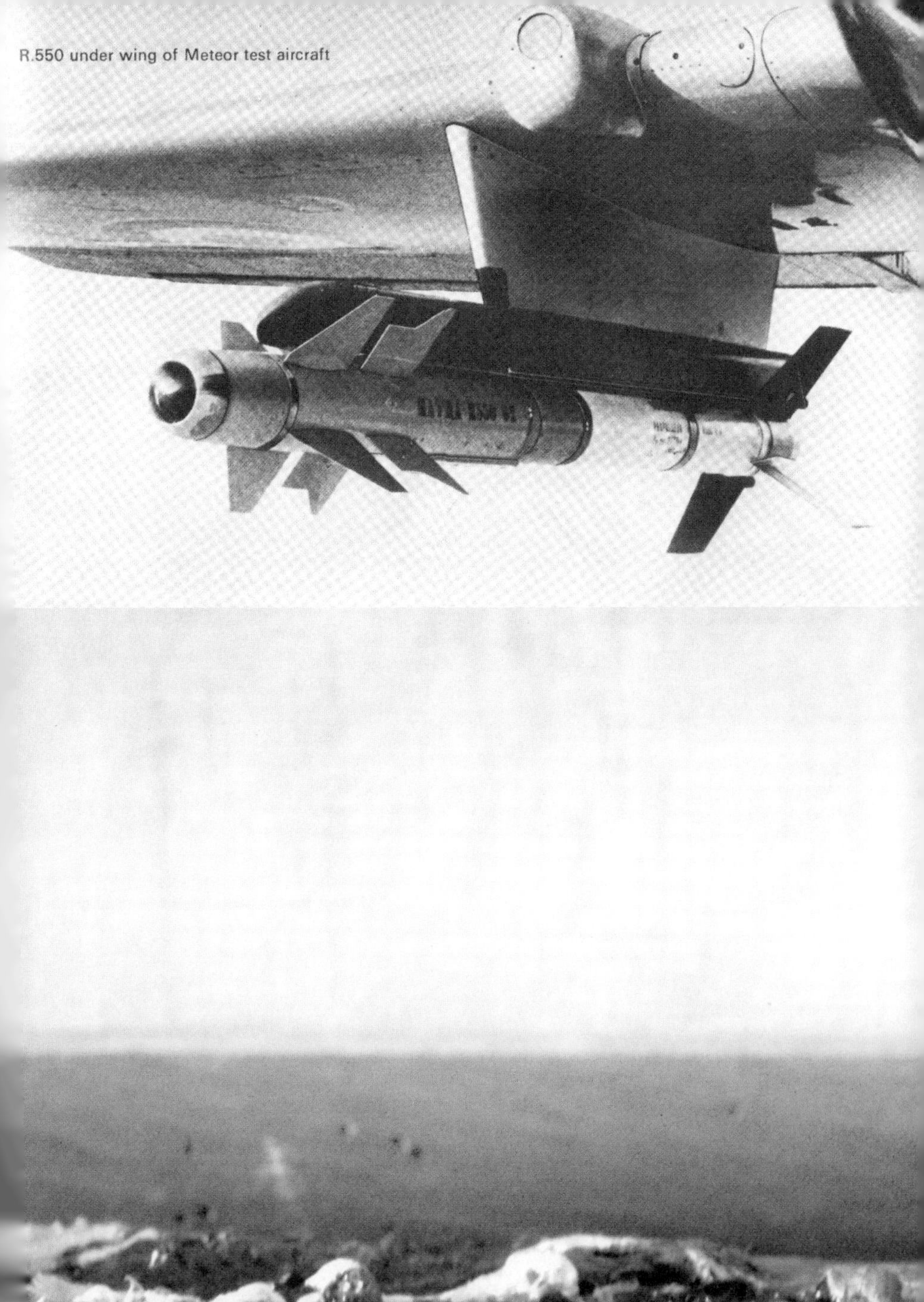

R.550 under wing of Meteor test aircraft

The main units of the system comprise a four-round launcher trailer, an optical tracker and a power unit. Once the launcher has been loaded by two members of the five-man detachment, it can be left unattended and the system can be operated by one man at the tracker. When surveillance radar built into the launcher detects a target, an IFF interrogator determines if the latter is hostile. If it is, the launcher and tracker are aligned automatically in the direction of the target. The operator acquires the target optically in elevation and then tracks it by means of a joystick, with the launcher following the tracker as he does so. When the target is within range, as assessed by a computer the operator is informed and fires a Rapier missile. Flares on the missile are followed by a TV camera in the tracker, which measures deviations from the sightline. The computer uses these data to correct the missile's trajectory and keep it on course to the target. The complete weapon system, with nine additional missiles, can be towed and transported by two Land-Rovers and is air-transportable by two Wessex helicopters.

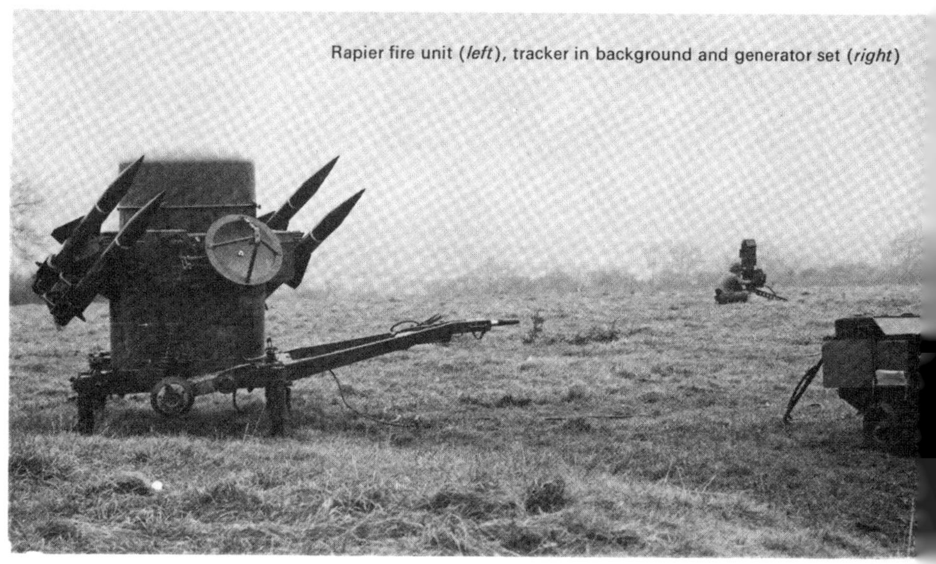

Rapier fire unit (*left*), tracker in background and generator set (*right*)

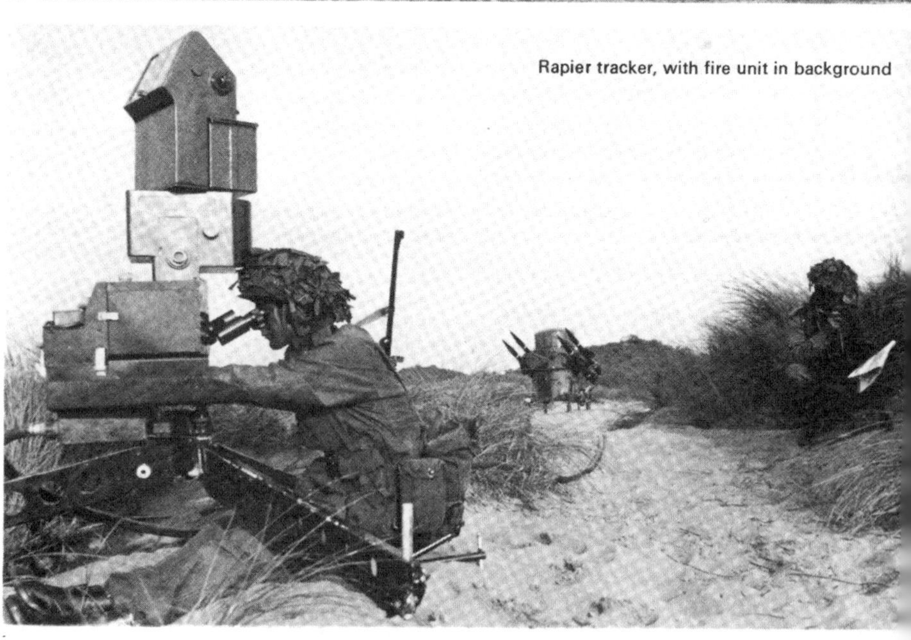

Rapier tracker, with fire unit in background

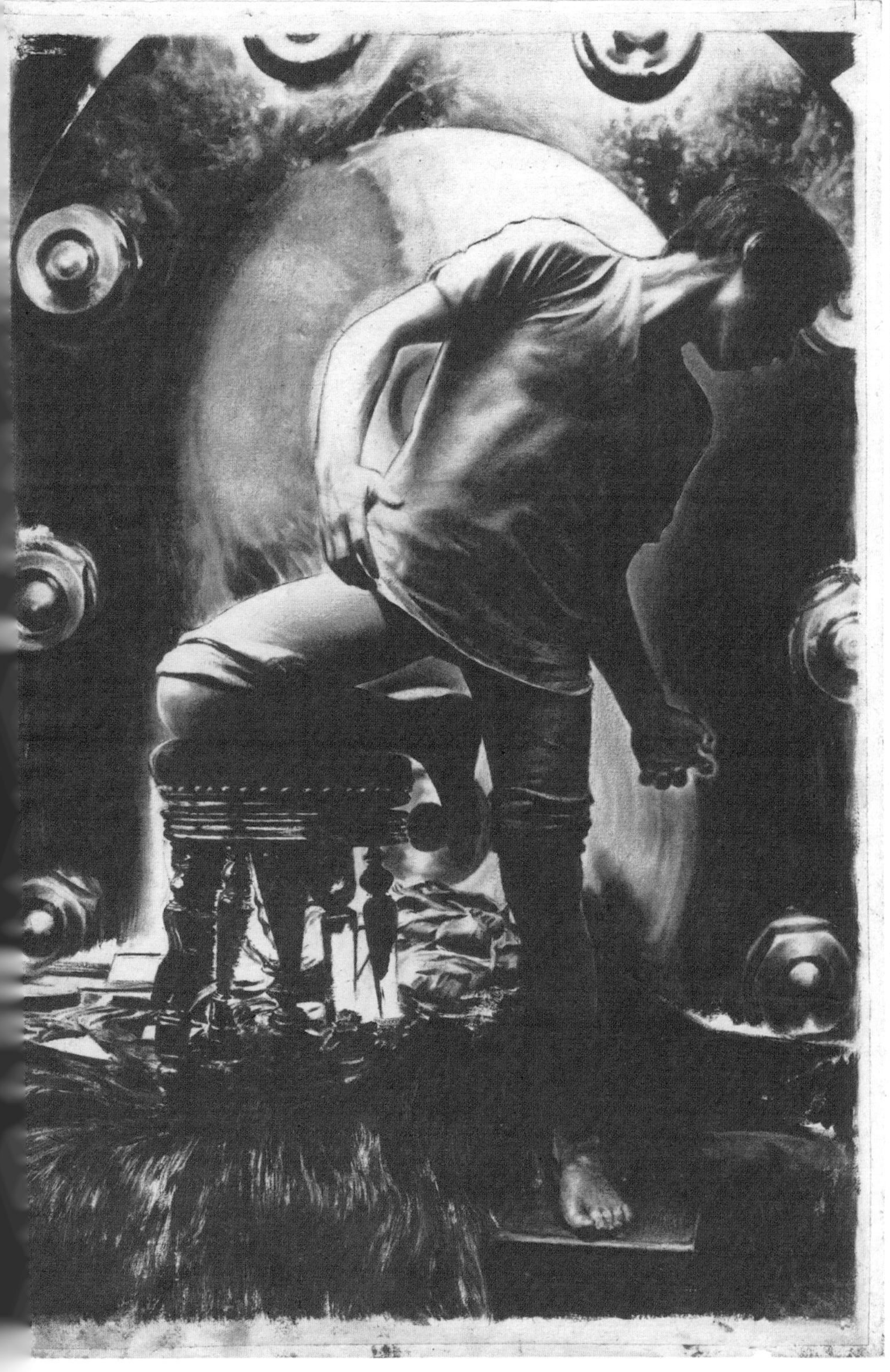

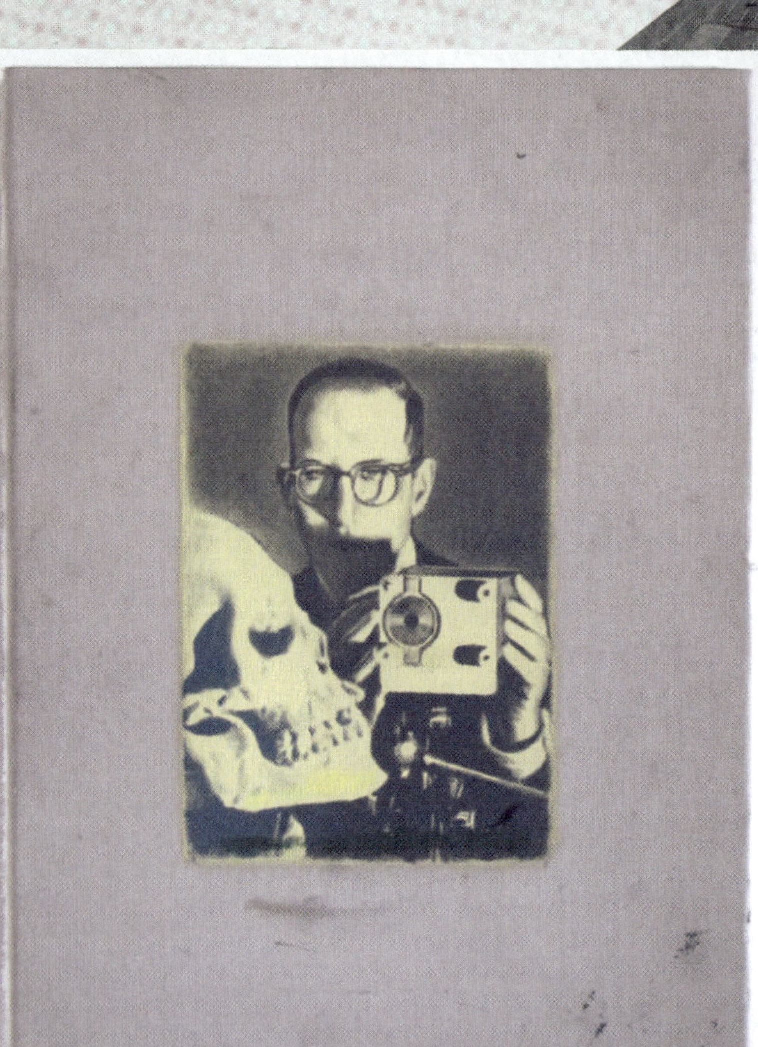

RBO5As under fuselage of Viggen

Sweden

gh degree of
make it poss-
ets situated a
er side of the
Saab claims
e used in an
radio link over
nals are trans-
sistant to jam-
of the missile
of terrain. The
ile so that a
mains aligned
fitted with a
being studied
ation.
began in 1960,
05A. An initial
ct was placed
AJ 37 Viggen
the lightweight
service.

Surface-to-surface or ship-to-ship missile. In service.

Prime contractor: Saab-Scania Aktiebolag.
Powered by: Turboméca Marboré IID turbojet. Two solid-propellant booster rockets power the launch carriage.
Airframe: Circular-section body which tapers towards nose and tail. Long tapered radome above nose air intake. Mid-set folding wings are swept at 30 degrees and fitted with end-plates and spoilers. Vee-type tailplane and elevators are supplemented by ventral fin, all swept at 30 degrees.
Guidance and Control: Stabilised initially. Terminal homing. Aerodynamic control by spoilers and elevators.
Warhead: High-explosive.
Length: 18ft 9in (5.71m).
Max body diameter: 2ft 2in (0.66m).
Wing span: 9ft 10½in (3.01m).
Launch weight: 1,985lb (900kg).
Performance: Secret.

Development and Service

This missile had its origin in the French CT.20 target drone, designed and manufactured by Nord-Aviation. The French company evolved combat versions known as the SM.20 and MM.20 for surface-to-water (sol-mer) and water-to-water (mer-mer) use respectively, and has stated that these could carry a 550lb (250kg) warhead over a range of 155 miles (250km). The Royal Swedish Navy awarded Saab a contract to develop a similar operational version of the CT.20 in 1959, followed by a production contract in 1965. Deliveries were completed by 1970, and the RB08A is now deployed with coastal defence batteries and on board two destroyers of the Royal Swedish Navy. In the latter case, the missiles are stored below deck and transferred by ramp to the launcher aft of the rear funnel when required for action. The Swedish-designed warhead is claimed to be highly-effective against invasion from the sea.

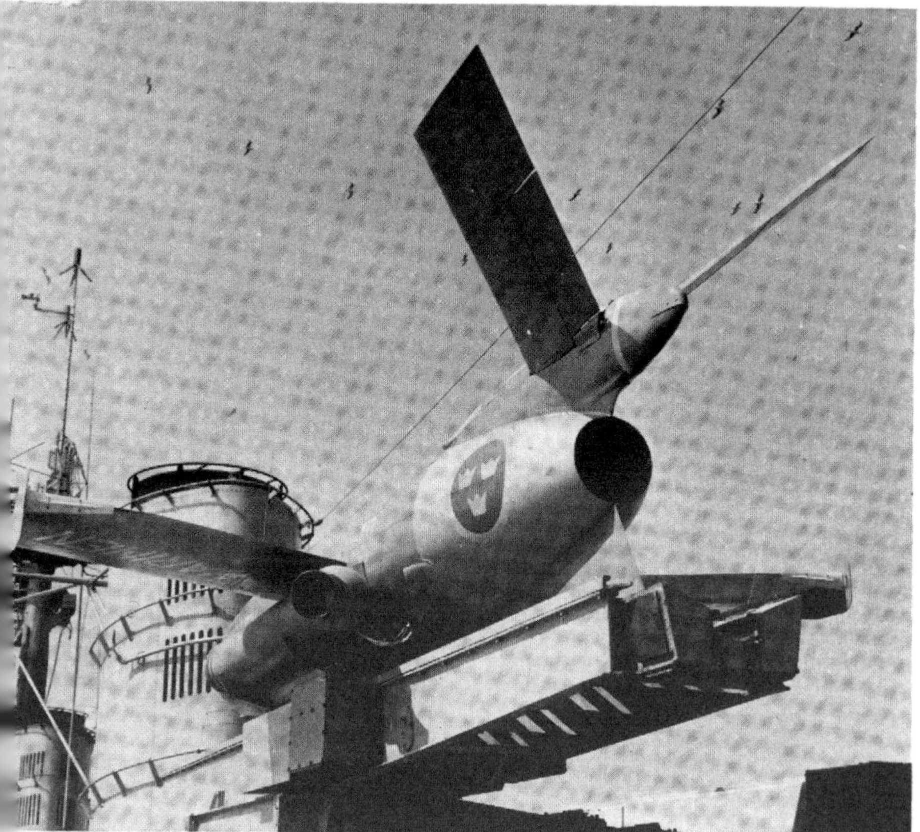

RB08A on board destroyer

Redeye (MIM-43A)
(Swedish Army designation RB69)

Shoulder-fired surface-to-air missile. In service.

Prime contractor: General Dynamics Corporation, Electro Dynamic Division.
Powered by: Atlantic Research Corporation dual-thrust solid-propellant rocket motor.
Airframe: Cylindrical body with flip-out cruciform tail-fins and nose vanes. Glass nose over infra-red seeker.
Guidance: Initial optical aiming, with infra-red terminal homing.
Warhead: High-explosive.
Length (container): 4ft 0in (1.22m).
Body diameter: 2¾in (7cm).
Weight of complete system: 29lb (13.15kg).
Cruising speed: Supersonic.

Development and Service

After satisfying the US Army as to the feasibility of such a weapon system, the former Convair-Pomona division (now Pomona operation of Electro Dynamic Division of GD) received a contract to develop Redeye in August 1959. Production began in 1964 and eventually reached the rate of more than 1,000 missiles per month for the US Army and Marine Corps. Each armoured, artillery and infantry battalion of the Army in Europe has a Redeye section composed of one officer, a sergeant and four to six two-man firing teams. Redeye is also a standard weapon in the Australian and Swedish Armies. Production was completed in the 1970 fiscal year.

Extremely compact, the weapon system consists simply of a sealed launch-tube, containing the missile, and a self-contained optical sighting/firing package attached to the tube. This makes it easily transportable by one man in a combat area, or in rough country, and it is effective against attacking aircraft at altitudes and ranges commensurate with the defence of Army field positions and Marine Corps amphibious operations. When the operator sights an enemy aircraft, he tracks it by means of the sight and energises the missile guidance system. A buzzer informs him when the missile is ready to fire. The boost charge propels the missile out of the launcher. When Redeye has travelled far enough to protect the operator from blast effects, the sustainer fires and propels the missile to the target.

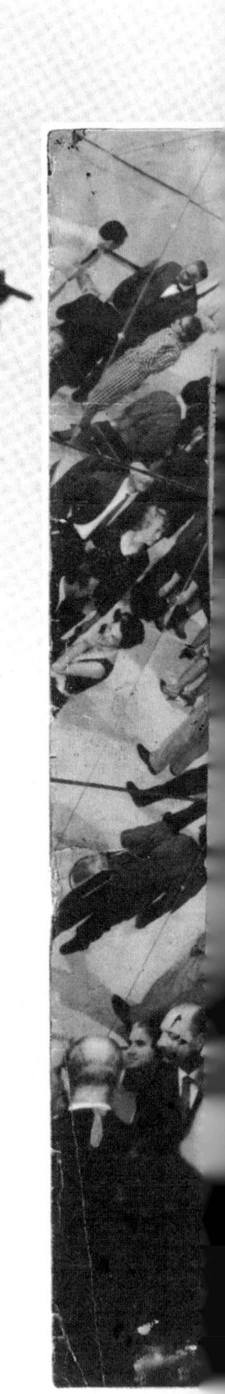

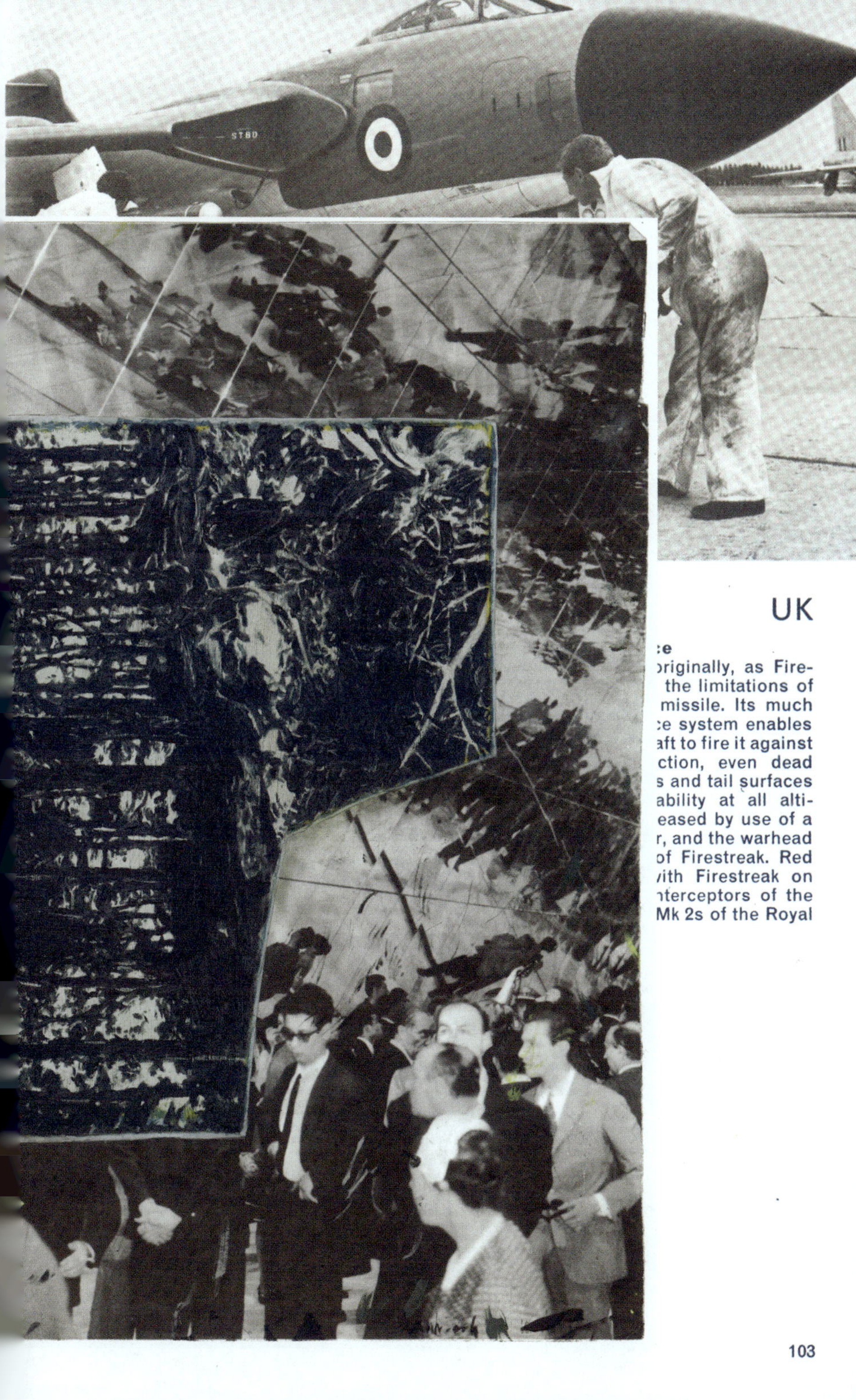

originally, as Fire-
the limitations of
missile. Its much
e system enables
aft to fire it against
ction, even dead
s and tail surfaces
ability at all alti-
eased by use of a
r, and the warhead
of Firestreak. Red
ith Firestreak on
terceptors of the
Mk 2s of the Royal

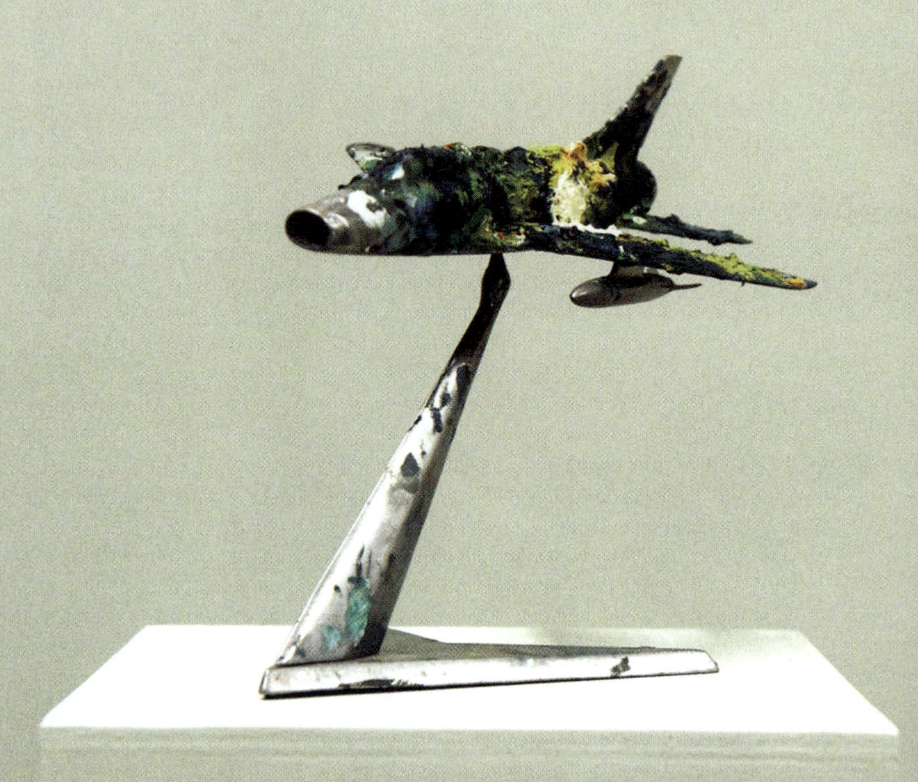

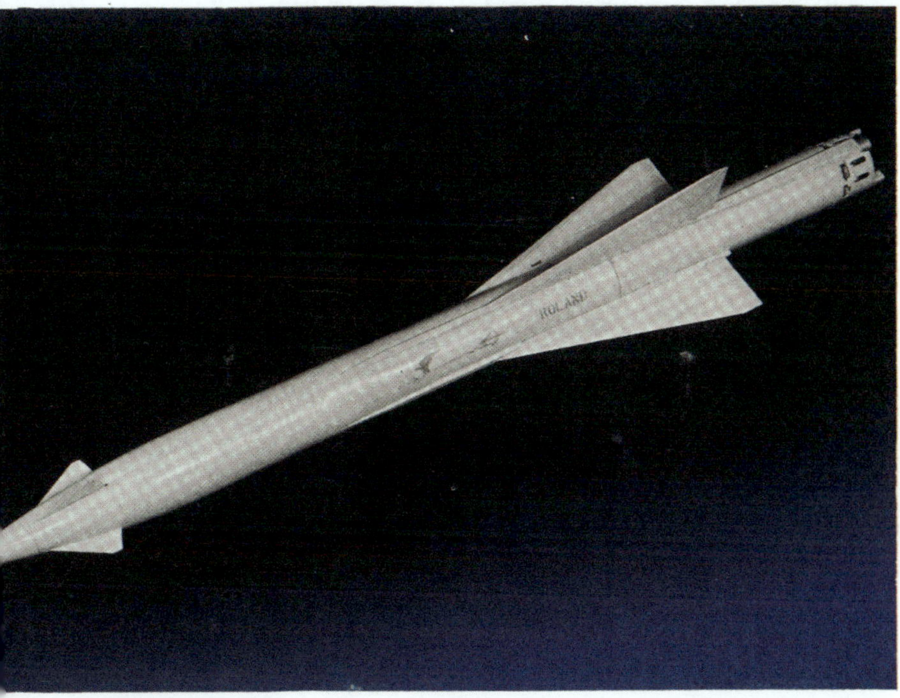

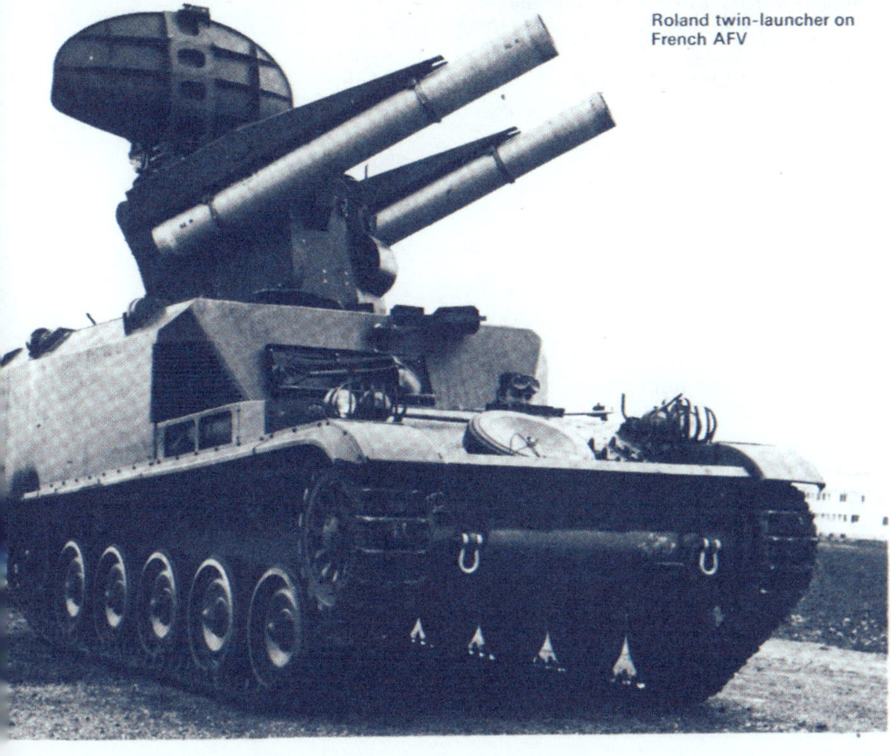

Roland twin-launcher on
French AFV

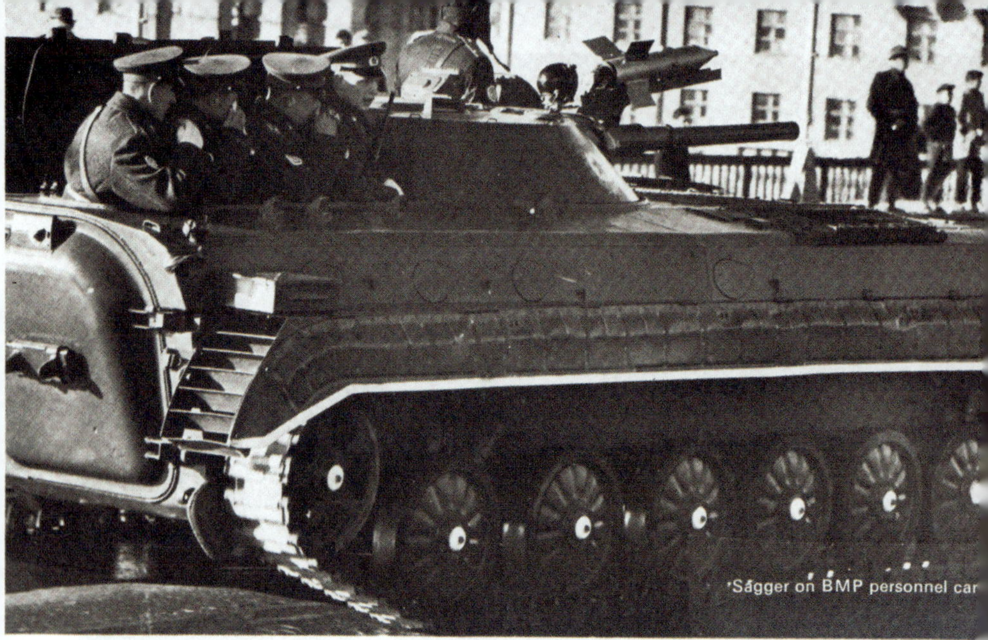

Sagger

Anti-tank missile. In service.

Powered by: Solid-propellant rocket motor.
Airframe: Short cylindrical body, with conical nose. Rear-mounted cruciform wings are swept near body of missile but unswept outboard. Wings fold for storage and transport.
Guidance and Control: Wire guidance.
Warhead: High-explosive.
Length: 2ft 6in (0.76m).

Development and Service

Latest of the three standard types of small wire-guided anti-tank missiles serving with the armed forces of Russia and its allies, 'Sagger' was first displayed publicly in May 1965. It was shown then on a six-rour launcher mounted on the BRDM armoure amphibious vehicle which is used also as carrier for 'Snapper' and 'Swatter'. The insta lation is interesting, as the launcher protected during transport by an armoure cover plate that encloses it within the vehic When the launcher is elevated for actic the cover plate remains in place above t launcher, affording continued protection. single 'Sagger' is carried on a rail launch above the 76mm gun on the BMP eight-m armoured personnel carrier, first seen 1967 and becoming a standard vehic throughout the Warsaw Pact nations.

SAM-D

Surface-to-air weapon system. Under development.

Prime contractor: Raytheon Company.
Powered by: Thiokol TX-486 single-stage solid-propellant rocket motor.
Airframe: Cylindrical body, with pointed ogival nose. Cruciform tail control surfaces.
Guidance and Control: Command guidance, with semi-active terminal homing.
Warhead: High-explosive.
Length: 17ft 0in (5.18m).
Body diameter: 1ft 4in (0.41m).

Development and Service

Studies for a new surface-to-air weapon system known as SAM-D began in 1965, following earlier US Army study programm known as Field Army Ballistic Missile D fense System (FABMDS) and Army / Defense System for the 1970s (AADS-7 After evaluation of competing indus proposals, Raytheon was awarded in M 1967 a contract covering the first yea advanced development of SAM-D, which intended to replace Hawk and Nike Hercul Subsequent contracts have covered demc stration of the advanced guidance syste operation of the radar in its various moc and the aerodynamic capabilities of missile, leading to 1971 demonstrations of full capability of the fire control group.

The missile and its shipping/launch c

tainer are being developed by Martin Marietta Corporation under sub-contract from Raytheon. Several missiles in their containers will be carried by each SAM-D tracked launch vehicle, from which they will be fired either singly or in close-sequence salvos at selectable azimuths and elevations, as required. In the field, a fire section will be mounted on about four vehicles, including a fire control vehicle carrying radar, radar/weapons control computer, communications and power supply. The multi-function phased-array radar will detect targets, track them, and track and issue guidance commands to the supersonic missile in flight.

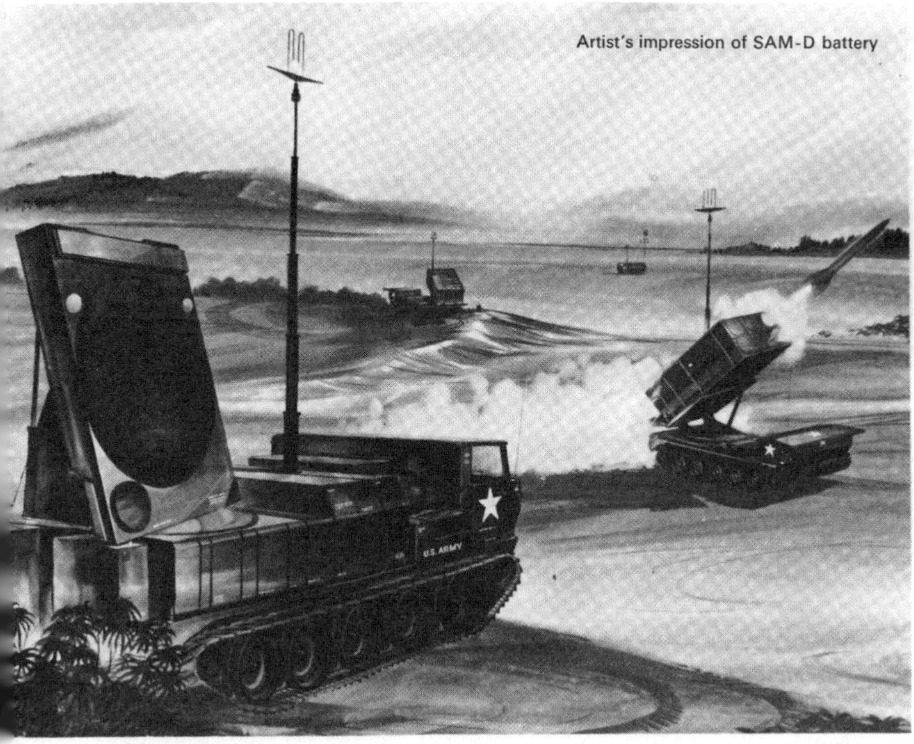

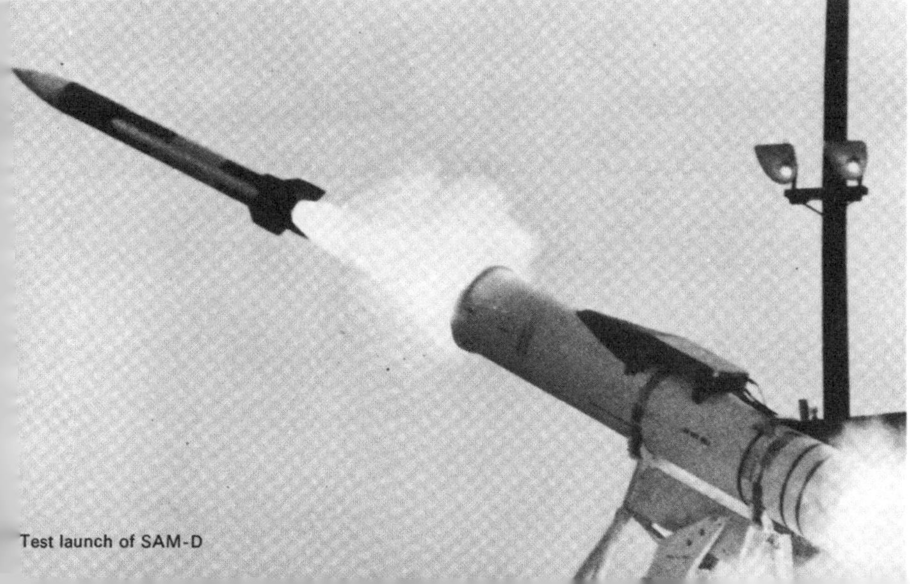

Artist's impression of SAM-D battery

Test launch of SAM-D

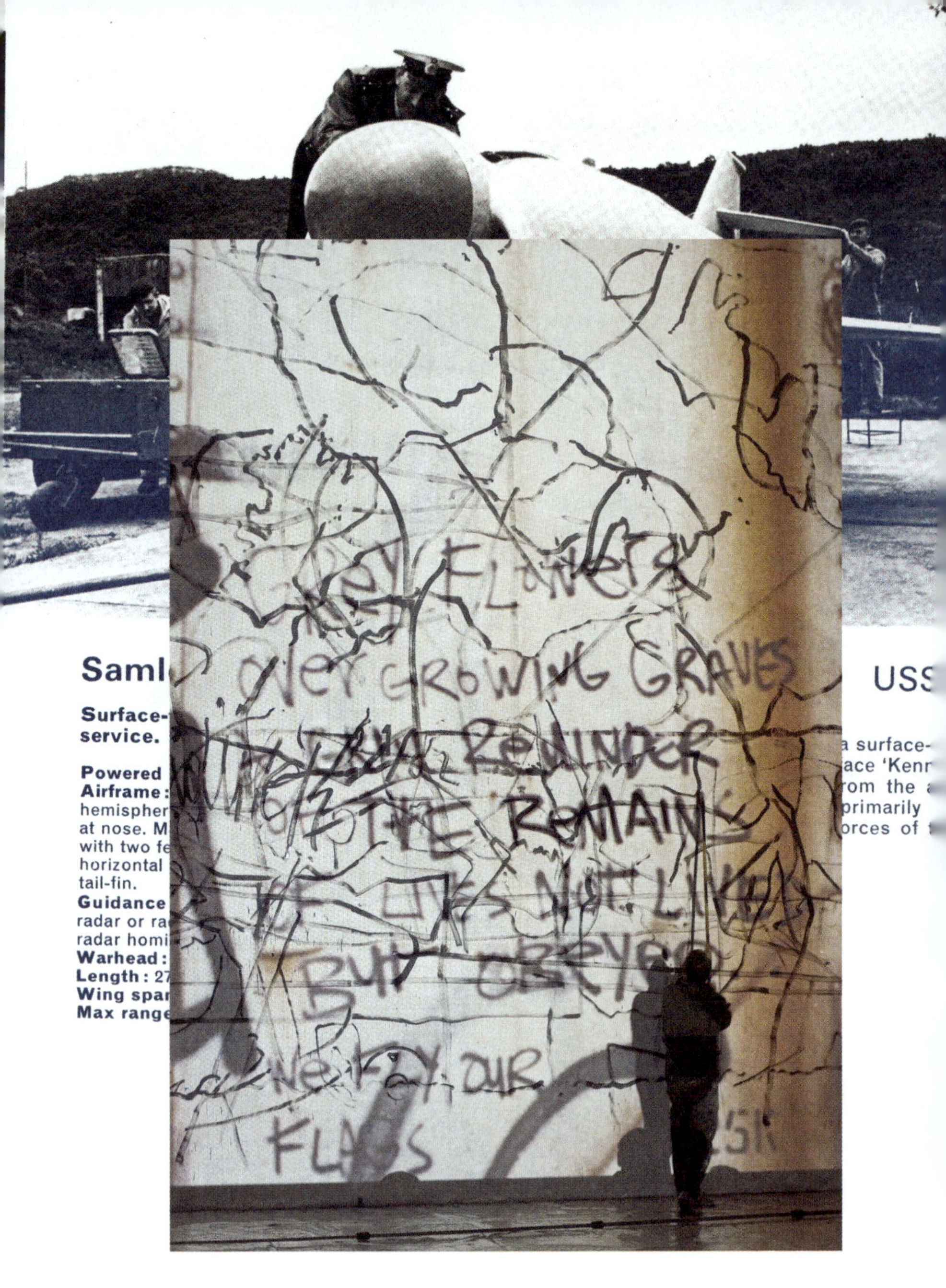

Saml

Surface-
service.

Powered
Airframe:
hemispher
at nose. M
with two fe
horizontal
tail-fin.
Guidance
radar or ra
radar homi
Warhead:
Length: 27
Wing spa
Max range

USS

a surface-
ace 'Kenn
rom the a
primarily
orces of

Sandal (SS-4)

Surface-to-surface intermediate-range ballistic missile. In service.

Powered by: One liquid-propellant engine. No
booste
Airfra
skirt ar
Pointe
Guida
guidan
trailing
rocket
Warhe
Lengt
Max b
Launc
Max s
Max ra

Devel
After
Germa
Union
becam
'Shyst
permit
was fi

November 1957. Its transporter was hauled
by a tracked vehicle carrying the launch
crew.
In 1961, a further-improved version was
vest
ving
e. It
its
al's'
of
lete
ther
port

ia's
ely,
nch
of
at
at
US
ted
the
and

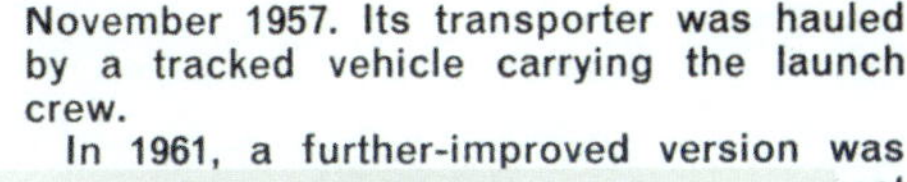

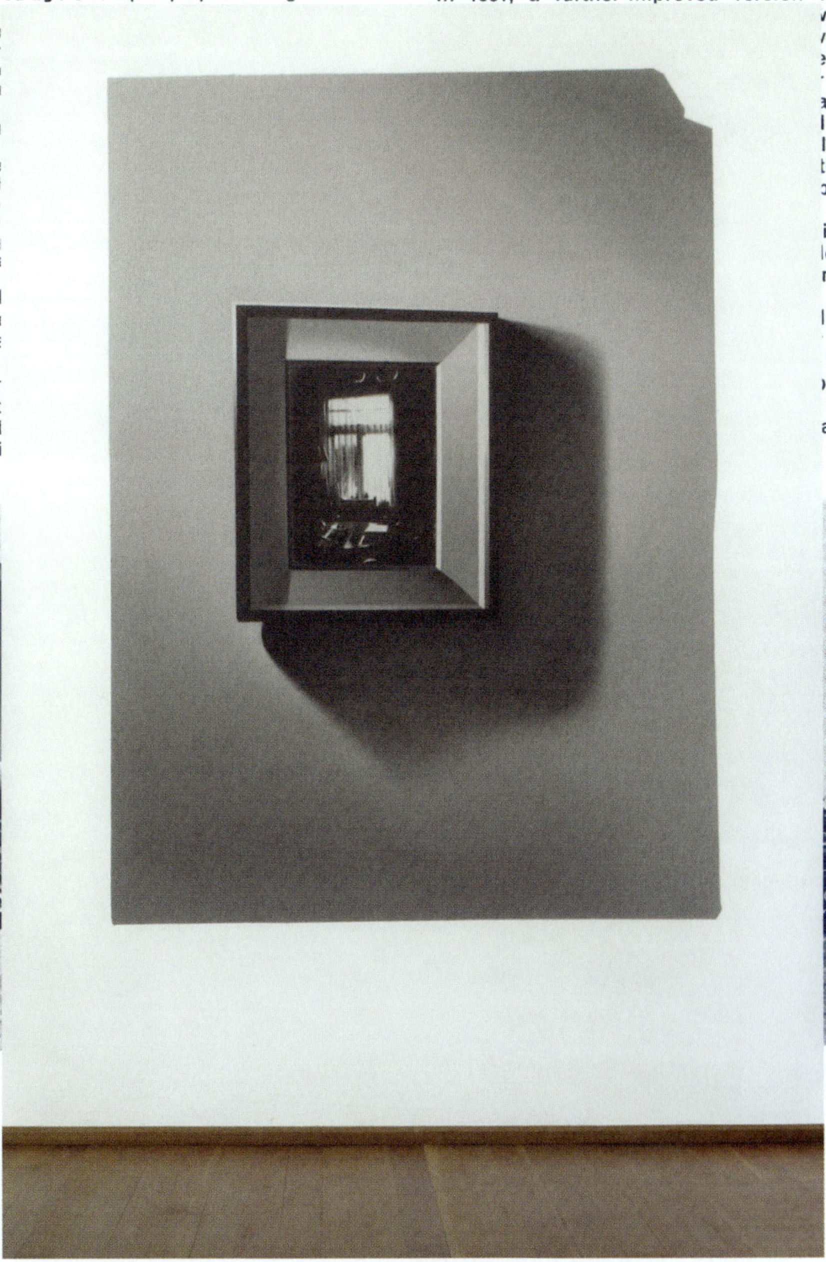

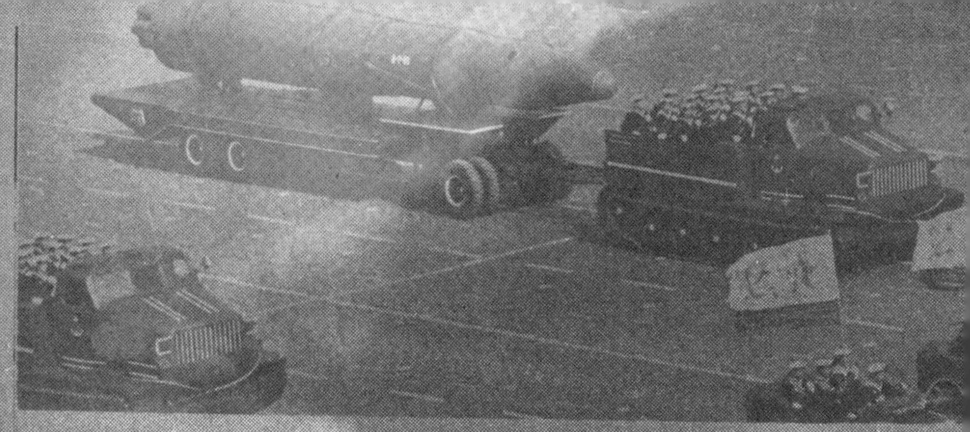

Sark (SS-N-4)

Underwater-to-surface or surface-to-surface missile. In service.

Powered by: Solid-propellant motors, with seven cylindrical first-stage nozzles.
Airframe: Probably two-stage missile. Basically cylindrical body, with second stage of slightly smaller diameter. Blunt conical nose-cone. No fins or wings.
Warhead: Nuclear.
Length: 48ft 0in (14.50m).
Max body diameter: 5ft 9in (1.75m).
Weight and Performance: Unknown.

US

Development and Service
This first-generation Soviet counterpart Polaris was first included in a Moscow parade on November 7, 1962. The commentator said that it could be fired either under water or on the surface. Projections on each side of the casing are assumed to be used to locate the missile inside its launch-tube.

Before the Soviet-Chinese diplomatic a single 'G' class submarine, with missile launch-tubes, was supplied by Russia to the Chinese Navy. The missiles carried this ship are said to have a range of at least 380 miles (600km) and may well be 'Sarks'.

Sasin (SS-8)

Exhibited as intercontinental ballistic missile. Not thought to be an operational weapon.

Powered by: Storable liquid-propellant rocket motors.
Airframe: Two-stage rocket. Both stages are cylindrical, with tapered fairing between first stage and smaller-diameter second stage. Blunted conical nose-cone. No skirt, fins or wings.
Warhead: Thermonuclear.
Length: 80ft 0in (24.40m).
Body diameter (first stage): 9ft 0in (2.75m).
Max range: 6,500 miles (10,500km).

US

Development and Service
Although this rocket was exhibited in several Moscow parades, from November onwards, it has not been seen recently there is little to suggest that it ever became an operational weapon. On the other hand it has a Western missile designation (SS-8) and the International Institute for Strategic Studies continues to list a total of 220 ICBMs of the SS-8 and similar SS-7 'Saddler' type in the current Soviet long-range missile force. If this were correct, these weapons could be expected to carry a thermonuclear warhead of about 5-megaton yield.

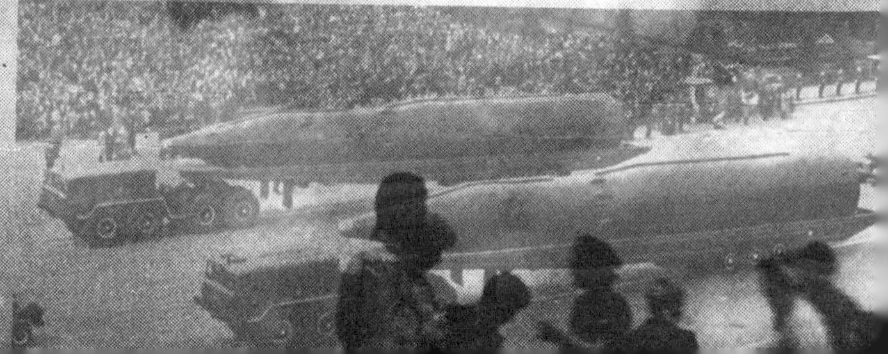

Savage (SS-13)

Intercontinental ballistic missile. In production and service.

Powered by: Three solid-propellant stages, each with four nozzles.
Airframe: Three-stage missile, with truss structure between stages. Each stage is cylindrical, of progressively-reduced diameter, with a flared skirt over its nozzles. Pointed conical nose-cone.
Warhead: Thermonuclear or nuclear.
Length: 66ft 0in (20.0m).
Body diameter (excluding skirt):
1st stage 5ft 6in (1.68m).
2nd stage 4ft 7¼in (1.40m).
3rd stage 3ft 2¼in (0.98m).
Max range: 5,000 miles (8,000km).

Development and Service

This Russian counterpart of Minuteman was first displayed in a Moscow military parade celebrating the 20th anniversary of the end of the second World War in Europe, on May 9, 1965. It is intended to replace the storable liquid-propellant SS-11 and up to 100 were thought to be operational in 1971. Firing trials down the Pacific range, from Tyuratam in Kazakhstan, are continuing. Two SS-13s tracked by America in November 1970 each delivered a single inert warhead over a range of about 4,500 miles (7,250km).

The top two stages of 'Savage' are used without the first stage in the 'Scamp/Scapegoat' mobile missile system.

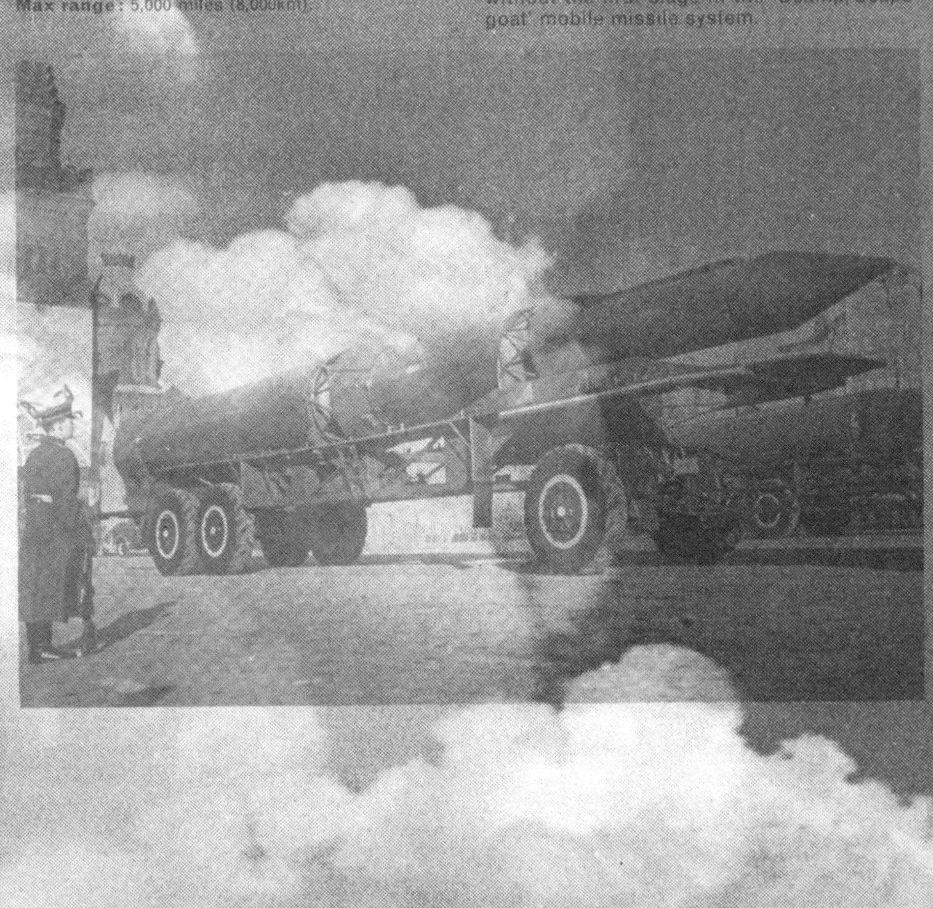

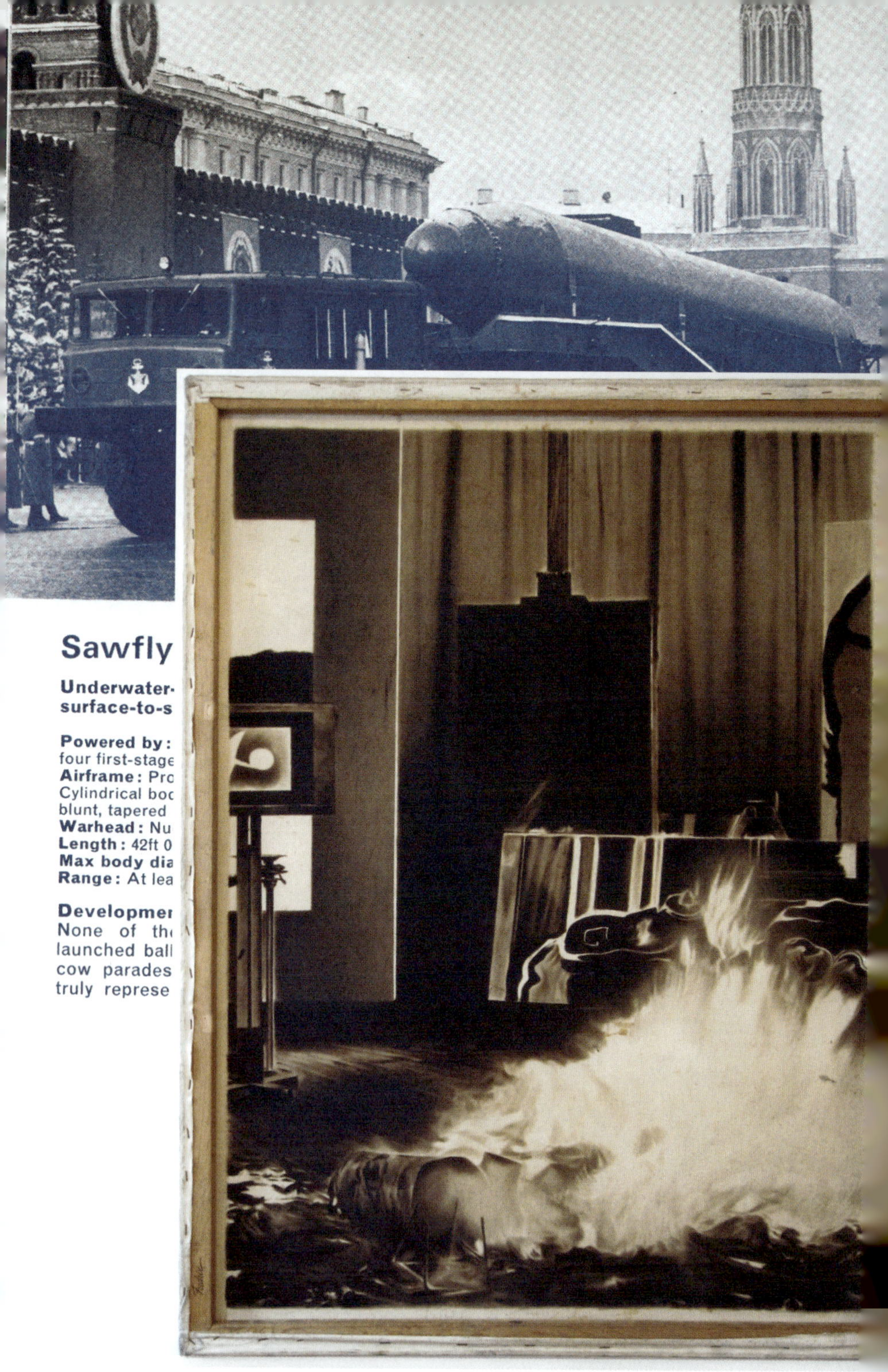

Sawfly

**Underwater-
surface-to-s

Powered by:
four first-stage
Airframe: Pro
Cylindrical boc
blunt, tapered
Warhead: Nu
Length: 42ft 0
**Max body dia
Range: At lea

**Developmer
None of the
launched ball
cow parades
truly represe

SCAD

USA

Subsonic cruise armed decoy missile. Under development

Powered by: Turbojet engine.
Guidance and Control: Inertial guidance system, with terminal assistance.
Warhead: Nuclear.
Design range: 975 miles (1,575km).

Development and Service
This projected USAF missile was inspired by the success of Quail (page 94). The basic subsonic cruise armed decoy (SCAD) version is intended initially as part of the ECM equipment carried by B-52 Stratofortress strategic bombers, and later for carriage by the swing-wing supersonic North American Rockwell B-1. An unarmed (SCUD) version has also been proposed.

Scaleboard (SS-12)

USSR

Surface-to-surface tactical missile. In service.

Powered by: Storable liquid-propellant rocket motor.
Airframe: Cylindrical body, with tapered nose-cone and either tail-fins or vernier engines at base.
Guidance and Control: Probably inertial guidance, set up before missile launch by means of equipment situated between two inner wheels on port side of transporter.
Warhead: Probably thermonuclear.
Length: 37ft 0in (11.25m).
Max range: 450 miles (725km).

Development and Service
First seen in November 1967, this mobile ballistic missile is about the same length as 'Scud-B' (page 120) and is transported on a similar MAZ-543 eight-wheeled erector-launcher. It is, however, of larger diameter than the 'Scuds', implying a longer range, and differs in being enclosed in a ribbed casing which is elevated with it into the firing position. No photographs have yet shown the missile without this casing. During transit, the driver of the vehicle occupies the left-hand cab at the front, with the launch operator and his control console in the right-hand cab and seats for at least three other members of the launch crew to the rear of these cabs. An increasing proportion of the total of 300 short-range ballistic missiles estimated to be in service with Soviet land forces is likely to consist of 'Scaleboards'.

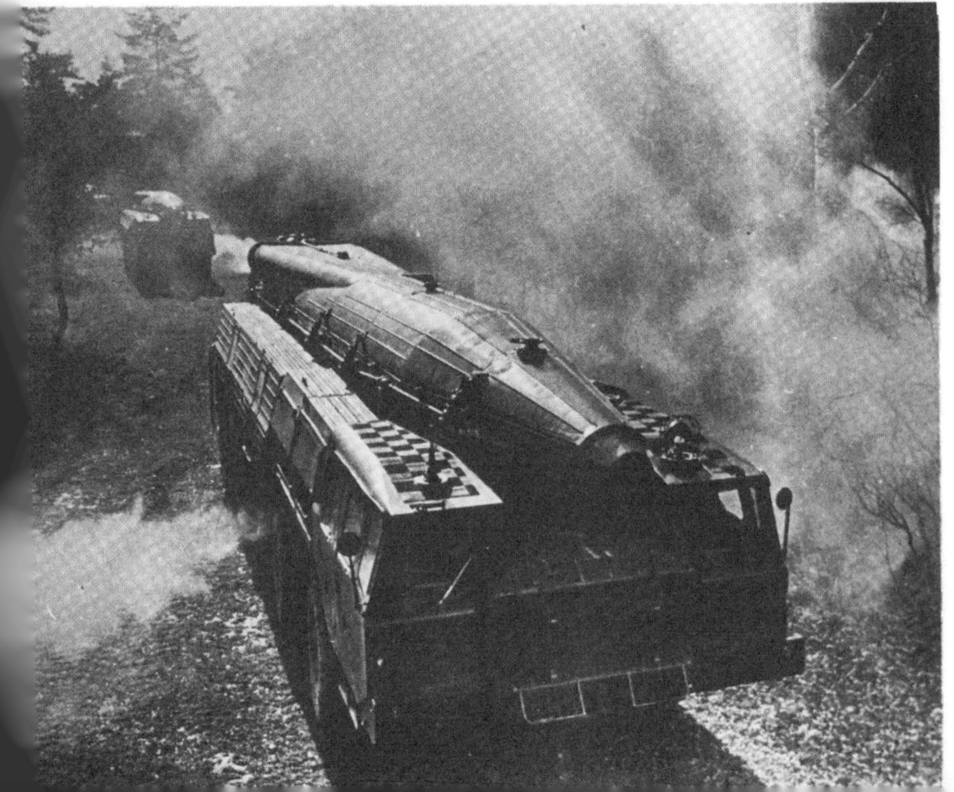

Scamp/Scapegoat (SS-14) USSR

**Mobile surface-to-surface ballistic
missile system. In service.**

The following data refer to the 'Scapegoat'
missile.
Powered by: Solid-propellant motors, with
four nozzles on each stage.
Airframe: Two-stage missile, with truss
structure between stages. Each stage is
cylindrical with a flared skirt over its nozzles.
Second stage has smaller diameter than first,
and is fitted with a pointed conical nose-cone.
Warhead: Thermonuclear or nuclear.
Length: 35ft 0in (10.6m).
Body diameter (excluding skirt):
1st stage 4ft 7½in (1.40m).
2nd stage 3ft 2½in (0.98m).
Max range: 2,500 miles (4,000km).

Development and Service

First included in a Moscow parade to mark
the 20th anniversary of the end of the second
World War, on May 9, 1965, this tracked
weapon system was nicknamed 'Iron Maiden'
by Western observers. This reflected the
fact that the missile is enclosed in a container which is made in two halves, split
horizontally and hinged. For firing, a massive
hydraulic jack on each side of the vehicle, at
the rear, raises the container to a vertical
position. The container is then opened and
moved away from the missile before the
latter is launched.

For several years the configuration of the
missile carried by the tracked erector/laun-
cher was not known; the complete weapon
system was therefore given the NATO
code-name 'Scamp'. The separate code-name
'Scapegoat' was given to a two-stage IRBM
first displayed on a trailer in 1967, which
appeared to consist of the top two stages of
the ICBM known as 'Savage' (see page 111).
Not until later did official Soviet films of
missile exercises reveal 'Scapegoat' to be

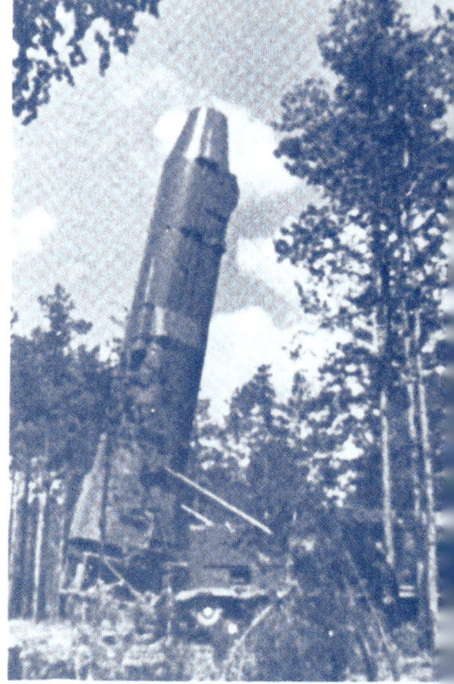

the missile carried inside the 'Scamp' container. The original type of tracked vehicle
has been superseded by an improved model
similar to that used in the 'Scrooge' weapon
system. Like the latter, 'Scamp/Scapegoat'
has been reported in operational service
near Buir Nor in Outer Mongolia, adjacent
to the Chinese frontier.

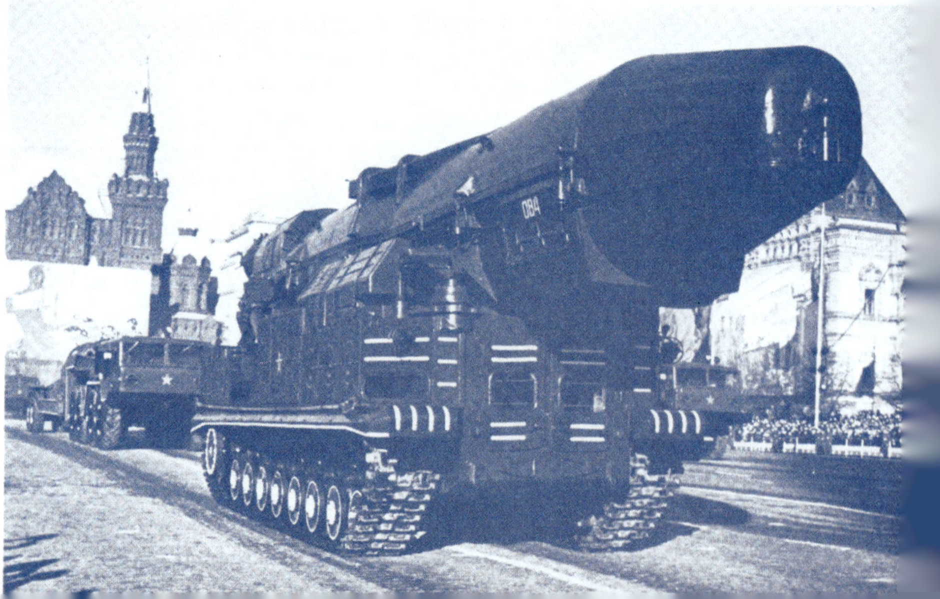

Scarp (SS-9/FOBS) USSR

Intercontinental ballistic missile, and fractional orbital bombardment system. In production and service.

Powered by: Liquid-propellant rocket motors. Ring of six first-stage nozzles is surrounded by four equi-spaced vernier nozzles.
Airframe: Cylindrical body of constant diameter, which tapers near the top to blend with cylindrical re-entry vehicle of much smaller diameter. Wedge-shaped fairings over vernier nozzles at tail. No fins or wings.
Warhead: At least three alternative warheads have been tested: a single 20/25-megaton charge; an unguided MRV comprising three separate re-entry vehicles, each with a yield of 5 megatons; and the FOBS 'space-bomb'. An MIRV warhead is under development.
Length: 113ft 6in (34.5m).
Body diameter: 10ft 0in (3.05m).
Max range: approx 5,500 miles (8,800km).

Development and Service

'Scarp' is the most formidable weapon that has yet been revealed anywhere in the world, with a thermonuclear warhead of 20/25-megaton yield. It was first exhibited in the Moscow parade of November 7, 1967, marking the 50th anniversary of the Communist Revolution. Four days earlier, the American Secretary of Defense had announced the existence of a Soviet 'space bomb' which was first tested, in the guise of the Cosmos 139 satellite, on January 25, 1967. During many subsequent tests, the inert 'space bomb' payloads have been sighted optically from the Royal Aircraft Establishment at Farnborough, and are estimated to be about 6ft 6in (2.0m) long and 4ft (1.2m) in diameter. The 'space bomb' version of 'Scarp' is known in America as a fractional orbital bombardment system (FOBS). This reflects the fact that the rocket puts its thermonuclear payload into an orbit about 100 miles (160km) above the Earth. At a pre-determined point, before completion of the first orbit, the payload is intended to be slowed by retro-rocket so that it will drop precisely on to its target.

As an alternative to its single very large warhead, the standard SS-9 ICBM can carry a simple, unguided multiple re-entry vehicle (MRV) made up of three separate smaller charges. During one test in 1970, observed by US reconnaissance satellites and naval vessels, an MRV travelled about 5,500 miles (8,800km) and re-entered the atmosphere with its three inert warheads dispersing to impact 80 miles (130km) apart—about the same distance that separates a cluster of three typical US Minuteman ICBM silo launchers. There is also reason to believe that 'Scarp' has been used as launcher for the Cosmos satellites which have intercepted and destroyed other test satellites in orbit. About one-quarter of the 1,200 Soviet ICBMs in service in late 1970 were SS-9s.

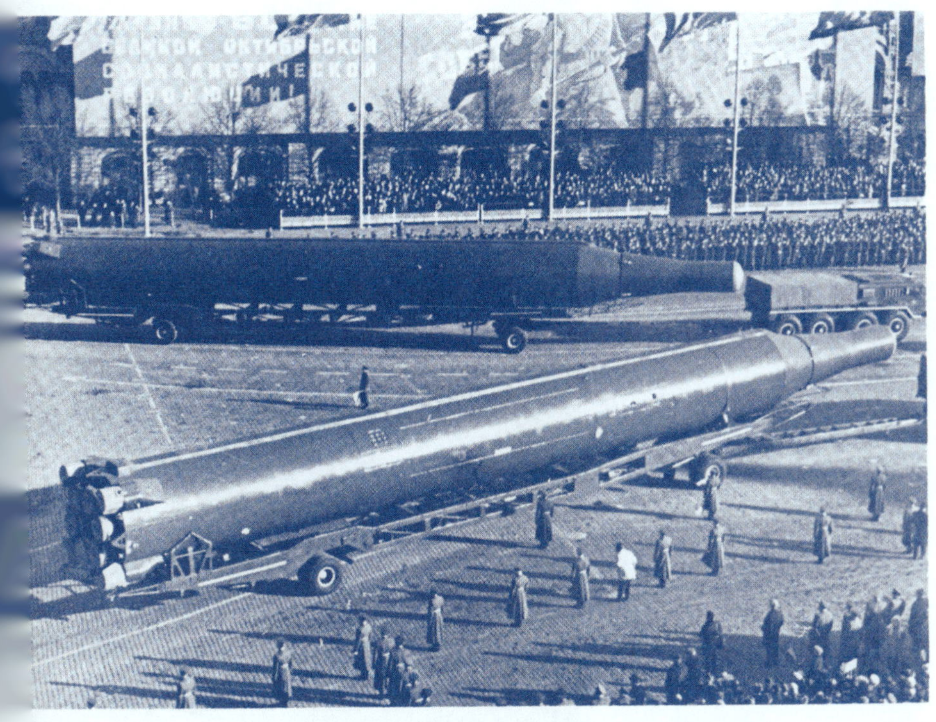

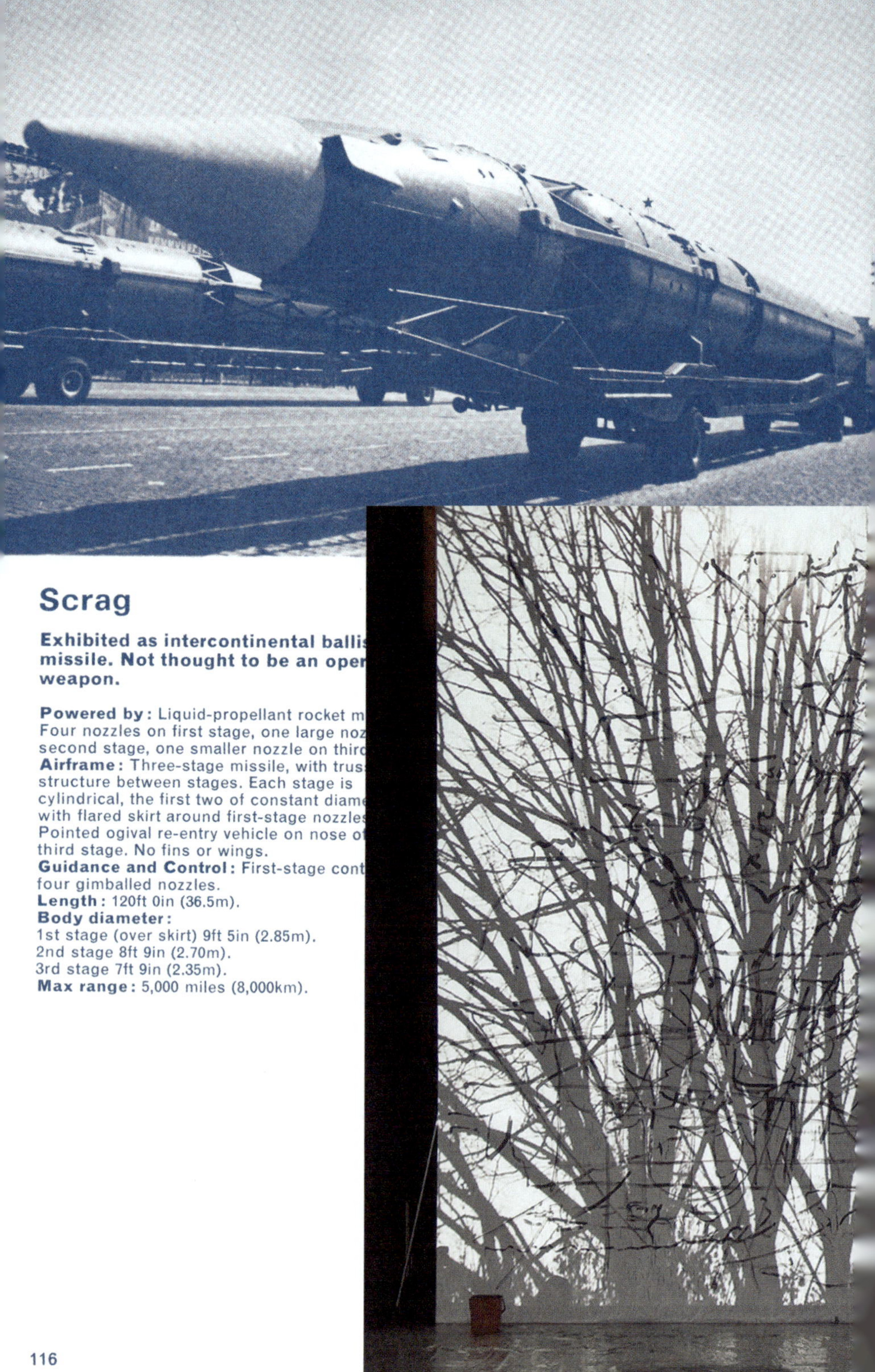

Scrag

Exhibited as intercontinental ballis
missile. Not thought to be an oper
weapon.

Powered by : Liquid-propellant rocket m
Four nozzles on first stage, one large noz
second stage, one smaller nozzle on thir
Airframe : Three-stage missile, with trus
structure between stages. Each stage is
cylindrical, the first two of constant diame
with flared skirt around first-stage nozzles
Pointed ogival re-entry vehicle on nose o
third stage. No fins or wings.
Guidance and Control : First-stage cont
four gimballed nozzles.
Length : 120ft 0in (36.5m).
Body diameter :
1st stage (over skirt) 9ft 5in (2.85m).
2nd stage 8ft 9in (2.70m).
3rd stage 7ft 9in (2.35m).
Max range : 5,000 miles (8,000km).

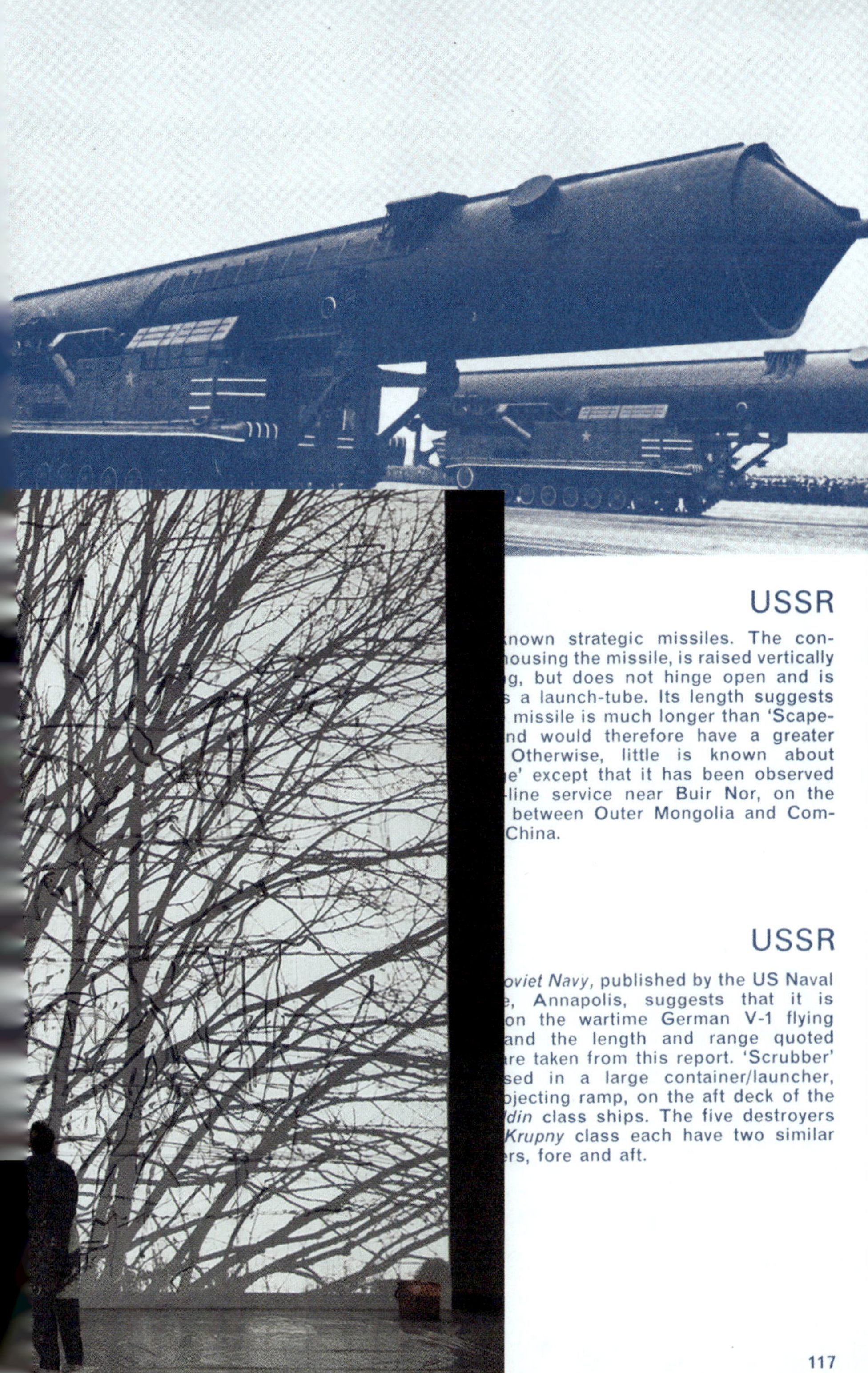

USSR

known strategic missiles. The con-
housing the missile, is raised vertically
g, but does not hinge open and is
s a launch-tube. Its length suggests
missile is much longer than 'Scape-
nd would therefore have a greater
Otherwise, little is known about
e' except that it has been observed
-line service near Buir Nor, on the
between Outer Mongolia and Com-
China.

USSR

oviet Navy, published by the US Naval
e, Annapolis, suggests that it is
on the wartime German V-1 flying
and the length and range quoted
re taken from this report. 'Scrubber'
sed in a large container/launcher,
ojecting ramp, on the aft deck of the
ldin class ships. The five destroyers
Krupny class each have two similar
rs, fore and aft.

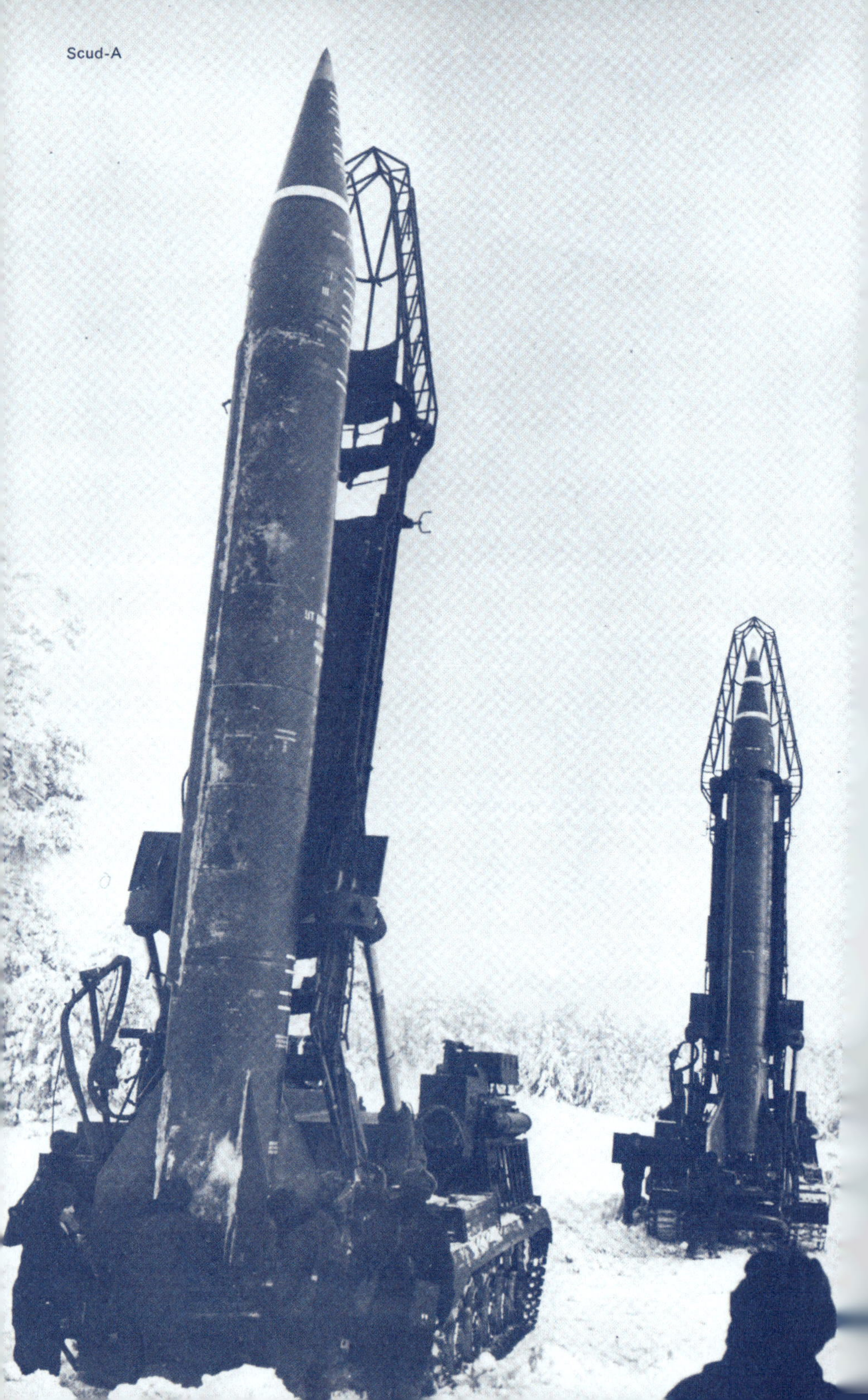
Scud-A

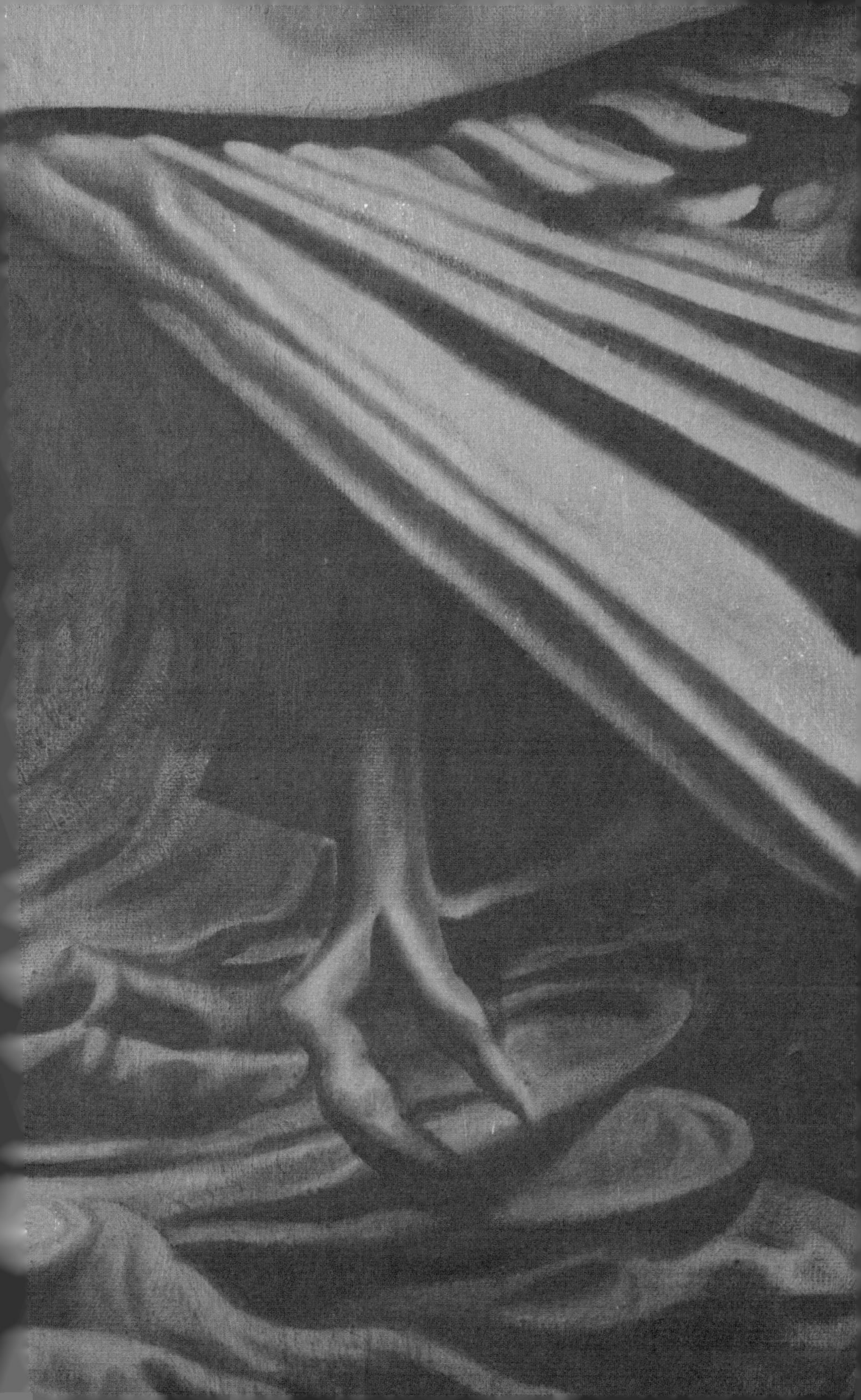

Scud-B (SS-1c)

Surface-to-surface missile. In service.

Powered by: Storable liquid-propellant rocket motor.
Airfra
structu
pointec
Guida
inertial
surface
Warhe
Lengt

Development and Service
Enlarged to provide increased propell
tankage, and hence longer range, this
proved 'Scud' first appeared in Novem

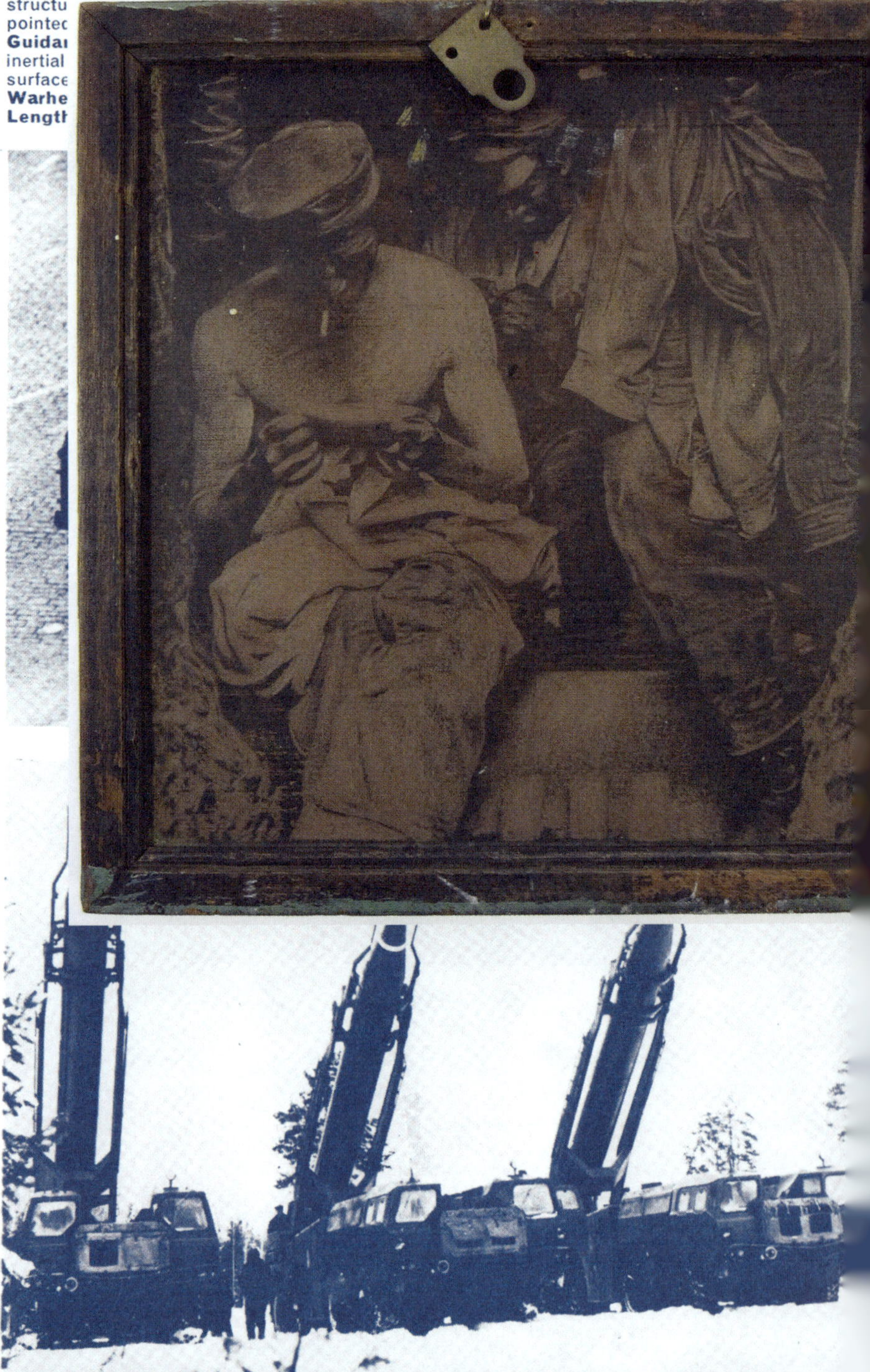

Seacat (Swedish Navy designation RBO7) UK

Surface-to-air and surface-to-surface ship-based close-range missile. In production and service.

Prime contractor: Short Brothers and Harland Ltd.
Powered by: IMI two-stage solid-propellant rocket motor.
Airframe: Basically-cylindrical body, changing to wider and more square cross-section on forward portion and with a pointed ogival nose. Pivoted cruciform sweptback wings, indexed at 45 degrees to fixed cruciform tail-fins, two of which carry tip-mounted tracking flares.
Guidance and Control: Radio command, with visual or radar tracking. Control by pivoted wings.
Warhead: High-explosive, with contact and proximity fuses.
Length: 4ft 10.3in (1.48m).
Max body diameter: 7.5in (19.05cm).
Wing span: 2ft 1.6in (0.64m).
Weight: Approx 150lb (68kg).
Max range (estimated): 2.2 miles (3.5km).

Development and Service

Seacat has proved one of the most widely-exported guided weapons in the world. Its development started under a contract awarded in April 1958. Within four years sea trials were underway from HMS *Decoy*. Today, in addition to the Royal Navy, a total of 14 other nations deploy this small and highly-manoeuvrable close-range weapon system on their naval craft. Production continues and Seacat is expected to remain in service well into the 'eighties.

Simplest of many different fire control systems in service is the Mk 20, in which the standard four-round launcher is controlled by two men in a director unit. One rotates the director so that the second (the aimer) can pick up and track the target through binoculars. The launcher is 'slaved' to the director in azimuth and elevation, with the result that missiles enter the aimer's field of vision soon after launch. The aimer guides each missile to the target by means of a small joystick, using flares on the missile as a tracking reference. The Mks 21 and 22 radar systems provide auto-follow of the target, permitting both visual and 'dark' firings. Sweden and Chile use a Dutch M4/3 radar system; Argentina uses an Italian system. Bofors of Sweden have developed a combined gun/missile system for Germany, with Seacat providing the missile element. Brazil and Iran utilise a lightweight Seacat system, with three-round launcher, which can be accommodated on vessels as small as fast patrol boats and minesweepers. In addition Seacat missiles are used in the Tigercat and Hellcat weapon systems.

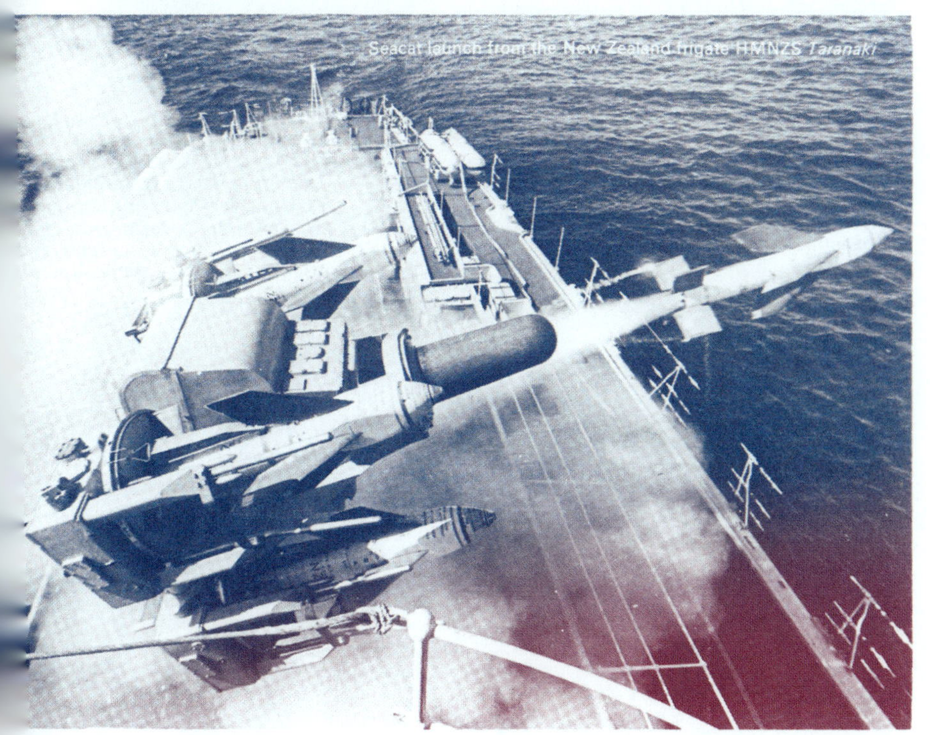
Seacat launch from the New Zealand frigate HMNZS *Taranaki*

Sea Dart (CF.299)

Ship-based surface-to-air and surface-to-surface missile. In production.

Prime contractor: Hawker Siddeley Dynamics Ltd.
Powered by: Rolls-Royce Odin ramjet and tandem jettisonable IMI solid-propellant rocket booster. Between-stage vents enable the Odin to be started prior to staging.
Airframe: Missile has cylindrical body with four interferometer aerials around nose intake for ramjet. Rear-mounted long-chord cruciform wings indexed in line with cruciform tail control surfaces. Larger-diameter cylindrical booster has cruciform fins that fold forward while the missile is on its launcher.
Guidance and Control: Marconi semi-active radar homing guidance. Control by tail surfaces.
Warhead: High-explosive, with EMI proximity fuse.
Length: 14ft 3½in (4.36m).
Body diameter: 1ft 4½in (42cm).
Launch weight: 1,210lb (550kg).
Range: At least 19 miles (30km).

Development and Service

Development of Sea Dart (originally CF.299) was started in 1962, to provide a weapon that would represent a major improvement on Seaslug and yet be compact enough to install on ships smaller than those fitted with the earlier missile. Choice of a ramjet sustainer has made Sea Dart a genuine area-defence weapon, capable of intercepting aircraft and air-launched or surface-launched missiles at both very high and extremely low altitudes, with added effectiveness against surface targets. Firing trials have been underway since 1965, confirming that the weapon system offers a rapid launch-rate and the capability of dealing with many targets simultaneously. Production was initiated in 1967 and the first ship to be fitted with the Sea Dart system is the guided missile destroyer HMS *Bristol*, which has a twin-launcher. A similar launcher is being fitted on each of the four destroyers of the new *Sheffield* class, and on two further ships

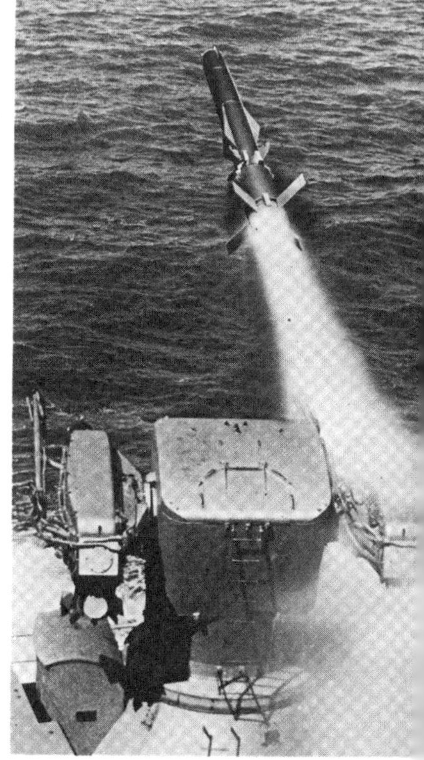

of this class for the Argentine Navy. Sea Dart system utilises a surveillance ra two Marconi Type 909 tracking/illumina radars, a Vickers twin-launcher and hand system, a Ferranti computer for target se tion, data handling, missile launch and flight control, and Plessey Radar operati room display equipment.

Sea Indigo Italy

Ship-based surface-to-air short-range missile. Under development.

Prime contractor: Sistel—Sistemi Elettronici SpA.

Development and Service
Sea Indigo is a navalised version of Indigo (see page 59), with modifications to suit it for the change of role. It can be utilised in launching systems with either automatic or manual reloading, with the latter recommended for ships of under 500 tons displacement. Indigo's Super Fledermaus fire control system is replaced by the Sea Hunter type specified for Sistel's Sea Killer missile systems.

Sea Killer Mk 1 Italy

Short-range surface-to-surface ship-launched missile. In service.

Prime contractor: Sistel—Sistemi Elettronici SpA.
Powered by: Solid-propellant rocket motor, rated at 4,410lb (2,000kg) st.
Airframe: Cylindrical light alloy body with ogival nose-cone. Pivoted cruciform wings mounted mid-way back on body and indexed in line with cruciform tail-fins.
Guidance and Control: Guidance by beam-riding/radio command, in conjunction with radar altimeter. Control by movable wings.
Warhead: High-explosive fragmentation type, detonated by impact/proximity fuse.
Length: 12ft 3in (3.73m).
Body diameter: 7.87 in (0.20m).
Wing span: 2ft 9½in (0.85m).
Launch weight: 370lb (168kg).
Max speed: Mach 1.9.
Max range: 6.2 miles (10km).

Development and Service
Known for a time as Nettuno, this missile is carried in a five-round launcher on board the Italian Navy's fast patrol boat *Saetta*. It is a fully developed operational weapon and can be integrated with existing naval fire control systems such as the Contraves Italiana Sea Hunter 2 and the Contraves AG (Switzerland) Sea Hunter 4.

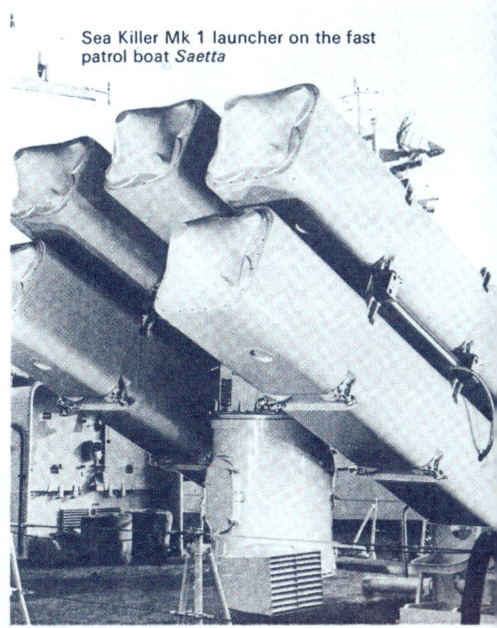
Sea Killer Mk 1 launcher on the fast patrol boat *Saetta*

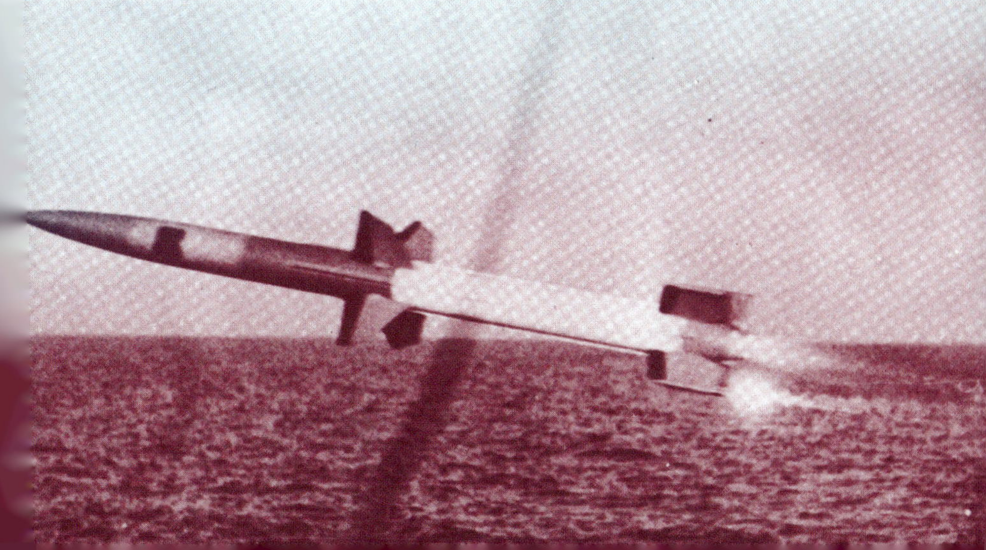

Sea Killer Mk 2

Italy

Surface-to-surface ship-launched missile. Available for service.

Prime contractor: Sistel—Sistemi Elettronici SpA.

Powered by: SEP 299 solid-propellant booster, rated at 9,702lb (4,400kg) st for 1.6 seconds, and SEP 300 solid-propellant sustainer, rated at 220lb (100kg) st for 73 seconds.

Airframe: Cylindrical light alloy body, with ogival nose-cone. Pivoted cruciform wings of rectangular shape mounted mid-way back on second stage and indexed in line with cruciform tail-fins. Tandem booster with large rectangular cruciform fins indexed in line with second-stage surfaces.

Guidance and Control: Guidance by beam-riding/radio command, in conjunction with radar altimeter. Control by movable wings.

Warhead: High-explosive, with impact/proximity fuse. Designed to penetrate steel armour.

Length: 14ft 9in (4.50m).
Body diameter: 7.87in (0.20m).
Wing span: 2ft 9½in (0.85m).
Launch weight: 530lb (240kg).
Max range: 11.5 miles (18.5km).

Development and Service

This Mk 2 version of Sea Killer is a two-stage missile, with tandem booster, enabling it to carry a heavier warhead and giving greatly increased range, at a high subsonic cruising speed. Flight trials have been under way since mid-1969, followed by the first weapon system qualification trials in mid-1971. Sea Killer Mk 2 can be integrated with the same Contraves shipboard systems as the Mk 1 version.

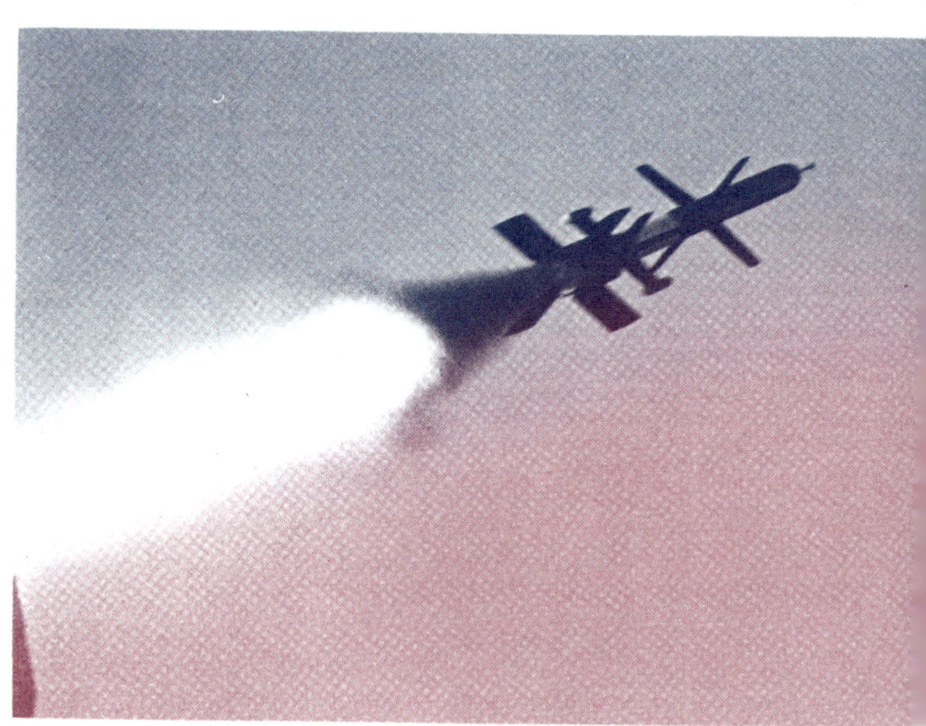

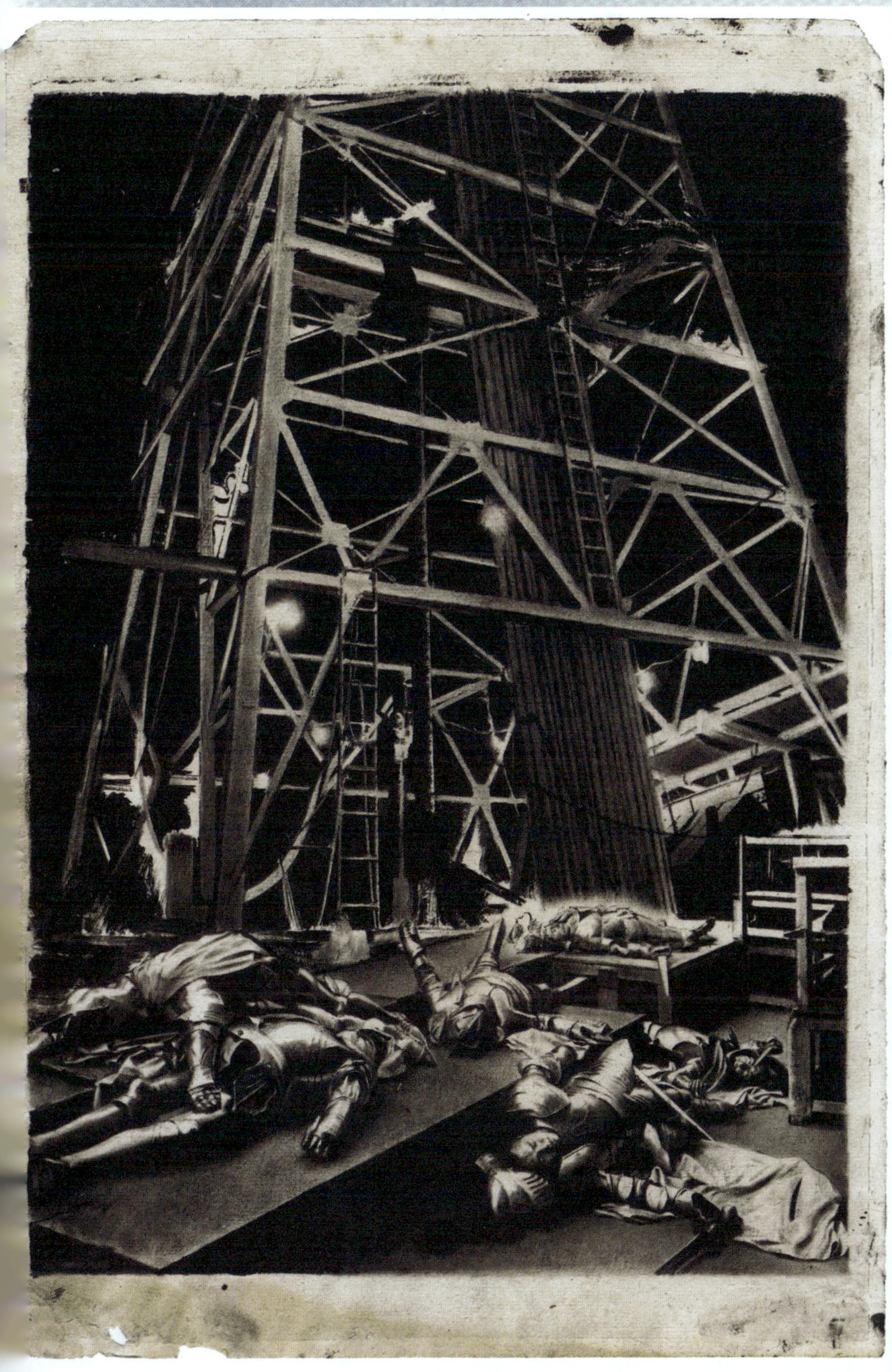

ary targe
formatio
with the
carriers
carry the

also a
eloped b
panies i
d Norwa
968. This
njunction
launcher
ital com
m and
nufactur

e USA i
which wi
to Spar
ilable fo
.

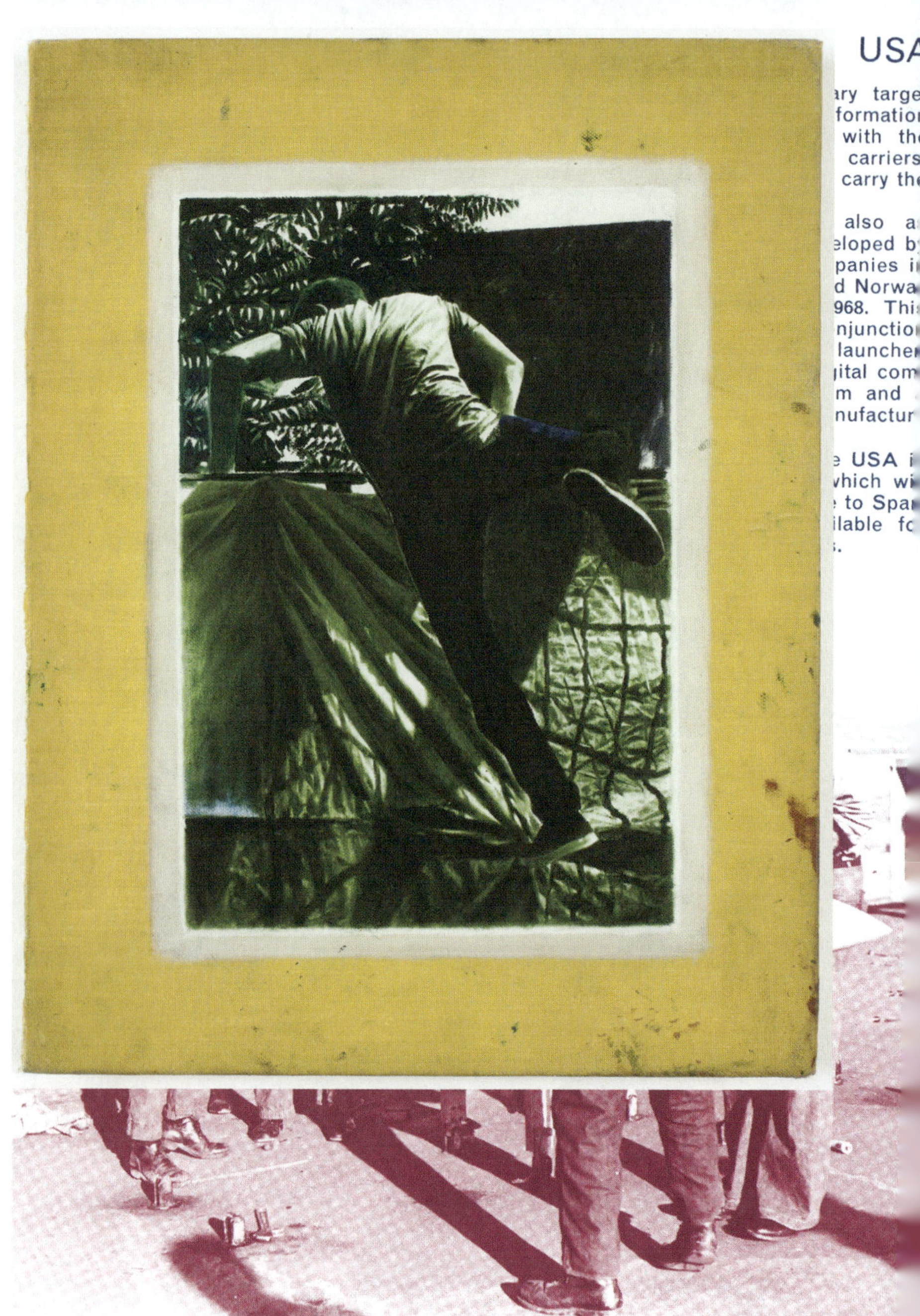

Sea Sparrow on the amphibious assault ship USS *Okinawa*

Seawolf

Close-range surface-to-air and surface-to-surface missile. Under development.

Prime contractor: British Aircraft Corporation, Guided Weapons Division.

Development and Service

BAC received a contract in June 1967 to develop an advanced surface-to-air weapon system which was then designated PX430 and is now known as Seawolf. Intended as a follow-on to Seacat (page 121) it will be an all-weather system, giving greatly improved defence capability against supersonic anti-shipping missiles and aircraft, and will be suitable for surface-to-surface use against ships and hovercraft. Marconi have responsibility for the entire electronics system, including surveillance radars, target tracking radar, missile gathering and guidance TV and data handling equipment.

Few details of the Seawolf missile are yet available, although development is at an advanced stage. It has been stated officially that the missile embodies techniques already used successfully in Rapier (see page 97) and that once a target has been identified as hostile all subsequent phases of launch and guidance are automatic. The Vickers-designed Mk 25 Mod O launcher has six rectangular launch-tubes.

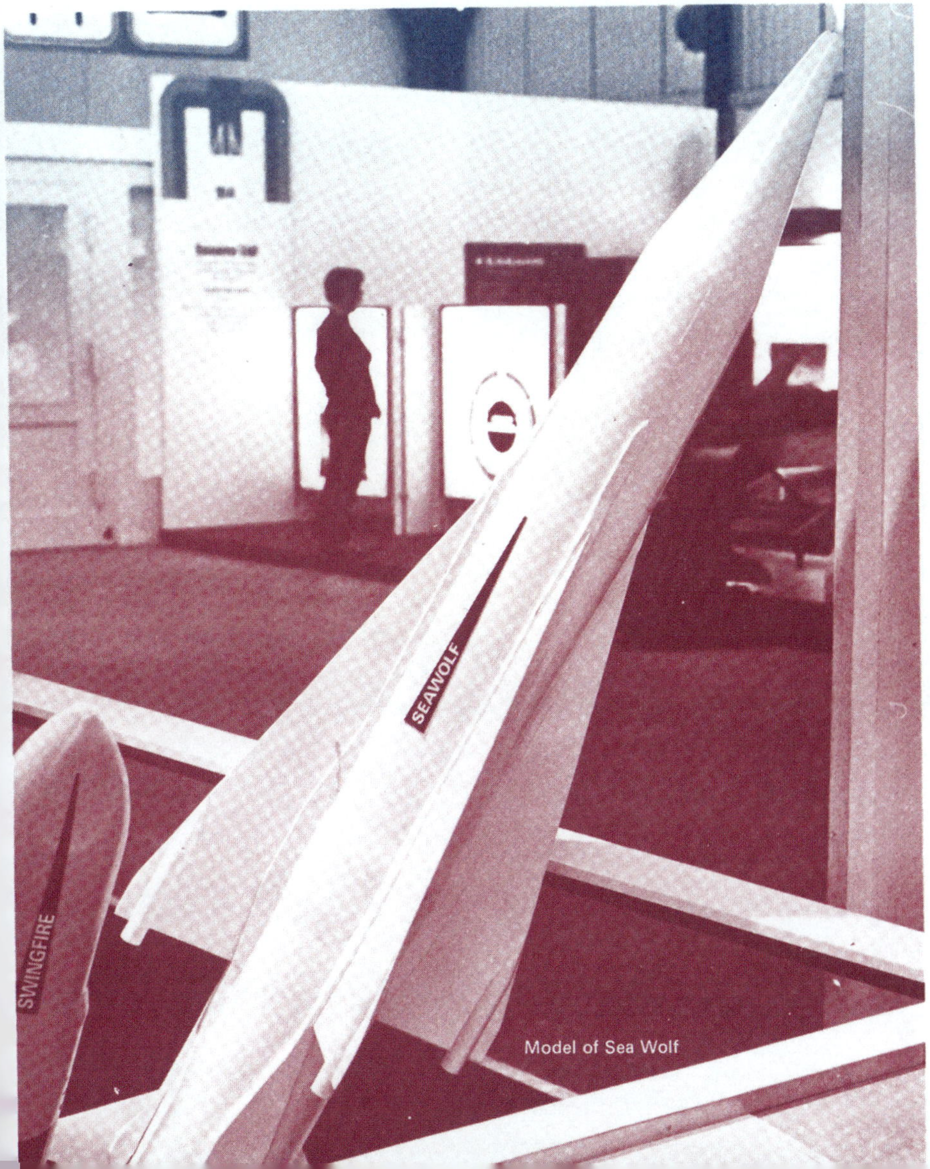

Model of Sea Wolf

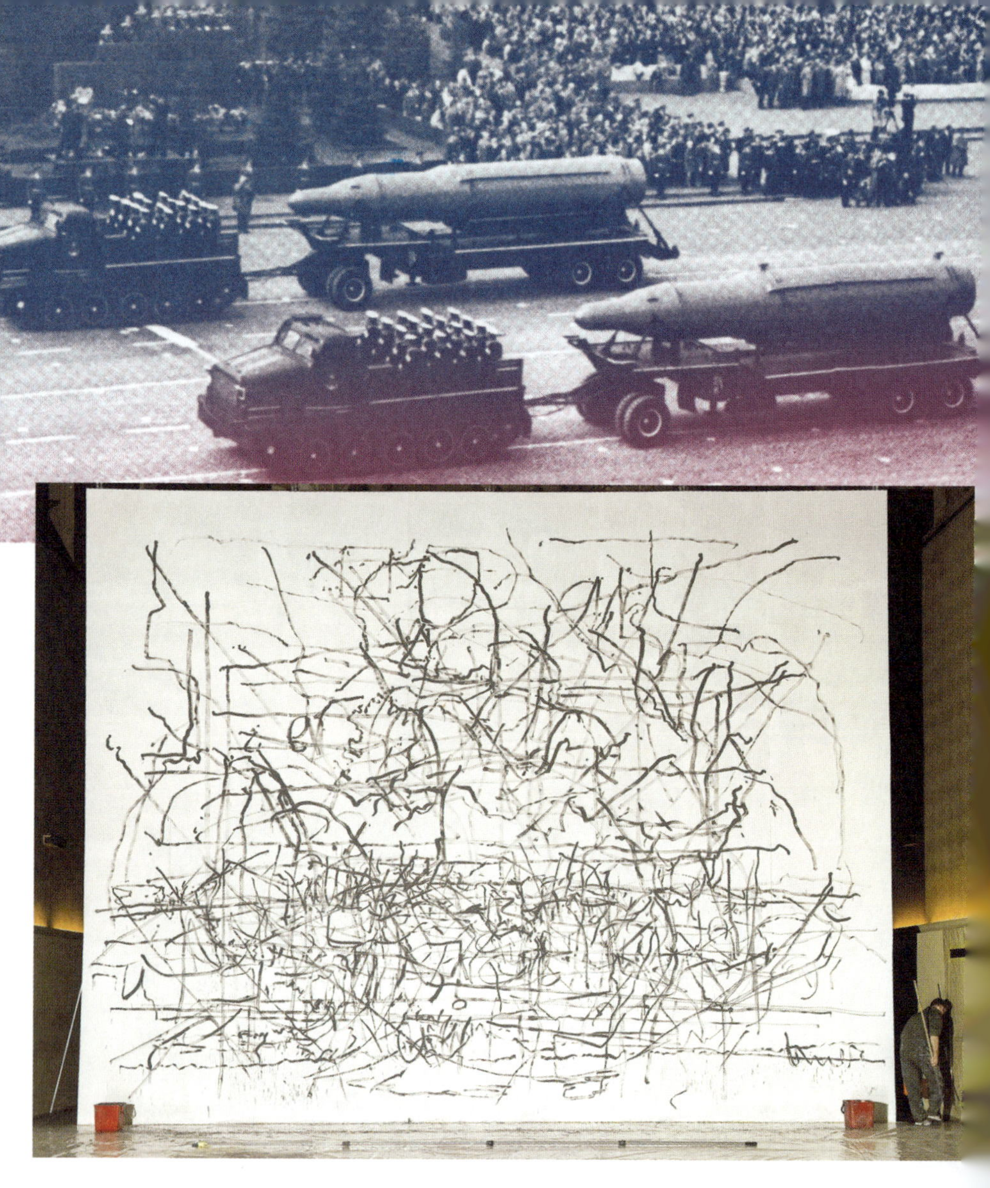

Sergeant (MGM-29A) USA

Medium-range surface-to-surface field artillery missile. In service.

Prime contractor: Sperry Rand Corporation, Univac Salt Lake City.
Powered by: Thiokol M-100 solid-propellant rocket motor, rated at 45,000lb (20,400kg) st.
Airframe: Cylindrical steel body. Cruciform tail-fins have small control surfaces hinged to trailing-edges and linked to jet-deflection vanes operating in rocket efflux. Pointed nose-cone.
Guidance and Control: Inertial guidance system made by Univac Salt Lake City. Control by hinged tail surfaces and jet-deflection vanes.
Warhead: Alternative nuclear or high-explosive.
Length: 34ft 6in (10.51m).
Body diameter: 2ft 7in (0.79m).
Fin span: 5ft 10.2in (1.78m).
Launch weight: 10,100lb (4,580kg).
Range limits: 28-85 miles (46-135km).

Development and Service

Sergeant was developed as a more mobile, quicker-reaction replacement for the earlier liquid-propellant Corporal artillery missile. Deliveries began in 1961 and it became operational in the following year. About 500 are thought to equip US Army units, with a further 100 in service with the West German Army. They are air-transportable, and each can be emplaced and fired in a few minutes by a six-man crew.

In recent years, since production ended, Univac Salt Lake City have concentrated on improving the efficiency of the weapon system. Faster count-down and firing rate resulted from introduction of a new digital computer, which replaced several of the original items of ground equipment. By integrating the functions of other electronic equipment, it was possible to dispense with two vehicles, so that each Sergeant battery now needs only one $2\frac{1}{2}$-ton truck and three semi-trailers.

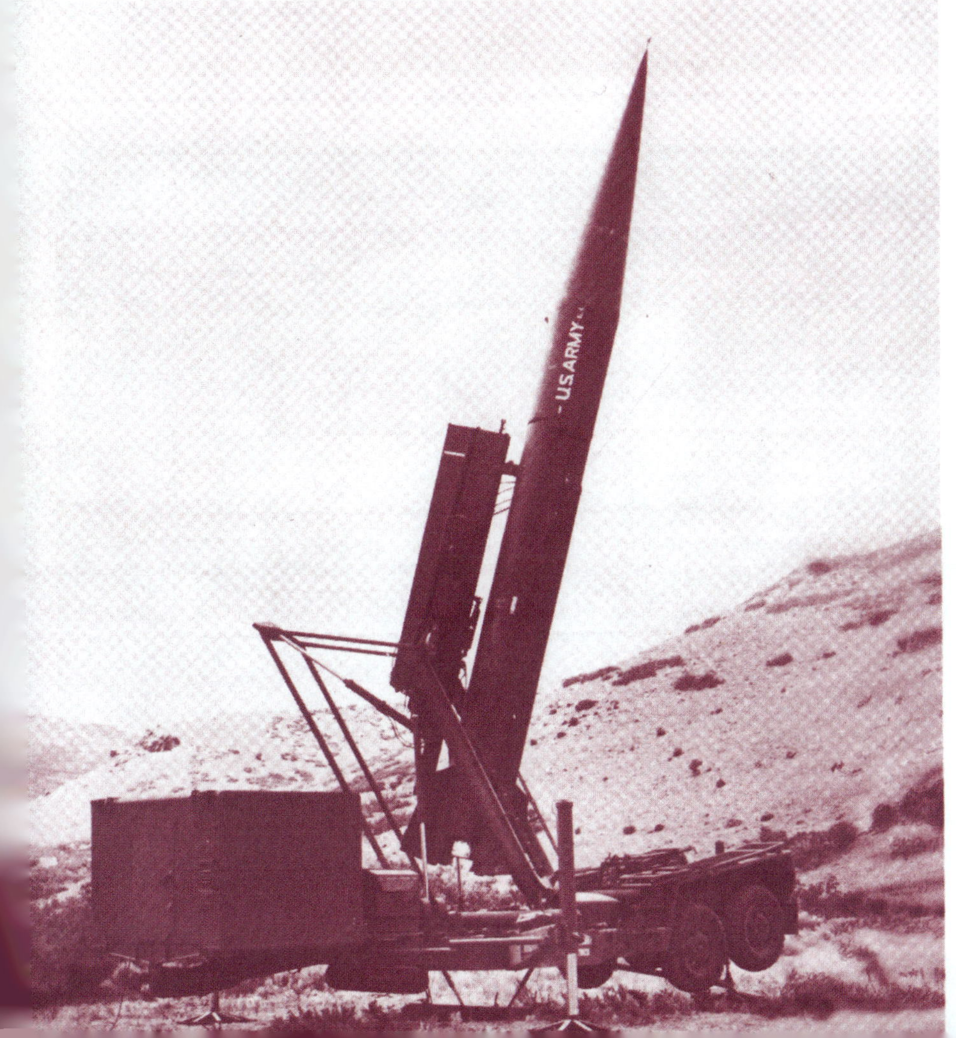

Surface-to-surface cruise missile. In service.

Powered by : Ramjet or turbojet cruise motor, plus two large solid-propellant JATO boosters.
Airframe : Basically bullet-shape body, probably with two short-span hinged wings at mid-point and with pointed ogival nose-cone. Two jettisonable boosters under tail, to each side of large ventral fin.
Guidance and Control : Active radar homing system.
Warhead : Probably nuclear.
Length : 35ft 9in (10.9m)
Max speed : Mach 0.95.
Max range : 230 miles (370km).

Development and Service

Cruise missiles of the subsonic 'flying bomb' type continue to serve in important roles in the Soviet armed forces. None is more formidable than 'Shaddock', which is carried as a standard weapon by many surface ships and submarines. Latest available non-classified data suggest that the four large destroyers known to NATO as the *Kresta I* class each carry four 'Shaddocks' in two twin launch-tubes, without reload capability.

This armament is more than doubled on the four destroyers of the *Kynda* class, each of which has four launch-tubes in a side-by-side cluster on the foredeck and four more on the after deck, almost certainly with eight more missiles in store for a second strike. At least 59 submarines are thought to be armed with 'Shaddock'. The nuclear-powered 'E I' and 'E II' classes carry six and eight missiles respectively; the 'J' class carry four each; and the converted 'W' class each carry two or four in what are known as longbin containers. About 100 more 'Shaddocks' are believed to be land-based.

'Shaddock' has never been revealed in public and the above description is based on what can be seen through the open ends of missile containers mounted on trucks which have taken part in parades through Moscow. The drawing is based on one which appeared in an official East German magazine, but has been modified to conform with known details of the nose and tail configuration. No details of the air intake for the cruise engine are known, but this could be annular like that of 'Ganef' (see page 43).

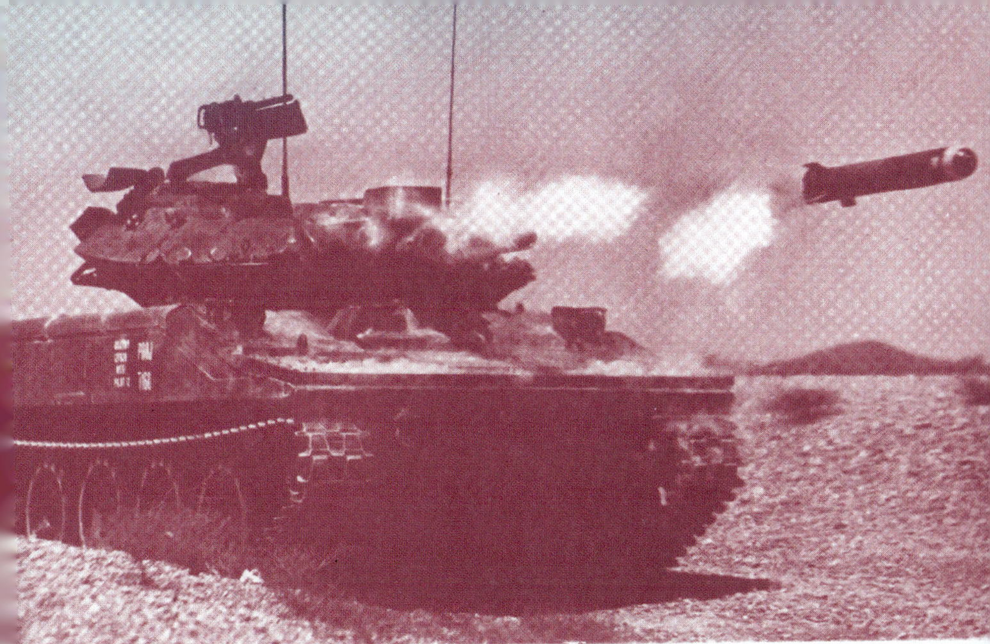

hillelagh (MGM-51A) USA

**ghtweight army close-support missile.
service.**

me contractor: Philco-Ford Corporation,
ronutronic Division.
wered by: Amoco Chemicals single-stage
d-propellant rocket motor.
frame: Round-nosed cylindrical body, with
r slightly swept flip-out tail-fins.
idance and Control: Aeronutronic
mmand guidance system, with infra-red
cking. Control by sustainer exhaust deflection.
rhead: Octol shaped-charge.
gth: 3ft 9in (1.14m).
dy diameter: 5.95 in (152 mm).
nch weight: 60lb (27kg).

velopment and Service
ilco-Ford claim that Shillelagh was built
greater numbers than any previous US
ded missile. It is unusual in being fired
m a gun/launcher that can also fire con-
tional ammunition. This makes it an ideal
weapon for tanks and other armoured fighting vehicles, and it has been carried by
General Sheridan AFVs of the US Army since
1967, including extensive overseas deployment. Other vehicles equipped with Shillelagh
include the American M-60A1E1/E2 battle
tank and the new XM-803 (MBT-70) main
battle tank.

After firing Shillelagh, the gunner has only
to keep the target centred on the cross-hairs
of his telescopic sight. An infra-red missile
tracking/command system associated with
the sight detects and corrects any deviations
of the missile's flight path from the line-of-
sight to the target. Shillelagh provides
greatly increased fire-power for use against
all types of armoured fighting vehicles, troops
and fortifications. It has been tested in an
air-to-surface role from a Bell UH-1B helicopter, in conjunction with a stabilised sight
developed by Aeronutronic.

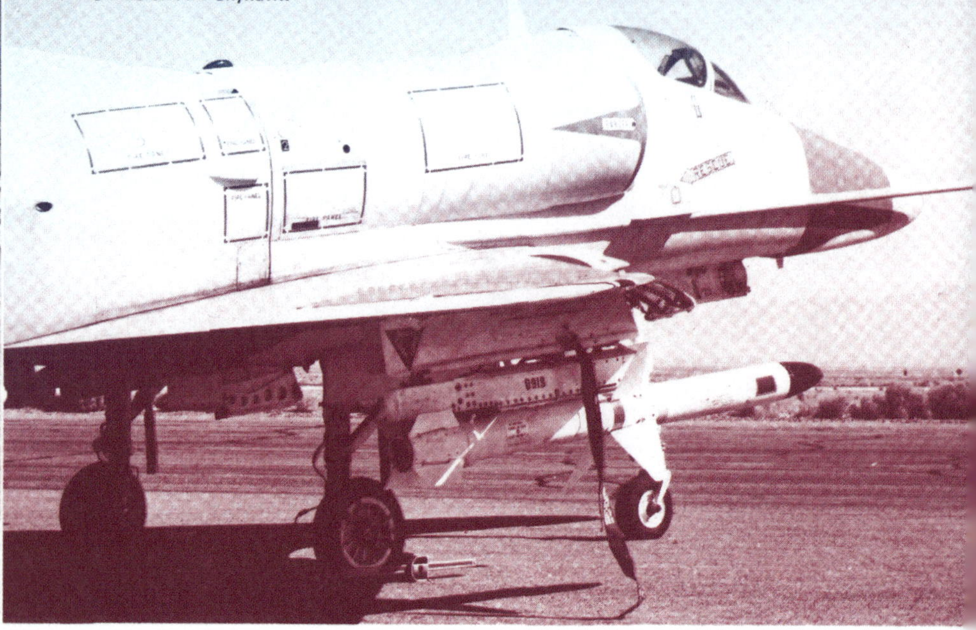

Shrike (AGM-45A)

US

Supersonic air-to-surface anti-radar missile. In production and service.

Prime contractor: Naval Weapons Center, China Lake, California.
Powered by: Rocketdyne Mk 39 Mod 7 or Aerojet Mk 53 solid-propellant rocket motor.
Airframe: Slim cylindrical body with ogival nose. Pivoted cruciform wings mid-way from nose to tail, indexed in line with cruciform tail-fins.
Guidance and Control: Passive homing head by Texas Instruments. Control via pivoting wings.
Warhead: High-explosive.
Length: 10ft 0in (3.05m).
Body diameter: 8in (20.3cm).
Wing span: 3ft 0in (0.91m).
Launch weight: 400lb (182kg).
Max range: 10 miles (16km).

Development and Service
Shrike was developed initially under acronym ARM (anti-radar missile), to h on enemy radars. The need for such a v pon was underlined by the war in Vietn where it became increasingly importan knock out or jam the North's warning missile/aircraft guidance radars during US air offensive. Delivery to US Navy car based attack squadrons began in USAF squadrons also adopted Shrike standard penetration aid, and it bec operational in Vietnam in 1966. Produc for the USAF and US Navy continues, many improvements have been introdu through the years to increase the weap effectiveness. One version supplied to Israeli Air Force is said to have a se head designed specifically to home on radars supplied to Egypt with Soviet 'Gu line' and 'Goa' missile systems.

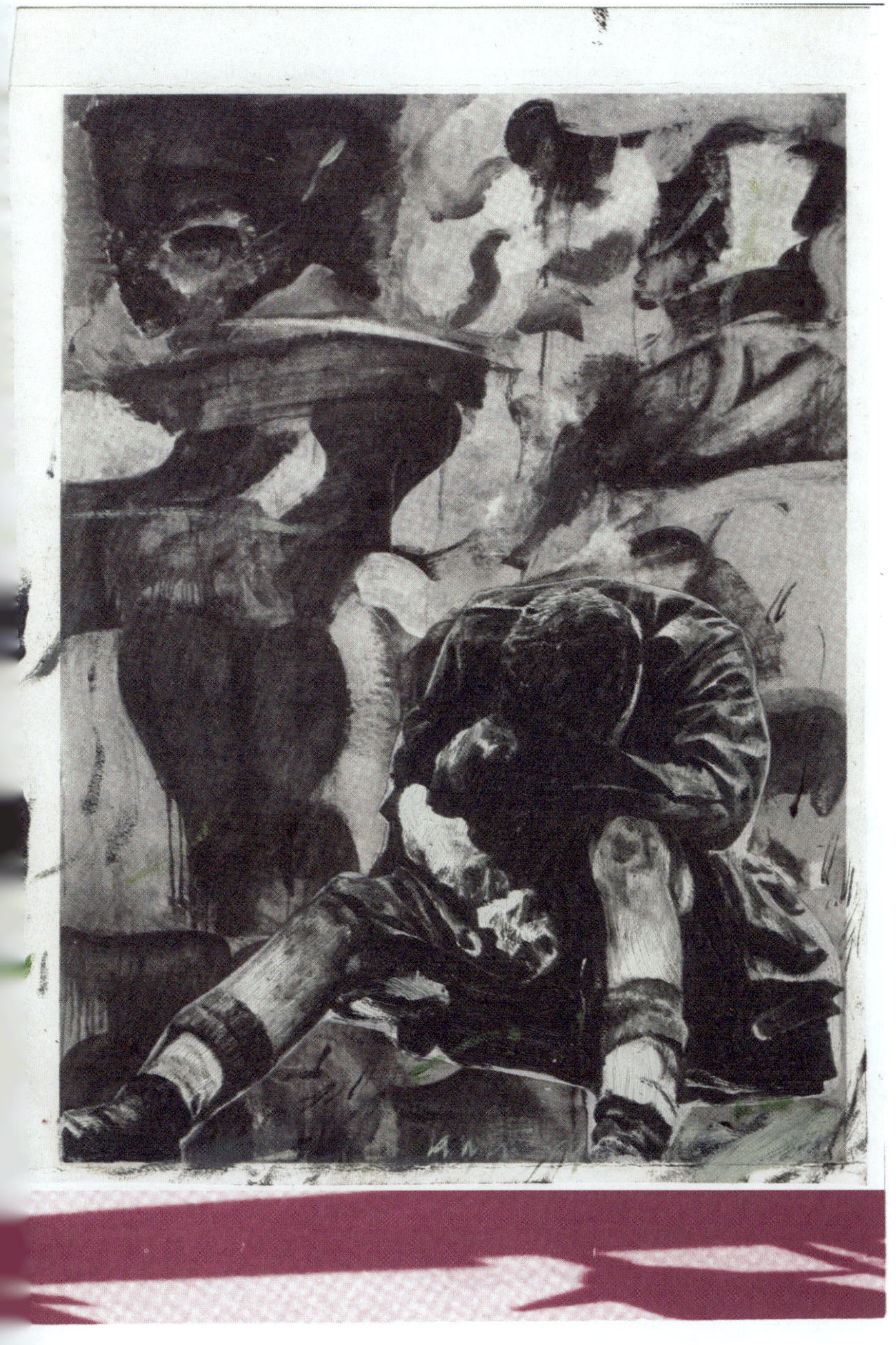

Sidewinder 1C (AIM-9)

Air-to-air missile. In production and service.

Data for AIM-9D.
Prime contractor: US Naval Weapons Center China Lake, California.
Powered by: Rocketdyne Mk 36 Mod 5 solid-propellant rocket motor.
Airframe: Slim cylindrical body, with tapering and rounded nose. Nose control surfaces are of longer chord than on the 1A version, and the cruciform tail surfaces have increased leading-edge sweep.
Guidance and Control: Raytheon infra-red homing (Motorola semi-active radar guidance on AIM-9C). Control via foreplanes.
Warhead: High-explosive.
Length: 9ft 6½in (2.91m).
Body diameter: 5in (13cm).
Span of tail-fins: 2ft 1in (0.64m).
Launch weight: 185lb (84kg).
Max range: over 2 miles (3.5km).

Development and Service
Sidewinder 1C was developed in two versio to offer higher speed and greater range th the 1A series. The AIM-9C radar-homi version is in production by Motorola. T infra-red AIM-9D is manufactured by R theon for the US Navy and UK, but is yet used by the USAF. Sidewinder 1C operational also in the US Army's Chapar surface-to-air missile system (see page 2

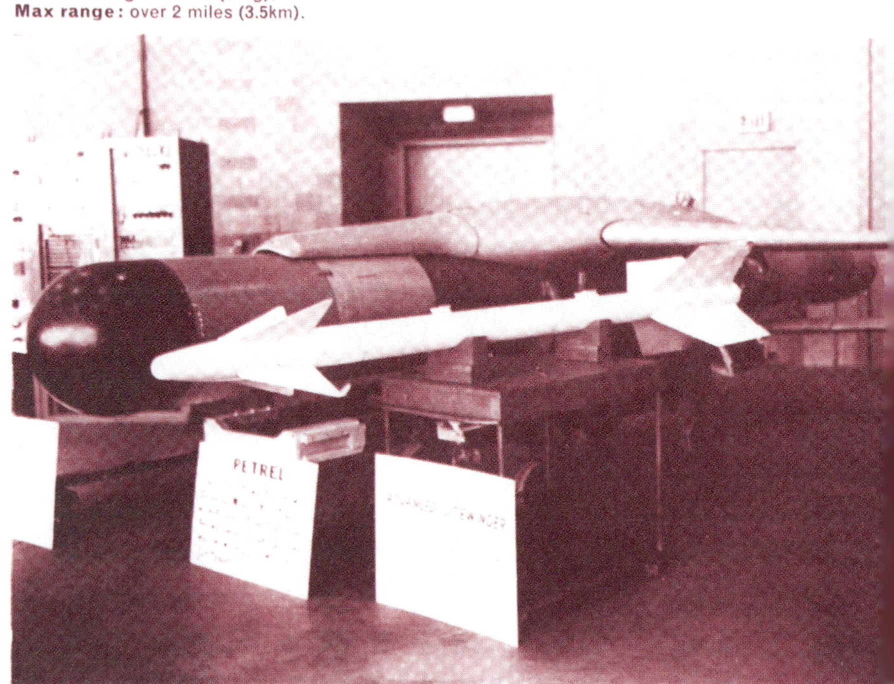

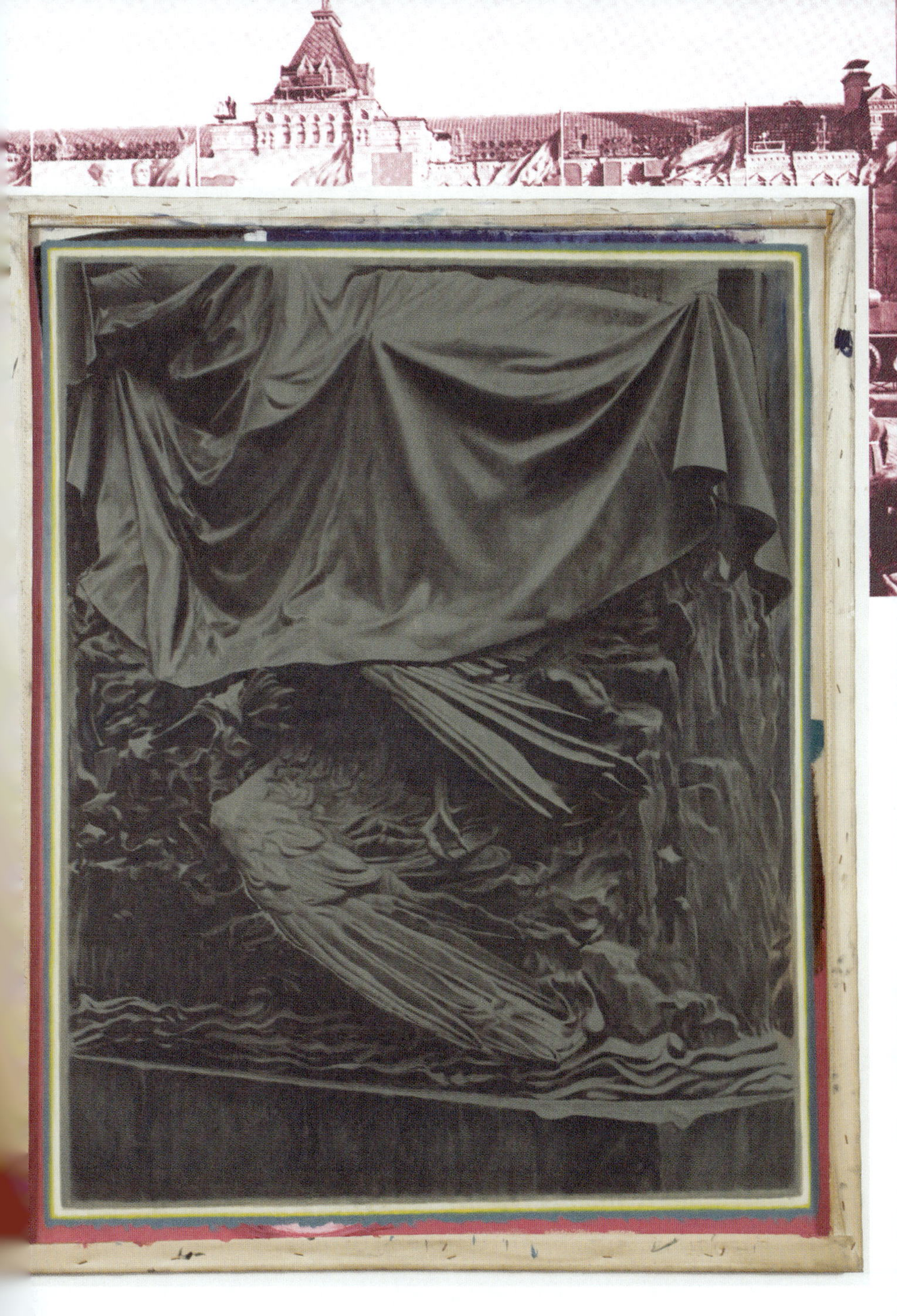

SLAM

Ship-launched missile system. Under development.

Prime contractor: Vickers Ltd, Shipbuilding Group.

Development and Service
The acronym SLAM signifies either sub-marine-launched air missile or surface-launched air missile system. In its initial form, the weapon system is being developed for compatibility with the *Oberon* class of submarines; but SLAM could be retro-fitted or built into almost any type of underwater or light surface craft for short-range defence against aircraft, helicopters and enemy surface craft. It consists of a cluster of six Blowpipe missile launchers (see page 26) surrounding an electronic package on a pylon mounting. Equipment in the electronic package includes a TV camera, gyro-stabiliser and some missile control equipment. After launch, each missile is guided by joystick by an operator in the ship's control room, who keeps both missile and target centred on a TV monitor. Preliminary trials of SLAM had been completed by January 1970.

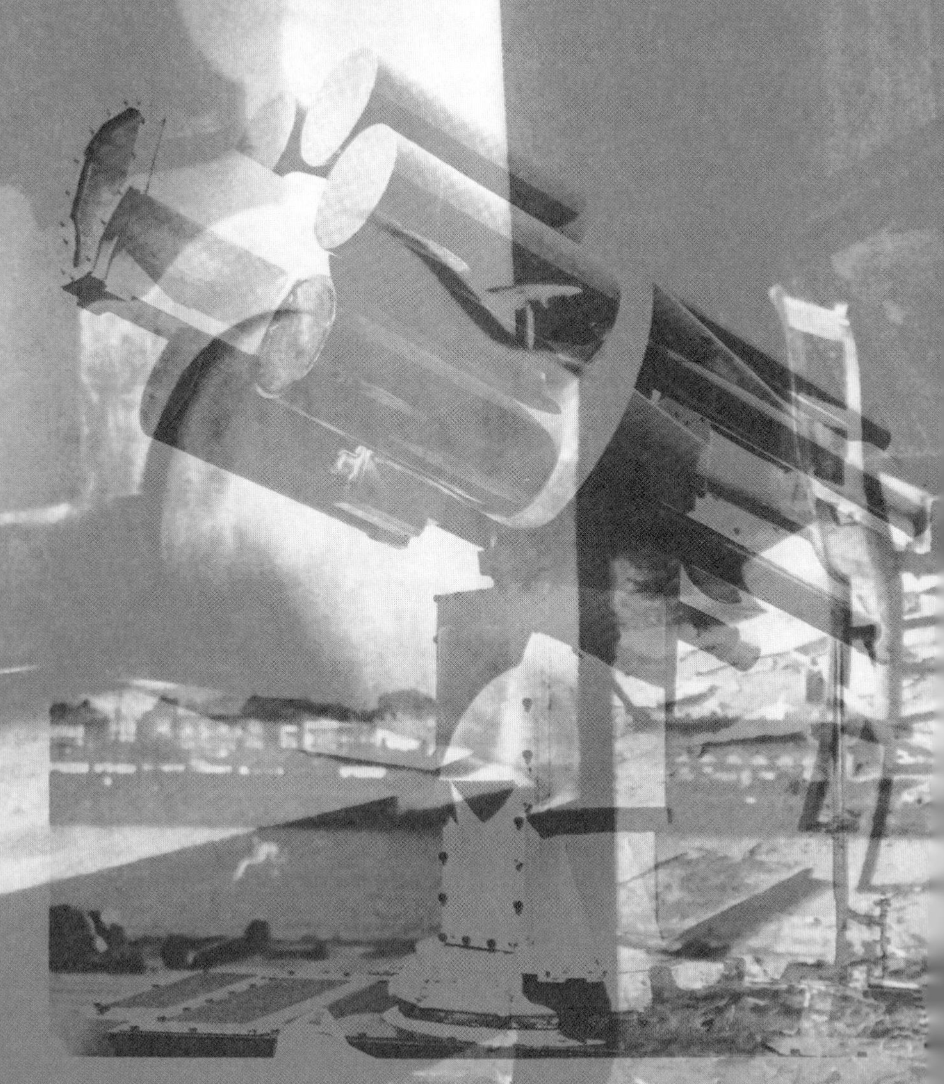

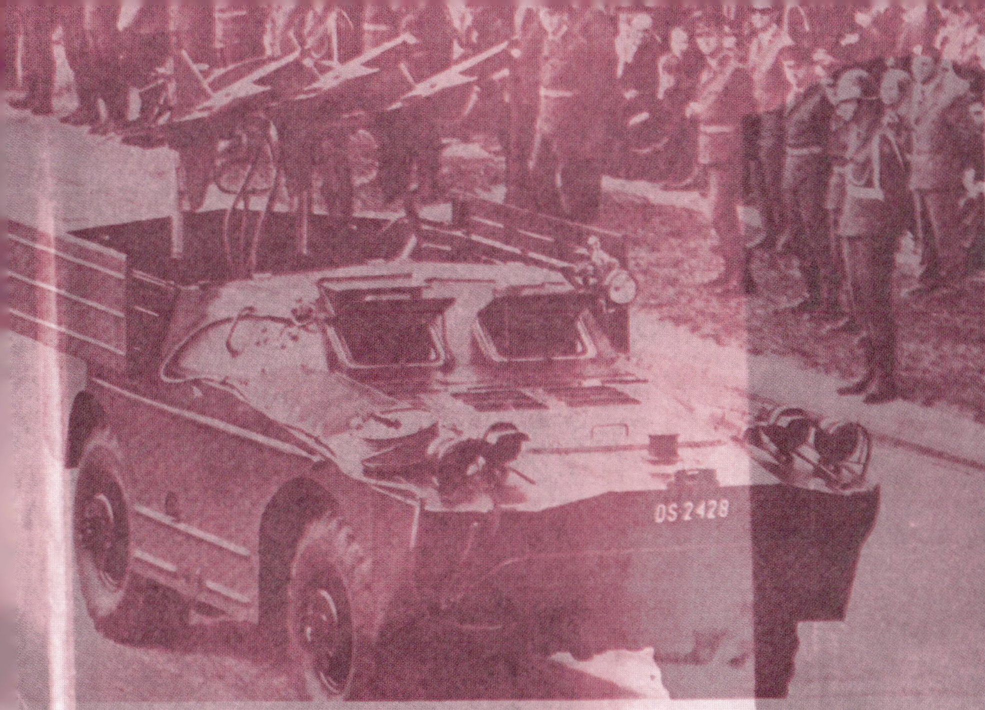

Snapper

...ight anti-tank missile. In service.

...owered by : Solid-propellant rocket motor.
...irframe : Short cylindrical body with conical
...ose-cone. Rear-mounted cruciform wings of
...elta shape, each with one or two vibrating
...poilers mounted in its trailing-edge.
...uidance and Control : Wire-guided and
...in-stabilised. Control by means of spoilers.
...arhead : Hollow-charge, weighing 11.5lb
...25kg), with contact fuse. Capable of
...enetrating 13.7in (35cm) of armour.
...ength : 3ft 8½in (1.13m).
...ody diameter : 5.5in (0.14m).
...ing span : 2ft 5½in (0.75m).
...aunch weight : 49lb (22.25kg).
...ruising speed : 120mph (323km/h).
...ax range : 7,650ft (2,330m).

Development and Servic...
Like 'Guideline' and 'Atol...
the better-known Soviet...
examples were captured by...
during the 1967 June War. 'Snapper' is a
first-generation anti-tank weapon, similar
in configuration to Western missiles such as
the Nord SS.10 and MBB Cobra. In its initial
operational form, as captured by Israel,
'Snapper' was carried on a quadruple launcher
by a GAZ-69 jeep-type vehicle. Control was
by joystick, and the operator kept the missile
aligned on target during flight with the aid of
tracking flares mounted on two of the wings.
Standard transport/launch vehicle in the
Soviet Army is now the armoured, amphibious BRDM, which carries a retractable
three-round launcher.

LIST OF WORKS

IAN TWEEDY
CRISIS

A selection of works from 2009 to 2012
over various pages of the original title
Missiles of the World, 1972

Published by cura.books
Design: Ian Tweedy & Andrea Baccin

Printed in Italy

ISBN: 978-88-97889-07-6

CURA.BOOKS
MONITOR, Rome
UNTITLED, New York